CHORA: Intervals in the Philosophy of Architecture
Managing Editor: Alberto Pérez-Gómez

Volume 1 (1994)
Edited by Alberto Pérez-Gómez and Stephen Parcell
Volume 2 (1996)
Edited by Alberto Pérez-Gómez and Stephen Parcell

Chora 2: Intervals in the Philosophy of Architecture

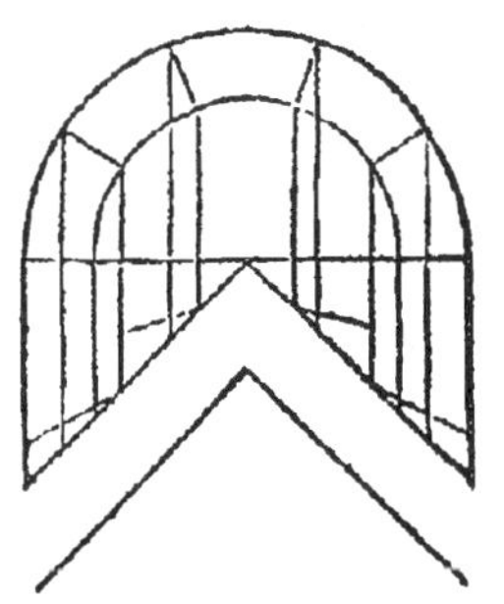

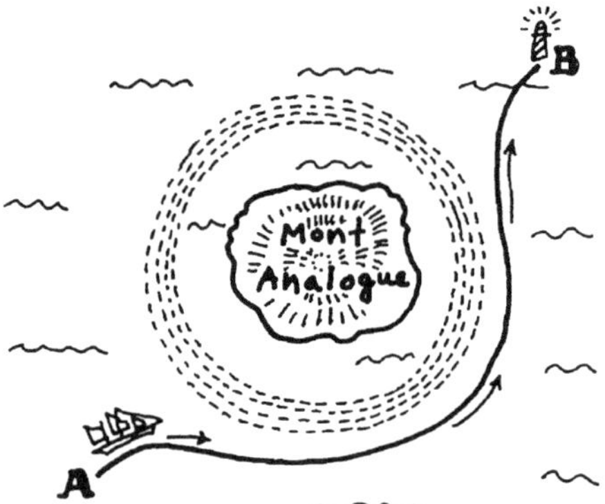

Intervals in the Philosophy of Architecture

CHORA

VOLUME TWO

Edited by Alberto Pérez-Gómez and Stephen Parcell

Published for the History and Theory of Architecture
Graduate Program, McGill University by
McGill-Queen's University Press
Montreal & Kingston • London • Buffalo

ISBN 0-7735-1406-6 (cloth)
ISBN 0-7735-1407-4 (paper)

Legal deposit third quarter 1996
Bibliothèque nationale du Québec

Printed in Canada on acid-free paper

National Library of Canada Cataloguing:

Chora (Montreal, Quebec)
Chora: intervals in the philosophy of architecture
Annual.
1994–
ISSN 1198-449X
ISBN 0-7735-1406-6 (bound: v. 2) –
ISBN 0-7735-1407-4 (pbk.: v. 2)
1. Architecture – Philosophy – Periodicals. I. McGill University.
History and Theory of Architecture Graduate Program.
NA1.C46 720′.1 C94-900762-5

Typeset in Sabon 10/13 by Caractéra inc., Quebec City.

Contents

Preface

CHORA, the Greek word for space, is the title of a collection of books devoted to exploring the potential of architecture beyond conventional aesthetic and technological reductions. Amid an unabated scientism and an irrelevant nihilism, in which the alternative to rationalist and functionalist building practices of modernity is often an empty formalism, CHORA offers a forum for pondering other possibilities. Is it conceivable to affirm the specificity of architecture *vis-à-vis* both technological building and the mass media, while avoiding futile nostalgic turns? Can we recognize a truth being revealed in our architectural tradition and a hope in our presence as embodied human beings, while rejecting the dangerous delusions of absolute, transparent truth and logocentric power?

Architecture is at a crossroads. If its role as the stage for the perpetuation of human culture is not recognized and redefined, its demise would be inevitable. The work of the architect, a work of imagination, cannot be simply a dominating gaze, a solipsistic play of mirrors, or an act of the will to power. It may yet be something different, something that must be explored, and that may, as reconciliatory action, point to a referent *other* than itself. In a world where the media establish new paradigms of communication approaching the ephemeral nature of embodied perception and the primary orality of language, architecture may indeed be able to carry intersubjective values, convey meaning through metaphor, and embody a cultural order beyond tyranny or anarchy.

CHORA 2 continues to offer ample space to meditate on the possibility of such an architecture, capable of both respecting cultural differences and acknowledging the globalization of technological culture. The essays in this volume continue to operate from *within* the discipline of architecture, while furthering an interdisciplinary understanding. Karsten Harries provides a fresh and long-overdue reading of Heidegger's well-known essay, "Building Dwelling Thinking." Donald Kunze and Stephen Parcell consider possibilities of meaningful architectural space for a visual culture, continuing themes they addressed in CHORA 1. Further reflections on the spaces of literature, cinema, and architecture include an interview with French writer Alain Robbe-Grillet and articles by Dagmar Motycka Weston on the surrealist city, Tracey Eve Winton on the museum as a paradigmatic modern building, and Terrance Galvin on spiritual space in the works of Jean Cocteau. Jean-Pierre Chupin and Bram Ratner explore historical themes in their essays on French Renaissance architect Philibert de L'Orme and the Jewish myth of the Golem. Gregory Paul Caicco addresses ethical questions in his essay on the Greek agora and the death of Socrates, as does Lily Chi in her meditation on the critical issue of use in architectural works. A concern with architectural representation and generative strategies for the making of architecture is present throughout, especially in the essay by Joanna Merwood on the provocative *House* by British artist Rachel Whiteread.

While the main philosophical framework for CHORA stems from phenomenology and hermeneutic ontology, the architectural pursuits in this collection could be placed generally in the context of Continental European philosophy, which demands a fundamental redefinition of thought and action and a substantial rethinking of traditionally accepted values.

Socrates in the Agora

Gregory Paul Caicco

Chora

1.1 Attic sacrificial rite involving priest, acolyte, and victim pig; from Paris Louvre G112, Attic red-figure cup, late 6th century B.C.E.; outline drawing by author.

SACRIFICE IS THE OLDEST FORM of religious action.[1] If a person wished to draw near to the gods, as the priest Chryses did with Apollo or as Hektor and Odysseus did with Zeus, he could do so only after he had "burnt many thigh-pieces of bulls" (*Il.* 1.40, 22.170; *Od.* 1.66). Ancient piety rested on a foundation of killing, death, and eating. The victim's end coincided with a ritual scream at a point, between the knife and the altar, where the community and the Awesome were gathered.[2] By going through this "irreversible act," life was affirmed through direct confrontation with the "Holy" and, as a result, the participants ascended to a higher plane.[3] Without sacrificial action such as this, an ordered relationship with the gods and the cosmos would be impossible; a community would not only be placing its future prosperity in great danger but ultimately risking its survival into the next day.

In classical Athens, Socrates stands out as one who understood that meaningful existence depended on sacrifice. His self-denial and faith in the gods brought him to the centre of Athens' sacred precinct and enabled him to become a sacrificial offering himself. In this essay I shall explore the role of Socrates within the consecrated boundary where his philosophy and example were heard and seen: the Agora of Athens.[4] To this end, I shall first describe the Agora in symbolic and spatial terms, and then, through the more or less "authentic" Socratic fragments in Plato, Aristotle, Aristophanes and Xenophon, resituate Socrates' thought and activity within the Agora itself.

SACRED CENTRES: KNOSSOS AND THE AGORA

The concept of a "Holy site," in Mircea Eliade's view, invokes the symbolism of the centre; that is, the centre acts as an earthly meeting point between heaven and the underworld.[5] Usually present is an axial relationship with a symbolic mountain that is striking in its configuration or placement. Textual evidence and archeological data have enabled scholars such as Walter Burkert to reconstruct how ancient cultures participated at this centre. Before entering the sacred zone for a sacrifice, a ritual preparation took place. After a "willing" victim offered itself for capture and procession, all participants underwent a ritual purification: bathing, fasting, sexual abstinence, and prayer. At the site of an altar-stone a fire was lit and a wide circle was drawn to demarcate a sacred/profane boundary. Within the boundary the victim was cleansed, the scream began, and the emotional climax arrived with the death blow (fig. 1.1). Horror transformed later into pleasure when the animal was eaten. The leftover bones and skins were then used to preserve the memory of the sacrifice: the bones were arranged in the "proper order" on and around the altar, the skulls were displayed in a sacred place, and the skins were sometimes stretched as a roof over the altar or sold for the benefit of the cult.[6]

George Hersey claims that these "arrangements" are the earliest evidence of architecture and monument in history. They were the beginning of communal memory, reflection, and order: that is, the beginning of communication.[7]

Hunting, killing, and blood sacrifice occur during 95 to 99 percent of human history since the Palaeolithic era. By comparison, the 10,000-year history of agriculture is a mere drop in the bucket.[8] Many historians, Burkert included, suggest that animal sacrifice is rooted in human sacrifice and aggression between human beings. Because it is as easy to kill another hunter as it is to kill a fleeing beast, self-destruction has always been a threat to the human race. In many cultures, especially the Greek, the animal victim was regarded as another human, and was referred to as a "father" (Apollod. *Epit.* 3.22). Nevertheless, humans survived and grew because they developed cultural rules in place of their natural instincts. By following the behaviour of predatory animals, co-operation among human males permitted mutual success in the hunt. This same co-operation developed their rituals of sacrifice, of giving thanks to the animal or god for offering itself, and of sharing the meal with their dependents. The altar therefore became the centre of the culture, where the desire for monument and memory would be preserved in oral traditions, human burials, shelters, and other communal constructions.

One of the earliest Greek city/palaces, Knossos (2000–1700 B.C.E.), was founded on an even earlier sacrificial site.[9] Both the Mycenaean Linear B script and its archeological configuration consistently point to its dependence on sacrifice, not only for its religious unity but also for its military, political, economic and administrative agenda (fig. 1.2). The king of Knossos brought together all aspects of this power and fused them in his own person . Bearing the title of "wa-na-ka," or *wanax*, the king regulated all aspects of palace life since he was primarily responsible for its religious life.[10] Through his participation in the cyclical myth structure, he could direct the weather, control fertility, and indeed, demonstrate his special sovereign connection to the god. For instance, the Cretan legend of Minos recounts a requirement of the king to enter the cave of Mount Ida every nine years to undergo an ordeal that would renew his royal power through direct contact with Zeus (*Odyssey*, XIX, 179).

This palace-centred political system – what Homer called the *basileus* – enabled the Minoans to administer and regulate an immense territory through the various rural land owners. All this, however, came to an abrupt end with the Dorian invasion of Mycenae in 1200 B.C.E. The palace system was never to return, the term *wanax* disappeared, and indeed, writing itself vanished until the end of Greece's so-called Dark Ages in the ninth century. When it finally re-emerged, writing was no longer for the private service of a king but instead served a public purpose, allowing all aspects of political and social life to be disclosed equally to all people. This equality, in fact, was the basis of the polis, the palace's successor. What was once the King's all-encompassing power became split into two very distinct spheres: the *arche*, an elected political leader; and the *basileia*, a religious administrator limited to certain priestly functions.[11] Rather than single family rule (*gene*), the spirit of competition (*agon*), began to animate the political forum. Opposition and oratorical contests became the norm, and their theatre was the Agora, the public square, which had been a meeting place long before it was a marketplace (fig. 1.3).

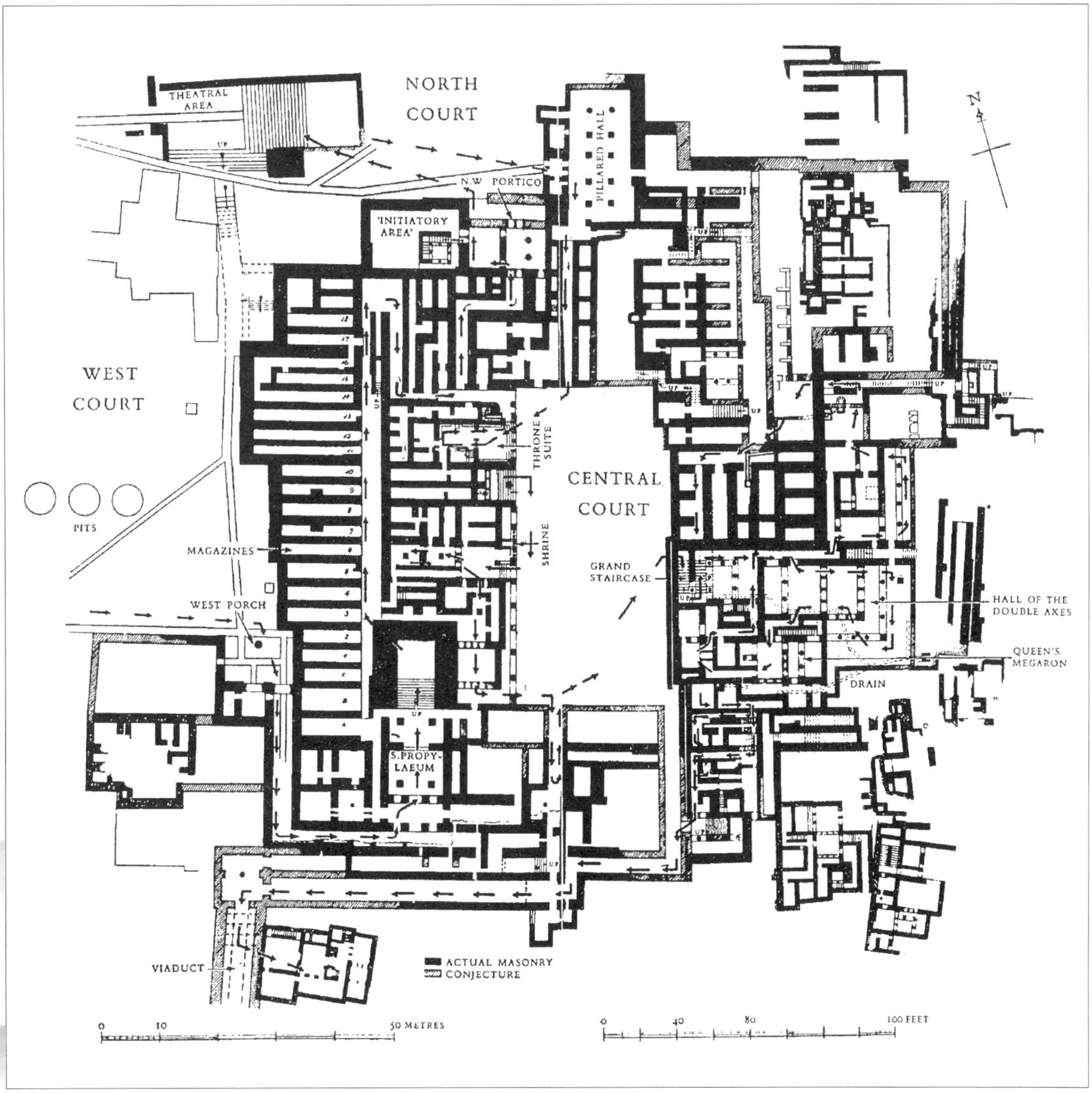

1.2 Palace at Knossos, Crete. Plan; from J.D.S. Pendlebury, *Handbook to the Palace of Minos at Knossos* (London: Macmillan 1933), plan 9.

The terms a Greek would have used to describe this space are striking: he would have said that certain deliberations, certain decisions must be brought *es to koinon* (to the commons), that the ancient privileges of the king and *arche* itself were set down *es to meson*, in the middle, at the centre.[12] This spatial image expresses the self-awareness acquired by a

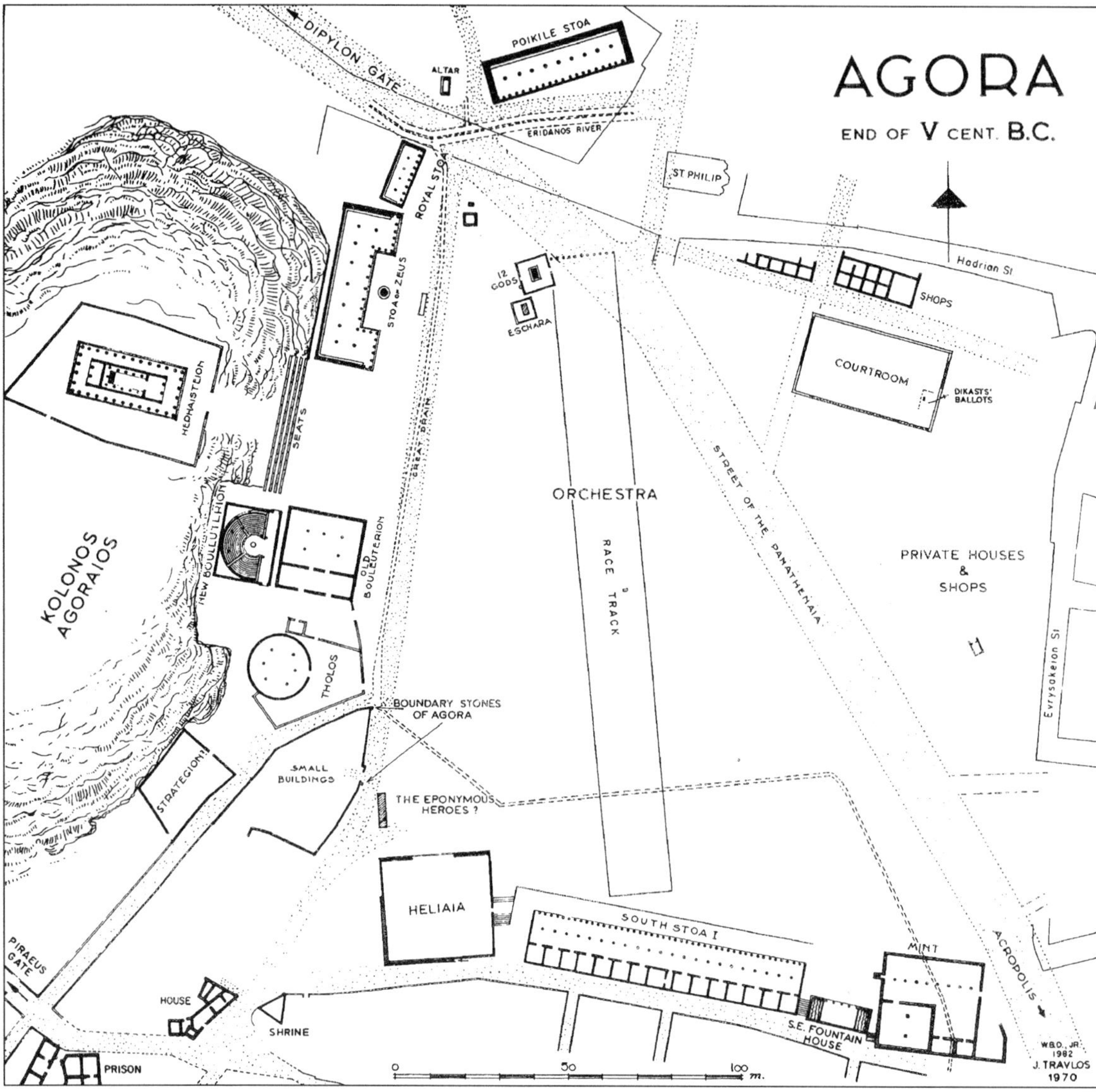

1.3 The Classical Athenian Agora, approx. 400 B.C.E.; from J. M. Camp, *The Athenian Agora: Excavations in the Heart of Athens* (New York: Thames and Hudson 1986), fig. 66.

human group, its existence as a political unit, and is of value not only by a comparison; it also reflects the creation of a social space that was altogether new. Indeed, urban buildings were no longer grouped, as before, around a royal palace ringed by fortifications. The city had become centred on the Agora, the communal space and seat of the *hestia koine* (the central or public hearth), a public area where questions of general interest were debated. As the palace was once enclosed within walls, so the entire polis had become surrounded by a wall, delineating a new protective and sacred boundary. The Acropolis became consecrated to the gods, and on the ruins of its palace were built freely accessible temples.

Interesting to note, however, are similarities between the plans of Knossos and the plan of the Agora of Athens, even though they were culturally worlds apart (figs. 1.2, 1.3). By overlaying both plans, at their different scales, one can find corresponding elements of the palace and the Agora in the same positions. Both were oriented orthogonally on a north-south axis leading to a mountain to the south that served as an *axon*, or sacred centre. Both had their processional entrance coming at the north-east corner, where the throne-room of the palace and the Royal Stoa of the Agora were located. On the eastern side of both plans was the political administration, while dwellings and shops abounded on the western side. Most important, however, was the central position of the large open square, toward which all activity was directed.

The central court of the Knossos complex was the ancient precinct of the sacrifice. Here, long before the palace structure was built, animals were brought to a simple altar stone to be killed and subsequently consumed, their bones becoming the first monument or architectural order to honour the dead. Once the site had evolved into a multi-faceted royal facility, where oral mythology was transformed into written decree, the sacrifice itself accrued many additional layerings. At its height, a "bull dance" preceded the offering and sacrifice of the bull. Young men and girls, facing death by the bull, seized the horns sacred to the goddess and leaped over the bull, propelled by the power behind the horns (fig. 1.4). In an effort to resurrect the hunt, the dance replayed both the real danger and the hunters' spiritual connection with the victim.[13]

The site of the Agora of Athens contains a late neolithic well that indicates habitation around 3000 B.C.E.[14] In the Mycenaean era, the Acropolis of Athens had a palace that is considered to be similar in plan and administration to that in Knossos. The Agora, situated just north of the Acropolis, became the area's primary burial ground and retained that function throughout the Dark Ages. With such strong associations with death, it is no wonder that the Agora was not only a sacred precinct, but an important, if not primary, sacrificial site. Victims were slaughtered at this spot and their remains were carried in procession up to the

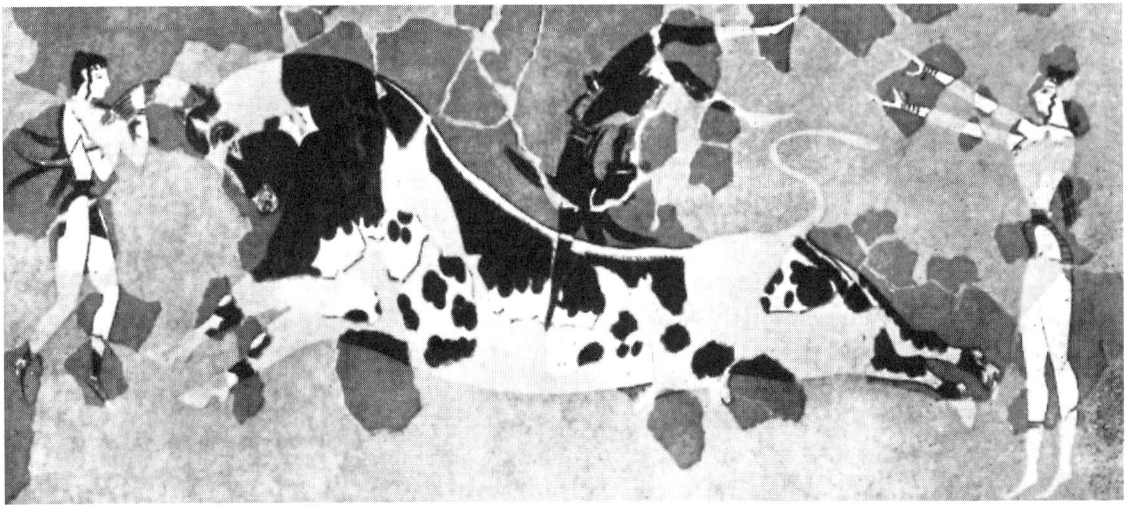

Acropolis to offer to the gods. After the collapse of the palace in the Dorian invasion, and following the Dark Ages, Athens rebuilt itself as an international power around the Agora. By 600 B.C.E., the great public square was officially marked out and the most important altar in Greece, the Altar of the Twelve Gods, was established at its centre. Only later did the great public buildings rise around the edges of the Agora.[15]

THE AGORA WITHIN SOCRATES' LIFE

Meaningful sacrifice depended on how well it revived the memory of the hunt, while expressing the community's gratitude to the animal or god for providing food. Over time, however, daily routine and the addition of subsidiary rites and observances made the sacrifice itself an empty formality, and the sacred zone became neglected. Furthermore, during the Dark Ages, sacrificial rites began to be questioned, as the god "to whom" the sacrifice was made began to seem merely an excuse for feasting by humans. All the god would receive were the bones, fat, and gall bladders. Hesiod said that the crafty Prometheus, the friend of humankind, did this to deceive the gods, and the burning of bones became a standard joke in Greek comedy (Hes. *Th.* 541). Pythagoreans and Orphics demanded that the lives of all creatures with souls be spared, and Empedocles was most vehement in attacking the cannibalistic madness of the traditional sacrificial meal (Emp. B 136–9). A

1.4 Opposite: Toreador fresco showing Knossos "bull-dance"; from Pendlebury, *Handbook*, plate 13.

1.5 Right: Discussion in Athenian palaestra (gymnasium). Red-figure vase found in a prison cell in the Agora; from Mabel Lang, *Socrates in the Agora: American School of Classical Studies at Athens* (Princeton, NJ: Institute for Advanced Study 1978), fig. 11.

student of Aristotle, Theophrastus, in his influential book, *On Piety*, explained animal sacrifice as a replacement for cannibalism, which had once been forced on tribes because of difficult times. Subsequently, a theoretical defense of sacrificial custom was virtually hopeless. Although Socrates lived a century before Theophrastus the early philosophical climate in which he was active had already developed doubts about sacrifice, cultic observances, immortality, and humankind's relationship to the gods.

Born in 470 B.C.E., Socrates spent his entire life, except for a brief expulsion, within the walls of Athens. Most of his time was passed in the Agora, where "he was always on public view; from early in the morning he used to go to the walkways and gymnasia, to appear in the Agora as it filled up, and to be present wherever he could meet people" (Xeno. *Mem.* I.1.10). According to the *Apology* of Plato, many of his discussions took place, near the "tables" in the open parts of the Agora, or in the shops, workshops, palaestra, and Lyceum that surrounded it (fig. 1.5). Although the Agora drew many people to buy and sell goods within its boundary, Socrates preferred to trade ideas.

For the Greeks, Socrates marked a turning point in the history of their philosophy. It was he who challenged the aphorisms and myth structures of an earlier philodoxy by initiating a search for true *episteme*.[16] In Aristotle's view, "There are two things which may justly be credited to Socrates, inductive arguments and general definition" (*Metaph.*

1078b27). Through induction, the mind is "led on" from the observation of particulars to the appreciation of general characteristics shared by all members of a class. The aim was to establish definitions as a foundation for fixed principles from which a philosophical discussion could begin. Concepts such as justice, goodness, courage, and temperance could then share a practical value in life.

One of the most important ideas explored by Socrates was the dictum "virtue is knowledge" (Xeno. *Mem.* 3.9.5). He associated this with two other concepts: that wrongdoing can be due only to ignorance and therefore must be considered involuntary; and that the primary condition of living well involves "care of the soul." On the one hand, the object of knowing virtue (*arete*) is to transcend all partial "goods" such as health, wealth, etc. to access a further end which embraces all "goods." On the other hand, this knowledge is a self-knowledge that strives to know the right and natural goal of one's life in its particular context. With these extremely high standards for moral action, death and sacrifice need not be feared if their purpose is to benefit the *psyche* of the person or the security of the community (*Prot.* 354a-b). When Socrates says that wrongdoing is ignorance, he reminds us that no human can have full knowledge of the consequences of an action, yet it is to this knowledge that we must strive (*Meno* 78a, *Rep.* 589c). Both sides of this ethical coin reinforce the need for humility and persistence in the pursuit of knowledge. In these ideas Socrates reveals an eminent practicality that is consistent throughout his philosophy: what is good is that which is *techne* – that which is directed only toward a desired end (*Prot.* 358b). As a result, this practicality inevitably places the care of one's *psyche*, the soul or seat of intelligence, beyond any physical concerns, and regards it as the chief activity of all humans.

In his life, Socrates made a sincere effort to "know himself" and to put that knowledge into practice. But how does one come to know one's own soul? Socrates would say that it is only by "understanding all that is divine – god and wisdom – that a man will most fully know himself" (*First Alcibiades* 133c). God (the divine mind) reflects the nature of the *psyche* more clearly than anything in the soul. Socrates must have believed these words, since his entire life's work, including his death, was guided by what both W.K.C. Guthrie and E.R. Dodds call "a deeply sincere faith."[17] Xenophon speaks of the meals Socrates often shared with his friends, which according to custom would be preceded by sacrifice and followed by libation to the gods; and he notes that Socrates "was frequently seen sacrificing on the public altars of the city" (*Mem.* I.2.49, *Gorg.* 485d-e, *Mem.* I.1.2). When answering the charges of impiety leveled at Socrates during his final trial, both Plato and Xenophon reported that he not only called upon the god of Delphi as a witness to his wisdom, but justified as a service to that god his unpopular practice of exposing the pretensions to wisdom in others.

Socrates' connection with the god or gods is twofold. First, from a young age, Socrates was in contact with a *daimonion*, a divine sign or spiritual guide, which prevented him from carrying out unwise decisions and guided him along other paths (*Apol.* 31c-d). Through this special and direct relationship with the god, Socrates acted with extraordinary confidence, trusting that his "voices" would warn him if he strayed. It was also reported more than once that Socrates had assumed a mystical, trance-like state, "going apart and standing still wherever he happens to be" (*Symp.* 174a). Once, on a military campaign, he became transfixed for twenty-four hours "and he stood there until it was dawn and the sun rose, then after a prayer to the sun he walked away" (*Symp.* 220c). With such single-mindedness and unwavering faith in his *daimonian's* assistance, Socrates admitted, "My service to the god has brought me into great poverty" (*Apol.* 23b). Nevertheless, he claimed that the little he had was "enough to satisfy my needs" (Xeno. *Oecon.* ii.2–4). This dutiful acceptance of his mission extended to all areas of his life, including his appearance: he regularly went barefoot, as well as "unwashed" (*Mem.* I.6.2). His passions and appetites, for sex as for food, were kept under strict control; temperance ruled all behaviours.[18]

A second important event connected Socrates further with the divinities. One of his disciples asked the Delphic oracle if anyone was wiser than Socrates, and the Pythia replied that there was no one. Socrates was shocked, "What can this god mean? What is his riddle? I know very well that I am not the least bit wise" (*Apol.* 21b). However one may look at this event, Socrates regarded it as the turning point of his life. His mission then became to discover, through a tireless interrogation of Athenians, whether any of them was wiser than he. While denying the role of a teacher, he preferred to include his friends as companions in his investigation, emphasizing the importance of self-knowledge and not supposing that one knows what one does not. Aristotle states that "it was the practice of Socrates to ask questions but not to give answers, for he confessed that he did not know" (*Soph. el.* 183b6–8). In Plato's *Theaetetus*, Socrates says, "I am so far like the midwife, that I cannot give birth to wisdom; and the common reproach is true, that though I question others, I can myself bring nothing to light because there is no wisdom in me" (*Theaet.* 150c-d). The metaphors of midwifery and "matchmaker" – assisting others with the birth that results from the "intercourse of mind with mind" – reveal his mission to serve others as a guide (*Rep.* 490b). By claiming ignorance, he enabled others to clear away their false thoughts and begin a hopeful, "co-operative search" for knowledge. Such a search implies an intellectual humility that is easily mistaken for arrogance, since the true Socratic is convinced of the ignorance not only of himself but of all humankind.[19]

SOCRATES' DEATH IN THE AGORA

When Socrates was young, an oracle promised his father that divine protection would come to Socrates through Zeus Agoraios, the chief god of the Agora (Plutarch, *de genio Socratis* 20). Socrates' belief in his consecrated mission shaped his life's work in the Agora of Athens. Convinced of his ignorance beneath the all-wise god, he fully accepted his role as a midwife or guide for others in search of truth, and expressed his beliefs not only in words but also in his decisions and actions. He freely accepted poverty, the ill will from his many opponents, and the discipline required for his training. Socrates even confessed that he married his shrewish wife not for love, but for the opportunity to tame her – as practice for the Agora debates (*Symp.* 2.10).

His religious vocation led him out into the political realm. In this way Socrates could have seen himself as a *wanax* figure – combining the religious gravity of the *basileus* with the ethical/political authority of the *arche*. Indeed, he once called himself the only true statesman (*Apol.* 31e). More important, however, Socrates accepted the sacrificial responsibilities that bound a *wanax* to his office: the ritual "ordeals" that the ancient Cretan Kings underwent for their people. Yet, Socrates surpassed that role in one respect – he resigned himself to a death sentence in accordance with his divine calling. The power of this acceptance has reverberated throughout history: once again a victim offered itself for capture and sacrifice by others. The gods have fed the people.

Indeed, the circumstances of Socrates' death, in 399 B.C.E., only serve to reinforce its deep connections to the most ancient rites of sacrifice. Judicial proceedings against Socrates took place in the Royal Stoa, where the *basileus* administered his religious responsibilities. In this case, Socrates appeared before the *King Basileus* and a jury of 500 on charges of impiety. Not only did Socrates challenge the state religion by following his "voices," but the rapid spread of his philosophy posed an insurmountable threat to the politics of the day – necessitating his removal from Athens.[20] When asked why he prepared no defence for the trial, Socrates replied, "Do I not seem to you to have been practicing for this throughout my life?" (Xeno. *Recoll.* 8.2). After the jury proposed death as his penalty, Socrates did not plead for banishment as someone who is guilty, but to be granted free meals in the Agora's Prytaneion (*Apol.* 36d). It is with this confidence that Socrates resigned himself to death in the ancient sacrificial precinct of the Agora. Indeed, when the opportunity to escape prison was presented to Socrates by Crito, even this he refused.

His sentence was delayed because of a city-wide proclamation for a period of ritual purity. He took this opportunity to discuss death and immortality with his friends – that is, to clarify or "purify" the final aspects of his thought. He solidified his belief that good would never be ignored by the gods, and to obey a divine call to death was, for Socrates, to do good. In the *Phaedo*, he proposed the immortality of the soul because it can perceive truth, goodness, and beauty, which are eternal (114d-e).[21] Humans can know god because they have in them something akin to the eternal which cannot die. Therefore, there is no reason to fear death, since the virtuous soul does not die but is absorbed into god, the supreme Mind and ever-renewing life (*Apol.* 40).[22]

Calm and steadfast to the end, Socrates then carried out two important symbolic acts. First, he volunteered to bathe himself, in contrast to the regular procedure of bathing the body after execution (*Phaedo* 116b). This seems to refer to the ancient practice of washing the sacrificial victim – a familiar custom since it was still being practised in Greece. Second, he refused to eat the customary "last meal," despite the urging of his friends (*Phaedo* 116e). This could be seen as a further purification through fasting, but it would make more sense for a "life-giving" meal to take place after the sacrifice. As the hemlock began to take effect, he laid himself out, as if upon an altar, and amidst the wailing of his friends, asked Crito to sacrifice a cock to Asclepius (*Phaedo*, 118). It was the Greek custom to make an offering to the divine healer after recovering from an illness. In his own eyes, Socrates was recovering rather than dying, entering into a "life more abundantly" and offering a final thanksgiving to the gods (fig. 1.6).

In pre-historic times, any new creation, any new music or building, required a ritual killing at its birth. "A house, a bridge, a dam will stay strong only if something lies slaughtered beneath it."[23] Thereafter, if the cult commemorated the original sacrifice (by repeating a ritual on that same spot, for instance), the tradition would retain its awesome, divine power. Socrates must have recognized the undercurrent of cynicism rising against the practice of sacrifice, as well as the more overt demythologizing of the gods. Instead he chose to believe in his god so fully that he would claim ignorance, undergo poverty, discipline, purification, and false charges – all in preparation to become a truly willing victim. He understood that the degree to which he entrusted his body to sacrifice is the degree to which meaningful existence could be sustained not only within the ancient configuration of the Agora but within the *polis* as a whole.

NOTES

1 Walter Burkert, *Homo Necans: The Anthropology of Ancient Greek Sacrificial Ritual and Myth.* (Berkeley: University of California Press 1983), 3.
2 Ibid., 5.
3 Ibid., 40.
4 While I propose to examine Socrates' symbolic participation in his locality, the debt that early Western philosophy owes to architecture in general has been successfully described by Indra Kagis McEwen. See *Socrates' Ancestor: An Essay on Architectural Beginnings* (Cambridge, MA: MIT Press 1993).
5 Mircea Eliade, *Cosmos and History: The Myth of the Eternal Return* (New York: Harper 1959), 12–17; Henri Frankfort et al., *Before Philosophy: The Intellectual Adventure of Ancient Man* (Harmondsworth, Middlesex: Penguin 1951), 30.
6 Burkert, *Homo Necans*, 3–6.

1.6 *The Death of Socrates* by David, 1787; The Metropolitan Museum of Art, New York. Reprinted in Barry S. Gower and Michael C. Stokes, eds., *Socratic Questions* (New York: Routledge 1992), fig. 6.1.

7 George Hersey, *The Lost Meaning of Classical Architecture* (Cambridge, MA: MIT Press 1988), 11–45.

8 Burkert, *Homo Necans*, 17.

9 Jean-Pierre Vernant, *The Origins of Greek Thought* (Ithaca: Cornell University Press 1982), 15–17.

10 Ibid., 29–30.

11 Ibid., 41–2.

12 Ibid., 47.

13 Vincent Scully, *The Earth, the Temple, and the Gods: Greek Sacred Architecture* (New Haven: Yale University Press 1962), 13; Walter J. Graham, "The Central Court as the Minoan Bull-Ring," *American Journal of Archeology* 61 (1957): 255–62.

14 John M. Camp, *The Athenian Agora: Excavations in the Heart of Classical Athens* (New York: Thames and Hudson 1986), 23.

15 Ibid., 38. On the origin of the *polis* see McEwen, *Socrates*, 79–89, and

Alberto Pérez-Gómez, "The City as a Paradigm of Symbolic Order," in *Carleton Book: Architectural Research by Faculty and Recent Graduates of Carleton University School of Architecture*, ed. Katsuhiko Muramoto and Stephen Parcell (Ottawa: Carleton University, School of Architecture 1986), 5–18.

16 On *episteme*, see Bruno Snell, *The Discovery of the Mind: Greek Origins of European Thought* (New York: Harper & Row 1960), 136–85.

17 W.K.C. Guthrie, *Socrates* (London: Cambridge University Press 1971), 163; E.R. Dodds, *The Greeks and the Irrational* (Berkeley: University of California Press 1966), 93.

18 Dodds, *Greeks*, 64–76.

19 Guthrie, *Socrates*, 129.

20 Ibid., 63.

21 Concerning the *Phaedo*, Nicole Loraux presents an interesting argument for Plato's textual presentation of Socrates' body as a metaphor for a discourse on immortality. For Plato, the ideal philosopher such as Socrates engages in *melete thanatou*, an archaic shamanistic "practice of death," in order to separate the soul from the body. See "Therefore, Socrates is Immortal" in *Fragments for a History of the Human Body* 2, ed. Michel Feher (New York: Urzone; Harvard University Press 1989), 13–45.

22 See Guthrie's argument for Socrates' belief in immortality, 153–64.

23 Burkert, *Homo Necans*, 39.

On the Use of Architecture: The Destination of Buildings Revisited

Lily H. Chi

Chora

THE DEMISE OF FUNCTIONALISM as a normative doctrine in architecture has long been a matter of common opinion, and yet is still difficult to speak of the "use" of architecture without being seized by one or the other side of an old polemic: the argument between utility and poetry, necessity and art. It would seem timely, in our exciting/bewildering context of endless possibilities and positions, to give some thought to this area of the mundane.

The belief that the use of a building and its expression in built form should be a central concern of architects emerged relatively recently in Western history. While for Vitruvius, *utilitas* comprised but one branch of architectural work collinear with *venustas* and *firmitas*, the *destination* or *purpose* of a building became increasingly the focus of debates on architectural principles and form during the eighteenth century. By the end of the century, the tenet "An edifice should present a character fitting to its destination" had become a common trope in architectural treatises. The expression communicates to us a familiar enough intent: to regulate form and ornament to purpose or programme. Beyond this general intent, however, lay starkly different attitudes about the use of a building, about what and how architectural form expresses, and about how "fitness" is judged.

It is instructive that the use of buildings should become a topic of critical interest for architects at a time of great turmoil in Europe's urban and political landscape. That the topic might be conceived at variance from the idea that Form follows Function suggests ever more acutely that the use of architecture might be considered not as a transcendent concept (as in, for example, the proposition that "function" is what distinguishes architecture from sculpture) but as a *historical construction*. That is, the various ways in which the use of architecture is named and discussed throughout history might not be homologous, but suggestive of different ways of conceiving the inhabitation of buildings.

My interest in revisiting these earlier ideas of architectural use derives from two observations. The first is the aforementioned suspicion that, despite much exciting exploration in recent architectural work and pedagogy, the use of architecture remains strangely obfuscated behind restrictive and unquestioned associations. The provocative play of similarity and difference between the concerns of eighteenth-century architects and those of contemporary culture will prove fruitful for defamiliarizing what often seems self-evident. The second observation is borrowed from a prominent nineteenth-century architectural pedagogue who suggested that the issue of use is tied intimately to the question of the public domain in modern culture: that is, to the question of the extent and limits of modern architecture's "legibility." Quatremère de Quincy's reflections in this area suggest that the use of architecture remains pertinent not only to architectural practice, but also to architectural thinking. The work of historical reflection here is thus also a thought experiment, "an exercise of oneself." As Michel Foucault put it, "The object [is] to learn to what extent the effort to think one's own history can free liberate thought from what it silently thinks, and so enable it to think differently."[1]

Drawing upon the discourse concerning architectural character in eighteenth-century France, I will discuss four traits in the thinking of architectural use at that time in order to reflect upon our own practices in this area. The first is the relationship intimated by Quatremère de Quincy between use and modern public space; the second concerns the tendency towards comprehensive, rather than specific, designations for the use or programme of architecture; the third, the meanings of the idea of *caractère* and the implications of its appropriation in architectural theory; and finally, the limits of the "characterization" of architectural use which distinguish it from the emergent idea of *utilité* in the early nineteenth century. The emphasis will be placed not on how buildings have been used and/or designed, but on how the use of architecture was broached and made into a critical topic – and what this may imply in defining a field of practice.

QUATREMÈRE DE QUINCY ON USE AND MODERNITY

A remarkable observation on the cultural conditions of modern architectural work can be found in an 1832 architectural dictionary – remarkable because the assertions of its author, Antoine Chrysostôme Quatremère de Quincy, might well be made in the late twentieth century.[2] In this, his second essay on architectural character, Quatremère reflects on the expressive capacity of architecture in his time. He avers that it is folly to expect contemporary architecture to achieve the moral and physical force so admired in the architecture of antiquity. Equally folly is the pretension to originality in architectural expression. This last remark is particularly curious, as we live in the wake of Romantic and

2.1 Jean Jacques Lequeu, design for a cowshed from *L'Architecture civile* (bequeathed to Bibliothèque Royale, 1825). From Philippe Duboy, *Lequeu: An Architectural Enigma* (Cambridge, Mass.: MIT Press 1987); copyright, Thames and Hudson, 1986.

avant-garde movements for which creativity *is* originality. For Quatremère, however, expression is an issue of reception as much as intention. As impact or effect, expression relies not only on the architect, but also on the cultural and historical situation of architecture. In Quatremère's estimation, grandeur and originality belong to the vigour and vitality of sentiment in humanity's youth – that state of simplicity which human reason/will cannot resuscitate. Hence, these two qualities are "historical"; reflection can seek a better understanding of them, but they cannot lead to a "didactic theory."

In this picture of an aging, diluted culture, simplicity has no place because it would not sate the taste for novelty. Similarly, an ambition to achieve distinctiveness or originality in this "prolonged age of art" would be merely polemical; apart from "accidental" occurrences of genius, such vainglory would produce only "caricatures." What *is* within the province and responsibility of the contemporary architect is the legibility of each building's *destination*, its use.

Quatremère's essay is both a poignant expression of the brooding melancholy of the end of the eighteenth century and a prophetic statement of things to come. In his writings, as in those of many others who lived through the French Revolution, the world had aged immeasurably through the excesses and apparent irrationality of events at the turn of the century. The heroic image of human reason and action seemed to have been irrevocably tarnished in the process, and was supplanted by a palpable anxiety over the apparent relativism in all matters moral and artistic. Quatremère revisits here a popular eighteenth-century precept on architectural expression: the notion that a building should present a character appropriate to its purpose or destination. However, the subtle anxiety that underlay earlier expressions of this tenet is spelled out lucidly by Quatremère in an extraordinary observation: the domain of shared experience on which architectural expression relies has contracted to the immediate issue of use.

For a contemporary reader, this is a striking observation because it describes quite accurately the public geography of the later nineteenth and twentieth centuries. The world-in-common *has* become most comprehensively the world-at-hand, the world of everyday affairs and exchanges, whether one choses to describe it through sociological epistemologies such as utilitarianism, or through existential problematics such as Heidegger's polemic between "worldless instrument" and "worldly tool."

Quatremère's pessimism about the public site of architectural work in his own time would certainly find sympathy today. In a sense, the circumstances which made the Functionalist analogy such an attractive "solution" to the quest for authentic architectural form continue to describe contemporary experience. The use of architecture seems to be pertinent still – not only to architectural practice, but also to architectural reflection.

A question remains: *how* does this common world come to be described and inscribed in architectural work?

CHARACTERIZATIONS OF ARCHITECTURAL USE

Prior to the late nineteenth century, there was no single word for architectural use with the same force and universality that the word "function" would later command. The French term *fonction* was rarely used in architecture until the nineteenth century, and certainly not consistently until Auguste Comte made commonplace the biological analogy for the systemic study of societies. Jaques-François Blondel – that famous teacher of Ledoux, Boullée, and other prominent eighteenth-century architects – used many different terms in his *Cours d'Architecture* to refer to the use of a building. The word *fonction* appears at one point to refer to a concern about the presentation of a building: "The *function* of the pedestal in a [one-storey] building ... is not only to protect the first [level] from the humility of the ground, but also to expose advantageously a work whose art is so obligingly revealed."[3] What *fonction* may have meant to Blondel seems to approach what another architect said about it a few decades later. Francesco Milizia's theory of expression (translated into French around 1792) was already a paradigmatic world away from Blondel's, as he polemically and stridently advised architects to restrict architectural form to what can stand up to "the evidence of *necessity.*" Yet note the meaning of *fonction* in this passage: "It should be demanded of each room, you there, who are you? What do you do there? How are you fulfilling your *office*? Are you contributing something there to commodiousness? solidity? Do you fulfill your *functions* better than any other in your place?"[4] *Function* here cannot be understood in the light of mechanical or biological processes, but as Marco Frascari has pointed out, referred to a world in which the term still commonly indicated an *office* – a socio-political role. Thus, while rooms *ought* to fulfill their functions, this was conceived in the framework of a moral obligation, a duty – which is entirely different from the directive of a mechanistic analogy. The one intends a *deterministic* relation between two ahistorical, objective entities; the other is far more ambiguous.

Beyond this exchange, the terms and meanings for architectural use multiplied in number and density. J.-F. Blondel used the term *usage* interchangeably with *destination* to speak of the ultimate reference of all architectural expression or ordonnance: "All the different kinds of productions which belong to architecture, in having to carry the imprint of the particular *destination* of each edifice, should have a character which determines their general form and announces the building for what it is."[5] *Destination* was the most common eighteenth-century term for "intended use" in both England and France. The active tenor of this word is reflected in the common use of its verb form. Viel de Saint-Maux, in a treatise which proclaimed the "liturgical," ritual origins of architecture, rarely used the noun form at all.[6] The word *programme* existed in the eighteenth century, but again was scarcely used until the end of the century. J.-F. Blondel placed the term within a strictly pedagogical context by defining it as "the detailed statement of a project which a professor gives to his students to make them understand his intentions and the course which they should follow, in order to guide them to the appropriate expression for each *genre* of building."[7] For Blondel, *programme* was a more didactic, streamlined – that is, *already directed* – reference to the use of a building, in contrast to the apparently more neutral *destination*.

By the end of the French Revolution, *programme* had become a more common architectural term. J.-A. Coussin, writing two decades into the nineteenth century, still made use of the common eighteenth-century trope to proclaim that a building should be "above all, instructive," that it should "convey the *character* appropriate to its *subject*" and "move the spectator according to the aim that the *programme* proposes."[8] Note, first of all, the interchangeability of *caractère, programme,* and *sujet. Programme* was beginning to supplant *destination* as a more profession-specific term (while the latter continued to be used with respect to other art forms[9]), but it had not yet acquired the twentieth-century connotation as a pre-design document, a science and methodology in its own right. For Coussin and his contemporaries, *programme* meant something more like "subject matter," and was used interchangeably with *sujet* or *motif*. The use of a building was its theme.

But a theme for what? The second part of Coussin's statement echoes its predecessors in advocating that the building/character should *move the spectator* according to the aim of the programme. As a concept of architectural expression, *caractère* was more than a matter of formal composition: it had pathic intent. Throughout the century-long period in which architectural character was topical, accounts varied as to *how* and *what* architectural form evokes and provokes, yet all architects seemed to presume one consideration: the presence of a *spectateur* as sentient body and moral actor.

DRAMATIZATIONS

The term *caractère* played no small part in this commingling of questions concerning architectural expression with those concerning physiological and moral human being. Throughout its history as a trope, *caractère* consistently involved an inquiry of visible signs, impressions, types, or emblems as manifest faces of hidden conditions; and, at the same time, an inquiry of the moral realm, the workings of the soul, and the passions as pathic states.

"Character" writing was a popular seventeenth-century literary genre: a form of moral portraiture, described by some as an antecedent of the nineteenth-century novel. Its model at that time was a translation of Theophrastus' *Characters*, a late fourth-century work by a student of Aristotle. Thought to be part of a lost treatise on ethics, the *Characters* was a collection of the vices and virtues personified, and reflected the philosophy of ethics, rhetoric, and poetics which framed Aristotle's own presentation of character and characterization. This grounding of characterization in moral teaching was maintained in the Roman treatises on rhetoric, and passed on to Renaissance Europe through monastic and humanist pedagogy. In the seventeenth and early eighteenth centuries, the Aristotelian concept of moral character was challenged first by Renée Descartes' mechanistic model of the passions; and then by John Locke's epistemology, with its emphasis on the role of the senses in the formation of the self. Drawn into such divergent and competing discourses, the notion of *caractère* became the nexus of a complex of inquiries in the eighteenth-century: from physiognomy and anatomy to language and classification theories; from theatrical treatises to tracts on *les mœurs* (a budding social anthropology) to morals and morality, and political theory. It was, moreover, a common stand-in for Vitruvius' Orders and for Serlio's theatrical genres in treatises on architecture and gardening.

This made for a rich, complex, and intricate fabric of inquiries, intentions and meanings upon which ideas of architectural use and its expression were drawn. Up to and during the decades following the French Revolution, profession-specific terms such as *usage* or *programme* invoked this site which, for architects, was alight with the recognition that architecture exhibits *actors*.

Our edifices, above all the public edifices, should be, in some facet, poems. The

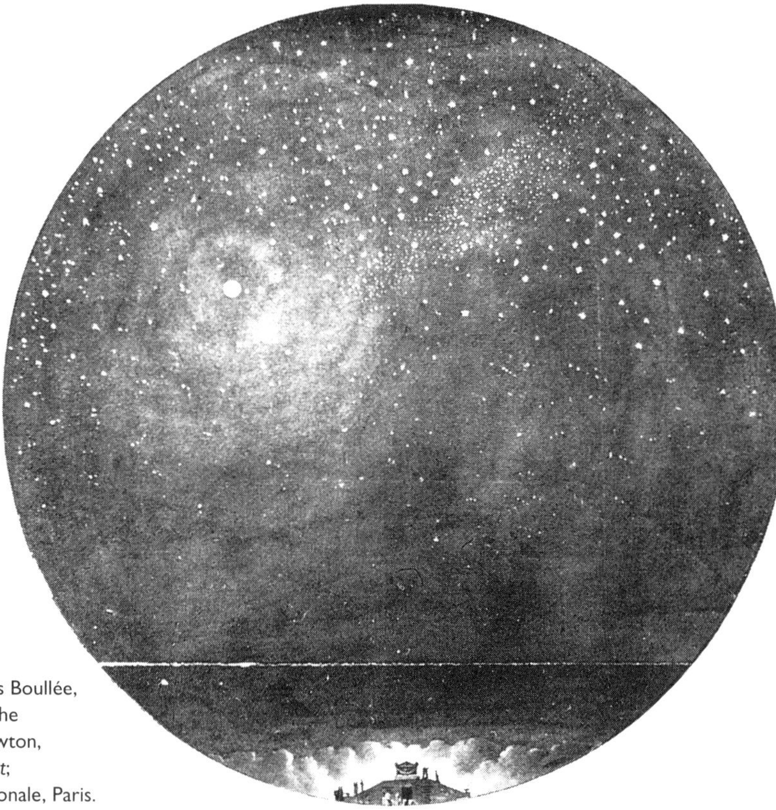

2.2 Étienne-Louis Boullée, interior view of the Cenotaph to Newton, from *Essai sur l'art*; Bibliothèque nationale, Paris.

images which they offer to our senses should excite in us sentiments analogous to the usage to which these edifices are consecrated ...

I do not know whether the architects of our modern temples had these thoughts in mind ... Does their art go so far as to induce a sense of veneration at the mere sight of their Temples? Are we afraid of desecrating them by recklessly setting foot there? Do they inspire the profound respect that results from religious belief? Do they have that quality of grandeur belonging to genius that surges forth and imposes itself on the onlooker, filling him with astonishment and wonder? Is the general impression that they surpass human capacities and are ... inconceivable? And, finally, have all the resources that nature has to offer art been tapped to endow the subject with the majesty it calls for? Such were my first thoughts on Temples.[10]

In Etienne-Louis Boullée's *Essai sur l'art*, the elaboration of architectural use became explicitly a work of *mise-en-scène*. Aided by the sensorial epistemology of Locke and Condillac, Boullée made of the architect a magus of cosmic *images*, a *metteur en œuvre de Nature*.[11] With knowledge of how regular geometries affect us sensually, the architect is able to produce the very sensations aroused by the most inspiring phenomena of nature. As his famous description of the Cenotaph to Newton demonstrated so remarkably, the work of architecture became effectively a choreography of nature's panorama opened up within a microcosmic, sensual site: the human body. Architecture had a dual responsibility in celebrating the spectacle of a magnificent universe, and in positioning at its centre: the *spectateur* as privileged witness-actor. The Cenotaph is but one famous example in a treatise which aimed not only to explain how architecture could be sensually profound, but also to illustrate this in detail – to define the images, or *caractères*, of the most important institutions of his time. Boullée seemed to find issue not with the programmes themselves, but with the muteness of their expression in the work of his contemporaries. Finding the key to sonority in the poetry of sensorial images, Boullée remade Paris' major institutions in words and images. The programmes became *sujets* which Boullée elaborated in metaphoric and allegorical depth before proceeding with his own architectural illustrations. To elaborate the meaning of a Palace of Justice, for example, Boullée suggested juxtaposing it with a prison: "It seemed to me that if I placed this august Palace above the shadowy lair of Crime, I should not only show to advantage the nobility of the architecture on account of the resultant contrast, but I should also have an impressive metaphorical image of Vice overwhelmed by the weight of Justice."[12]

In another example, Boullée sought out an appropriate si[gh]ting for the Palace of the Sovereign – one which would present a spectacle of immensity and inspire admiration – by developing the character of its surrounding wall into a small city formed by Palaces of the Princes. This reference to a wall being constituted by the people whose community it makes is repeated later in the treatise and recalls a long-standing tradition that Boullée himself did not discuss. The boundary of the *polis*, and later of the Roman *urbs*, was defined not only by the making of a physical barrier, but in the legislative acts which thereby defined a community – a body politic.[13] Architecture served to secure the spatial and temporal enduring of the playing field thus opened up between the inhabitants. Boullée's strategies for scenic effect reflected something of this sensibility. In the example above, and in others, he seemed to suggest that architectural expression was not just a matter of formal composition, despite elaborate theorizing on the evocative power of regular forms. The significance of places was gleaned from their being used, from the fabric of meanings which constituted their socio-political setting.

Boullée wrote at the end of the eighteenth century, already distant from the first authors who mused upon the idea of "characteristic expression." For Germain Boffrand, writing in 1749, there was no need to discourse upon how *caractère* works, no need to reiterate the meaning of certain institutions in narrative terms. Boffrand's *Livre d'architecture* conjured up a very different sort of spectacle. In Boullée, a silent, infinite universe played host to the institutions of Man through breath-taking imagery and illusionistic movement orchestrated for a lone spectator. If this experience seems more analogous to film than to theatre, Boffrand's world was more like a masked ball, a *comédie* of manners:

> Architecture, while seeming to have as its object the employment of material things, is subject to different genres which animate its parts [according] to the different *caractères* that it makes felt. An edifice, through its composition, expresses as in Theater whether the *scene* is Pastoral or Tragic, whether it is Temple or a Palace, a public edifice destined for a certain usage, or a private house. These different edifices, through their disposition, through their structure, through the manner in which they are ornamented, should announce to the spectator their destination; and if they do not do this, they offend expression, and are not what they should be.[14]

Boffrand's theatrical reference is significant because it suggests that, for him, architectural legibility did not rely on *innate* feeling. In contrast to the sensorialists' theory of correspondence between exterior visuality and interior sensation, expressiveness is accomplished instead through manifest signs and marks which are recognizable to everyone within an assumed language community. In Boffrand, this compendium of marks is given by the characteristic traits of the three Orders, which are akin to three *genres* of drama from which the architect must elaborate an expression appropriate to the use of a building. This notion of *appropriate* measure – as opposed to essential or exact correspondence – is key. It is not authenticity with respect to a hidden depth that measures the architect's success, but decorum to circumstance. This in turn requires the most exquisitely discerning sense of judgment – that which only instruction, knowledge of the world of manners and customs, can provide. Architecture, like dress and contemporary theatre, becomes the

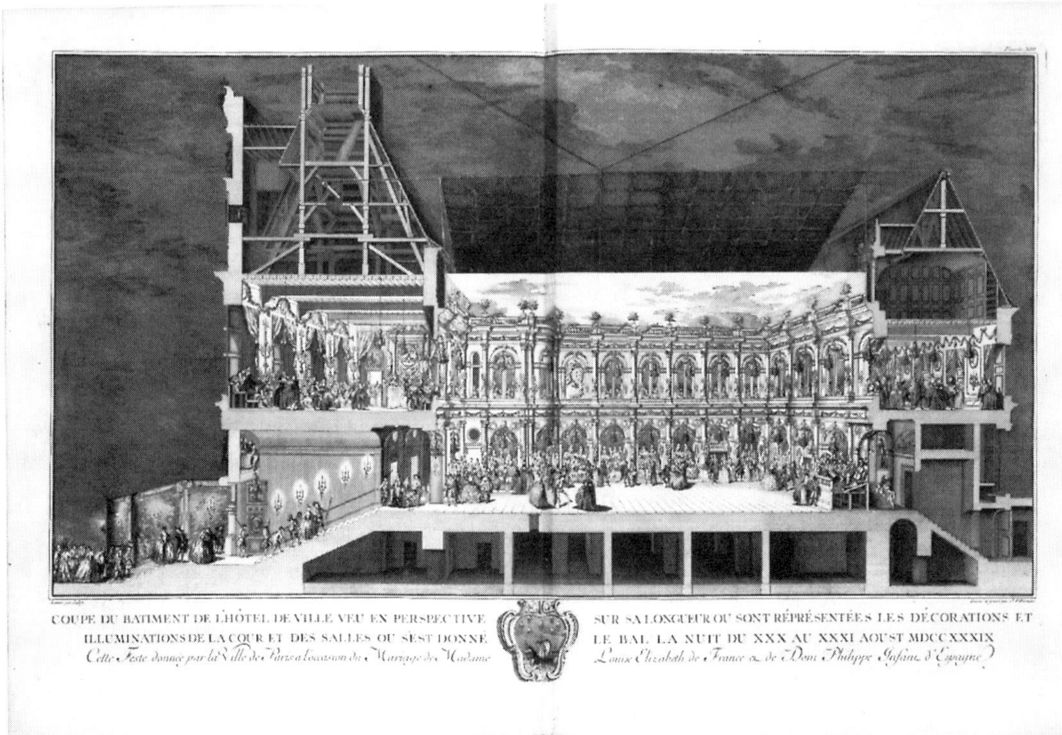

2.3 Royal marriage ball at the Hôtel de Ville, drawn and engraved by Jacques-François Blondel for his *Description des Festes données par la Ville de Paris* … (1740); Copyright Board of Trustees, National Gallery of Art, Washington, D.C.

playing-out of topical roles and situations.[15] In this still-Aristotelian social world, conventions – whether in manners or in ornamental genres – continued to carry public meaning in the staging of certain model comportments or virtues. The fact that this world was beginning to disintegrate – that for several decades, philosophers had been decrying and promising repair for this severance of appearance and essence, of bodily action and passion of soul – did not immediately empty the gestures and signs of their meaning.

At the close of the eighteenth century, architects could no longer assume such common, meaningful *topoi*. Boullée's rewriting of Paris' monuments reflected the prevalent concern that the three tropes of classical expression – in theatre as in architecture – were no longer adequate sites for the stories that were to be told. Claude-Nicholas Ledoux's treatise/programme/narrative epitomized this state of affairs.

LIMITS OF THE THEATRICAL PARADIGM

From Boffrand to Boullée and Ledoux, the articulation of architectural use changed noticeably. Boffrand invoked a richly populated world of competing desires and divergent tastes; Ledoux's ideal listener-actor was a solitary wanderer on a long journey. For Boffrand, architectural space found an analogy on the theatrical stage; for Ledoux, it was a literary page. Furthermore, if the three Orders sufficed as model plots for Boffrand, for architects after him, such plots must be unearthed (Viel de Saint-Maux), retold (Boullée), or foretold (Ledoux). Yet, in that they all relied on the term *caractère* to articulate their expressive theories, these architects continued to presume what I would call a *theatrical* concept of architectural use.

It was "theatrical" because the route from programme to expression involved analogy, metaphor, and especially, narration. In justifying their proposals for a particular character or expression, the authors relied consistently on scenographic references – whether borrowed or invented. In presenting their own designs this way, the architects offered up dramatic scenarios – stages of a sort – which they justified by referring to the actors and/or stories to be made visible thereupon.

By the early nineteenth century, not all architects would agree with Ledoux, Coussin, or Quatremère de Quincy about either architectural character or its concern for and *approach* to expression. A paradigmatic shift was taking place in the concept of architectural use and its relation to form. The emerging paradigm of "utility" retrospectively highlights two traits in the earlier theories of character – concerns which later writers seemed to consider unimportant.

The first trait is the assumption that *more than one expression* is possible for a given architectural programme, and that the issue for architects is how to make an *appropriate* choice. For Boffrand, a fortuitously ambiguous eighteenth-century notion of taste aided the architect in the choice between three *genres* of dramatic setting, whereas Le Camus de Mézières[16] and Boullée sought out painterly, narrative evocation to render mood and atmosphere. And while for Le Camus, the three Orders served as springboards for mythological and erotic inspiration, for Boullée, the four seasons emerged as expressive sites for architecture on a celestial scale. This demand for such "fine tuning" as only cultural etiquette could define, or for scenographic richness which only narration

2.4 Above: Jean-Jacques Lequeu, "Public house at the entrance to an admirable little forest," *Architecture civile*. From Duboy, *Lequeu*.

2.5 Opposite: Lequeu, "Public house," detail.

could render, highlights the emphasis on *particular circumstance* in their approaches to programmatic expression.

Such ambiguity and circuitousness became intolerable for some architectural pedagogues in the early nineteenth century. For L.P. Baltard, Professor of theory at the Ecole nationale supérieure des beaux-arts from 1818, a proper understanding of *utilité positive* – architecture's *raison*, the basis of its principles – makes the issue of diverse styles irrelevant.[17] History's panorama of varying forms puzzled him: "It is inconceivable as to how there can exist such remarkable differences among the forms, colours, and degrees of ornamentation of *objects of the same nature, consecrated to the same usages*, in times more or less distant from us."[18] Baltard concluded that this ignorance of "the laws of taste" must be caused by the imposition of moral and political institutions which either lacked the guidance of Genius, or were indifferent to its inspiration. Social institutions and custom are thus irrelevant influences hindering the arrival of the ultimate forms sanctioned by reason and nature:

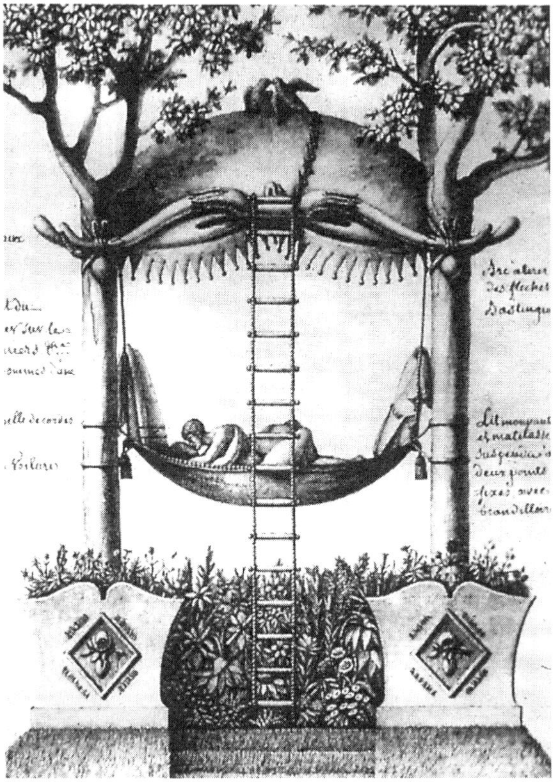

"Nothing is good but that which has the property of being useful, and there can be no beauty but in what is natural."[19] Baltard's ahistorical and acultural notion of *utilité* marks the dawn of a new concept of architectural use – a concept not far from the aspiring determinism of "Form follows Function."

The second distinguishing trait of character discourse is its foremost preoccupation with the question of *expression* – with the possibility of architectural eloquence, physiognomy, and/or legibility. As noted above it is not likely by accident that eighteenth-century architects came to adopt this term – itself a tradition of inquiry into impression and expression – to deal with their own version of relativism. In other words, the use of a building emerged as a critical topic in response to a crisis about architecture's "legibility." In the process, the use of architecture assumed *expressive* power.

By the second decade of the nineteenth century, this concern for expression was displaced by new formulations of architectural technique. Jean-Nicholas-Louis Durand, a professor at the École polytechnique, dismissed the preoccupation with *caractère* as a non-issue. The deterministic relation between architectural use and form hinted at by Baltard was made explicit by Durand in an 1813 work: "If one disposes an edifice in a manner fitting to the usage to which one destines it, will that not perceptively differentiate it from another edifice destined for another usage? Will it not naturally have a character and, furthermore, its own character?"[20] In pointing to what he saw as a redundancy in the *caractère*-use formulation, Durand was effectively excising the whole issue of expression and physiognomy from the realm of architectural design. There would be no need to worry about expression if one attends well to a building's use through the economy of composition offered in his teachings. The use of architecture could thus be conceived as a matter of formal composition without socio-political implications.

CONCLUSION: BEYOND FUNCTIONALISM?

The eighteenth-century's musings on the social origins and political contributions of architecture were, however, not entirely forgotten. Ironically, their potential was best understood not by architects at first but by social reformers such as Jeremy Bentham. Ironic because, appropriated for the purposes of social construction, architectural use in the Utilitarian model became insidious. It was to be effective by being decidedly *un*spectacular: a display of bodies divorced from the self-revelation of actors.

It is not necessary to repeat the critiques with which we are all familiar: the intrinsic ambiguities and contradictions masked by Functionalism's simple analogy of correspondence and determinism; the ahistoricality of a scientific pretension which proved even more untenable in fact than in theory.

More topical today are the politics of the Utilitarian concept of use underlying functionalism as a sociology. Hannah Arendt's post-war critique of the depoliticization of human affairs endemic to traditional tyrannies, as well as to twentieth-century "mass politics," suggested that functionalism was but one expression of a more global *leitmotif* in the modern age: the enframing human action within an ahistorical "process" analogy. In the same vein, and more well known today, is Michel Foucault's critique of panopticism – a term which he extends to describe

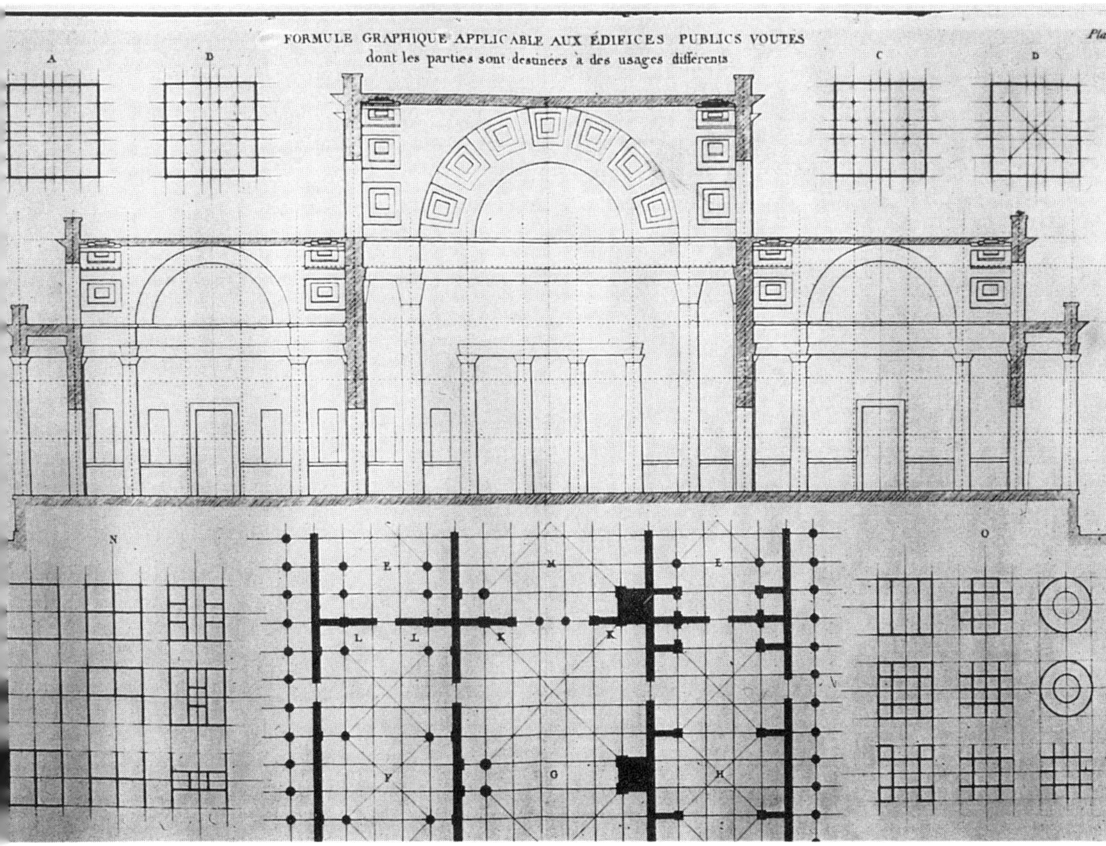

2.6 Jean-Louis-Nicholas Durand, "Formule graphique applicable aux édifices publics voutés…"; *Nouveau Précis* 1813.

not only Jeremy Bentham's model prison but a pervasive phenomenon in modern culture. Bentham's disciplinary model was an architectural machine: architectural space put to work as a strategy of surveillance. For Foucault, what makes panopticism distinct as a uniquely modern enforcement of non-reciprocal power relations is the *invisibility* of that power. Through Bentham, Foucault drew attention not only to the political dynamics which architectural space sets up, but also to the explicitly non-visual strategies which Utilitarianism has contributed to modern concepts of planning.[21]

The observations offered by Foucault and Arendt, among others, suggest that modern architectural work, understood as a configuration of human relations as well as spaces and forms, can operate in theory and practice like the proverbial two-sided coin. On the one hand, the

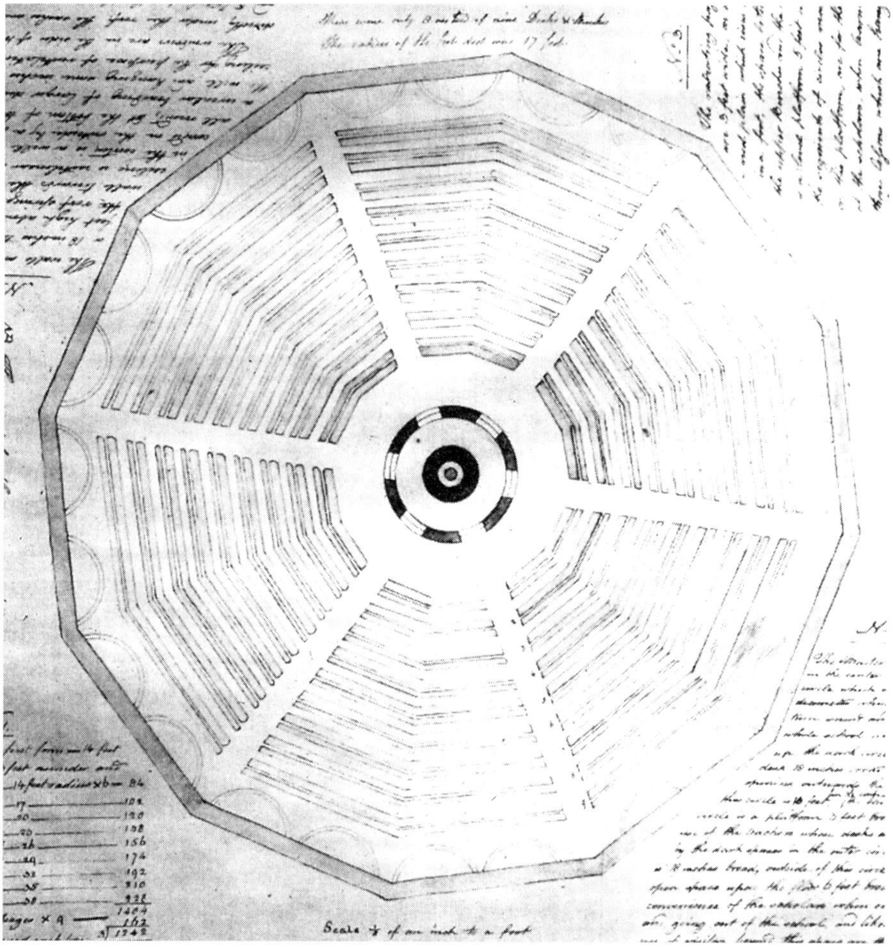

2.7 Jeremy Bentham, Chrestomathic Schoolhouse (1816), from Robin Evans, *The Fabrication of Virtue* (Cambridge: Cambridge University Press 1982).

planning and programming of social habitats are "predesign" problematics. On the other hand, the terms which architects have inherited from nineteenth-century sociology to refer to the inhabitation and use of architecture – terms such "function," "programme," and "use" itself – are cleansed of specific political or moral reference. Thus when architectural work becomes officially the representation of "function," it is not just "form" which is *deceptively* "value-free"; the thinking of architecture itself inherits a vast critical blindspot.

Today, the questioning and dismantling of modernist epistemologies such as functionalism are commonplace in architecture. In the main, the critique of modernism has focused on its representational framework: the logocentric geometry, the assumption of linear methodology and end-product, the reification of theory and practice, the hegemonic and reductive systemic thinking, etc. Recent experimentation with different strategies of working can be seen in some cases as an attempt to rediscover modes of inhabitation exempted from the concept of function. Insofar as the focus has been on the epistemology of representation, however, there remains a disturbing tendency to reduce the problem to *forms* of representation, to polemics which perpetuate in new guise the old divide between utility and poetics.

Regardless of how it is conceived, the use of architecture remains a site of modern communality. To go "beyond" Functionalism however, it would seem necessary to confront that heritage in an effort to demystify what has become a ubiquitous, remnant divide without a name. The idea of a building's *destination* giving way to architectural and human characters is helpful in offering a vision of architecture's being used as visible, sonorous spectacle – one open to both celebration and questioning.

2.8 Advertisement for an ideal kitchen, circa 1967.

NOTES

1 Michel Foucault, *History of Sexuality, The Use of Pleasure*, trans. Robert Hurley (New York: Random House 1986), 2: 9.
2 A.-C. Quatremère de Quincy, *Dictionnaire de l'architecture* (Paris 1832), 307. All translations by L. Chi unless otherwise noted.
3 J.-F. Blondel, *Cours d'architecture* (1771–1779), 2: xxxi.
4 F. Milizia, *De l'art de voir dans les beaux-arts* (Paris an 6), 75. Italics added.
5 Blondel, *Cours d'architecture*, 2: 229.
6 Viel de Saint-Maux, *Lettres sur l'architecture* (Paris 1787).
7 Blondel, *Cours d'architecture*, 4: lxxxiv.
8 J.-A. Coussin, *De l'origine de l'architecture* (Paris 1824), 41. Italics added.
9 As in, for instance, Quatremère de Quincy's *Considerations morales sur la destination des ouvrages de l'art...* (Paris 1815).
10 E. Boullée, *Essai sur l'art*, trans. H. Rosenau (London: Alec Tiranti 1953).
11 See, for example, Boullée's astonishing description of light in the Cenotaph to Newton, *Essai*.
12 Boullée, *Essai*.
13 For further discussion on the relation between *nomos*, custom or law, and city-wall, see H. Arendt, *The Human Condition* (New York: Doubleday 1959), J. Rykwert, *The Idea of a Town* (Cambridge, Mass.: MIT Press 1988), D.K. Kelley, *The Human Measure* (Cambridge, Mass.: Harvard University Press 1990), chaps. 1–3.
14 G. Boffrand, *Livre d'architecture* (Paris 1745), 16.
15 See, for example, Riccoboni, *L'art du théâtre* (Paris 1750).
16 Le Camus de Mézières, *Le génie de l'architecture...* (Paris 1780).
17 L.P. Baltard, *Notice sur l'organisation des bâtiments civils...* (Paris n.d.), 5.
18 L.P. Baltard, *Aperçu ou essai sur le bon goût dans les ouvrages d'art et d'architecture* (Paris 1841), 4. Italics added.
19 Baltard, *Aperçu*, 7 and 29.
20 J.-N.-L. Durand, *Nouveau précis*, (Paris 1813), 19.
21 Michel Foucault, *Discipline and Punish*, trans. Alan Sheridan (New York: Vintage Books 1979). See also Paul Rabinow, *French Modern: Norms and forms of the Social Environment* (Cambridge, Mass.: MIT Press 1989).

Hermes' Laugh: Philibert de l'Orme's Imagery as a Case of Analogical Edification

Jean-Pierre Chupin

> It is Hephaïstos, indeed, who causes alterity in the world to be inscribed in Harmony and friendship, and is responsible for the intertwining of all things here below, and doing so they interlace, through demiurgic relations, identity and alterity, harmony and division, communion and vexation. And this is what Apollo laughs about, Hermes laughs, laughs each one of the Gods, and their laughter gives existence to all beings in the world and gives strength to the relations.[1]

IT IS A HISTORICAL FACT, however strange, that architects often associate architectural creation with "divine" venture. From Plato to Vitruvius, and from Philibert de l'Orme to Le Corbusier, there is a recurrent and symbolic set of images that connects the architect's role and the intervention of a demiurge. Although for most historians these images are understood as common metaphors, they are rarely recognized as partaking in an overall analogical framework of thoughts. Beyond religious beliefs or dogmatic standpoints, it is this peculiar way of thinking about architecture called "analogical" that I will be exploring in this paper. Numerous analogies can be compiled in architectural texts; one could certainly imagine an atlas of such examples. However, while it is relatively easy to classify concepts – notions which are by definition "boxes" of meaning – it is more difficult to classify slippery notions such as analogies. In fact, an ambivalence accompanied by a serious lack of logical certitude explains why analogical thinking has an astonishing power to relate things and ideas, places and potentialities: in other words, an almost raging capacity to conjugate alterity. This paper is an hermeneutic and iconological exploration of Philibert de l'Orme's treatises of architecture. After introducing some of the most important emblems of sixteenth-century French symbolism, particularly in regard to a theory of winds and a philosophy of alteration, this essay will present some intertwined significations of analogical edification and their ancient connections to a theory of incorporation.

AN INTRODUCTION TO ANALOGICAL THINKING

Grasping elementary matter

The prevalence of logical and conceptual thinking still makes it difficult for us to imagine ways of designing outside the current scale of values imposed by scientific rationalism. It may be useful to return to the sixteenth century to study clear and genuine examples of creative analogical thinking in architecture. The case of Philibert de l'Orme is perhaps the most exemplary. As a Catholic priest, he could not simply think of himself as the Creator, instead he set his architectural "inventions" under the banner of Hermes-Mercury. To choose such a symbol already indicated an ambivalent theoretical attitude; while Hermes is the Messenger God who reveals divine intentions (and relations) to mortals, he also symbolizes a strong capacity to hermetically conceal any conjunction. Indeed, Philibert de l'Orme's treatises do not fall into the "speculative trend," a category coined by André Chastel referring to Pacioli, Alberti, or Filarete, whose writings anticipate action and give the illusion that practitioners already followed their instructions and recipes.[2] Both *Nouvelles Inventions pour bien bastir et à petits fraiz* (1561) and *Premier Tome de l'Architecture* (1567) are instructive amalgams of intentional "revelations" and "secrets." They were written by a recognized practitioner delivering his thoughts to a larger public, while displaying a characteristic prudence in respect to the reader; an imaginary student encouraged to consult the master whenever necessary.[3]

Today, beyond de l'Orme's prudent words, it is still possible to enter his "philosophical garden." An iconological analysis of the frontispiece which opens *Premier Tome* epitomizes the major emblems of his imagery concerning the art of edification (see fig. 3.1). Balancing the composition of the plate, two characteristic Platonic solids are depicted: an icosahedron and a dodecahedron. Emerging like flames from the top of candelabra, both solids stand not on one side but, curiously, each on one point. They both mirror the armillary sphere and the terrestrial globe that can spin about their respective imaginary axes. As suggested by their display, the regular solids will reveal themselves to be signposts of what could be labelled a qualitative thinking of materiality. Indeed, it would be improper to reduce Platonic solids to mere geometrical formulations often invoked by sixteenth-century artists. De l'Orme gives the regular solids a peculiar role in the invention of his architecture. The Hermetic imagery in his work must therefore be approached through a theory of the four elements (air, fire, earth, and water), the major arcana of pre-Newtonian mentalities.[4] In the Renaissance, regular bodies were clearly related to Elements. The two bodies chosen by de l'Orme are explicitly symbolic: the icosahedron was related to water, and the dodecahedron to air (or the cosmos). These geometric forms are not only emblems of the potential dynamism of matter, they are also symbols of *reciprocity* and *reversibility* , inasmuch as they can inscribe or be inscribed geometrically in any of the other Platonic volumes.[5]

Antoine Mizault was a physician and astrologer whose advice de l'Orme seems to have followed carefully.[6] His annotations in the margins of the *Premier Tome* reveal an emphasis on a cosmological unity inherent in the theory of the four elements.[7] Indeed, de l'Orme still inhabited an animistic universe – more specifically "vitalistic" – as did Paracelsus and Rabelais. For both these Renaissance physicians there was no doubt about the holistic quality of all manifestation, multiplicity being essentially one aspect of this quality.[8] Their attitude toward matter was qualitatively opposed to our common understanding, in which the material substratum is dead when it is not externally animated.[9]

This peculiar display of the icosahedron and dodecahedron among geometrical drawings and other symbolic devices in de l'Orme's frontispiece epitomizes an understanding of architectural invention as a qualitative transformation or transmutation. In a context in which the inanimate world is altogether alive, it is less surprising to accept that architecture, as edification, raises ontological questions of life and death. For this not to remain a simple justification of the architect's demiurgic role – a mere metaphoric device to distinguish it from the role of a master-mason – we must emphasize that in de l'Orme's philosophical context, analogy is not a simple stylistic ornament. Analogical thinking was a metaphysical endeavour, a vertical connection of the elements, best described by Plato in his *Timaeus* as a work of "proportion." To understand de l'Orme's search for "Divine Proportion," it is helpful to review Ficino's commentary on the *Timaeus* through Proclus, the last great systematizer of Greek philosophical traditions. His *Commentary on the Timaeus* was authoritative for most French humanists, from Guillaume Budé to the more obscure Loys le Roy, who gave us the first French translation of the *Timaeus* in 1551.[10] Proclus emphasized Plato's warning about the relationship between proportion and mathematical "precision": "All this Plato himself saw clearly, this is why he added 'as far as possible' (32B5) in order for you not to require the same absolute degree of precision in physical reasonings as in mathematics. Indeed, if you dare examine each of the Elements, you will see how much melting it contains. Air, for instance, is not only subtle, but it also has thickness, brumosity,

3.1 Frontispiece with Hermes/Mercury at the top of the composition; from Philibert de l'Orme, *Premier tome de l'architecture*, Paris, 1567.

moisture ... For it is necessary that the top of the inferior Elements be related to the base of the superior Elements."[11]

Since such a final assertion recalls the famous sentence of the *Emerald Table*, the Bible of Hermetists, it could be tempting to follow this radically alchemical path.[12] But this is not immediately necessary for Proclus gives us more clues to understand proportion in this epistemological framework. Proportion, wrote Proclus, understood in its full etymology, is a general weaving of things, an intertwining, it becomes the vehicle of a qualitative mixture: "Moreover, it must be observed that Plato here assumed and clearly indicated that he meant mediety or geometrical Proportion as we said (cf. op. cit.): The expression anaton auton logon is more particular to this one, this is why some called it analogia in the proper sense."[13]

This definition of proportion as analogy, demands a complete rethinking of the quest for divine proportions and consequently of the question of "body image" in the Renaissance. Analogy as an "agreement of ratios" is more than a mere correspondence; it is an agreement of one thing with another, a likeness of *relations* between elements, forms, bodies, and potentially between beings and gods. Both Philibert de l'Orme and François Rabelais participate in this analogical world in which conceptions of the imagination are all related, are considered to be alive, and all are thus sacred.[14]

This essentially explains why "*quick* silver," analogous embodiment of Hermes' powers, imprudently taken as a miracle remedy (literally in the form of mercury!), was considered to be the epitome of the general instability of things. The world was understood as a great "mixture" in which any inventive work was a mimetic *amalgam*: such a procedure was essential to alchemists, for it made an alloy of mercury with another metal. Amalgamation, on the other hand, was a process which allowed the extraction, with the help of mercury, of gold and silver from their gangue. With this shade of meaning between amalgam and amalgamation, we approach an understanding of mercury as an ambivalent and reversible herald of exegesis and hermeneutics.

For de l'Orme, mathematics was an equally sacred endeavour. In the sixteenth century, numbers had not yet lost their symbolic character and their *analogical* referents.[15] This historical meaning of proportion has been underestimated by some historians. Too eager to found their work on scientific systems of value, they have confronted difficult "contradictions" between ideal models and defective realizations.[16]

Deciphering astrological winds

De l'Orme read Vitruvius and Alberti. In the *Premier tome*, he carefully describes the theory of the four cardinal winds, with some classical advice concerning the orientation of rooms. However, he pretends to be more preoccupied, than these earlier writers, about the inhabitants' health. Consequently he strongly criticizes those who do not base their geometry on the analysis of the "winds."[17] We need to examine how this new approach of the "theory of winds" is reflected in de l'Orme's architectural animism; how could the permanent solidity and rather material presence of his architecture respond to the fluidity and evanescence of his ethereal imagination, whether moved by zephyrs or whirlwinds? One cannot study the dialogue between astrology and architecture in the Renaissance world without considering the spiritual content revealed by the stars as well as the fact that *soul* was synonymous with *breath*. With a contemporary positivistic point of view, one again will risk interpreting the most revealing analogies of pre-scientific consciousness as mere childishness.[18]

The French historian Jean-Marie Pérouse de Montclos has recently (1988) restored de l'Orme's treatises with their original pagination and engravings, and by doing so has showed that most historians working with the 1626 and 1648 editions were using distorted documents. We might not agree with Pérouse de Montclos' hypothesis that the heading in book 4 reveals de l'Orme's birth date, but we must recognize how crucial these engravings must have been for de l'Orme[19] (see fig. 3.2). A preliminary examination shows that the attributes and geometrical instruments, placed between the personified planetary signs, appear once more as complementary tools for a qualitative understanding of places. Like the caduceus, which was quite common in Renaissance iconology, the *horn* was a crucial symbol in de l'Orme's imagination. However unsatisfying, his description of another engraving gives some clues about these features: "We accompanied Mercury with his attributes which are the Caduceus and the Horn, only to signify that the architect will acquire fame and honor if he conforms to what we have already said."[20]

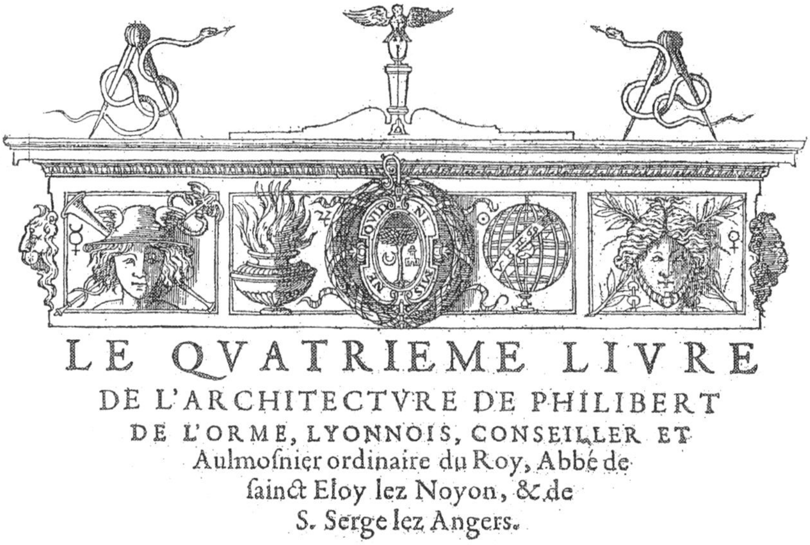

3.2 Heading in book 4 with the lions on each sides, and the moon, the "tree" and the tower in the central medallion; from de l'Orme, *Premier tome de l'architecture*, folio 86.

With this sibylline explanation preceded by a sentence from the Gospels inviting us to follow the prudence of the serpent and the simplicity of the dove, it is hard to be satisfied with the meaning de l'Orme gives here for the horn. As we will show, it needs to be related to his elaborate discussion of the *symbolism of winds* and his Neopythagorean understanding of soul as breath.[21] Such laconism needs further exploration.

Winds and foundations

If a building can share the *Anima Mundi*, as I have suggested in the discussion of elemental matter, it is not surprising that the laying of the foundation stone, as a starting operation, should be the symbolic act which establishes the potential significance and appropriateness of a building. In the *Premier tome*, de l'Orme insists on the fact that this task requires an investigation of "astrological houses"and of "cardinal winds."[22] In de l'Orme's understanding of architecture the world of forms is an "intertwining of winds." This makes the architect's role partly therapeutic and almost complementary to the role of the physician when his work takes into account even the light winds, the zephyrs, the exhalations and what he calls the *fumes*. As emphasized in the conclusion of the *Premier tome*, the "Bad Architect" has "little nose," for he does not have the intuition of good things[23] (see fig. 3.3). In other words,

3.3 Portrait of the *Bad Architect*, agitated and disguised; from de l'Orme, *Premier tome de l'architecture*, folio 281.

smell and consciousness are intimately related, especially for places which, like living beings, have their own breath – either fragrance or pestilential emanation.[24]

In the image of the "Good Architect," de l'Orme's elm (*orme* in French) extracts its life essence from the earth and transforms its branches into rounded clouds, mirroring the actions of the good Hermetic architect. Meanwhile, a storm is created by the ignorance of the "Bad Architect" (see figs. 3.3 and 3.4)! In de l'Orme's imagery, air is the flesh of movement and clouds are condensed souls.[25] As in Sandro Botticelli's *Primavera,* it is again Mercury who looks at the clouds and thrusts his wand into the sky to decipher the mysteries hidden behind the fog.[26]

While de l'Orme respected traditional teachings, he also wanted the apprentice to design his own instruments including the making of a *rose des vents*. Starting from the geometry of the square, he described sixteen winds; to those questioning such a number, he simply retorts that while sailors use thirty-two winds, Vitruvius decided to mention only twenty-four of them.[27] For de l'Orme the architects seeking to ground a building and thus to have knowledge of the winds must divide "the horizon of a place into as many parts as he wants to, since from all the points can come winds, which are nothing else than an exhalation, a vapor or smoke, driven and agitated laterally on the earth, and proceeding from various parts of the horizon."[28] De l'Orme recommands the freedom of the "bargee" who decides by himself the number of winds needed to build his horizon in order to travel in every country.

In de l'Orme's theory, there is no doubt about the interplay between macrocosm and microcosm. His statements lack fixity precisely because he does not have to be reductive; he does not imagine any architectural work outside this cosmological horizon. It is certainly problematic to talk about boundaries delineating macrocosm and microcosm in sixteenth-century cosmology. Apparent contradictions often spring from our own difficulty in understanding simultaneously (i.e., analogically) the various emblems that still connected humanity to the universe at the end of the Middle Ages. In the same way that the elements are not exclusive conceptual categories, the microcosm can also contain the macrocosm. This Hermetic message is often misunderstood by commentators who conceive it simply as a mathematical one-to-one relationship between planets and organs, without acknowledging its ultimate pantheistic

3.4 Portrait of the *Good Architect*, serene and generous; from de l'Orme, *Premier tome de l'architecture*, folio 283.

foundations.[29] But it would be equally erroneous to exaggerate the importance of teleological determinism in de l'Orme's imagery. Rather he "parallels" his invention of architecture with the demiurgic process that recreates the world. The sky within responds to the sky without, and so any building, when read as a matrix, becomes a Hermetic vessel in which the *Anima Mundi* takes on a specific shape. In this sense, buildings are analogous to the alchemical retorts described by Girolamo Cardano in his *De Subtilitate*, this other great character of Renaissance science. De l'Orme, along with Mizauld, speaks very highly of this work particularly while exploring the question of "fumes."[30] The various shapes of the retorts were supposed to induce movements and transformations, and their names are very revealing: along side the *Mariæ balneum*, there are the *Vas spirale*, the *Vasa recta,* the *Vasa mutua* and, above all, the *Vasa reciproca*, which is a re-enactment of the interplay and inside-out unfolding of macrocosm and microcosm[31] (see fig. 3.5).

De l'Orme's cosmology was therefore much more organic than intellectual, for as M. Tuzet writes: "It was an old doctrine, this parallel between microcosm and macrocosm. But we see its meaning changing. For people in the twelfth century, it was a question of intellectual correspondences: It was in God's mind that the scheme of Man could match the scheme of the world. But for people of the fifteenth and sixteenth centuries, this parallel becomes a participation, a deep substantial unity, an organic relation, in which man is not subordinated; he is the bond, the core of the world."[32] In such a context, man was understood not simply as some reduced "microcosm." Philibert's theories about winds can be grasped only with reference to this understanding of the human body.

Listening to silent bodies (with noisy winds)

Understanding proportion as analogy also allows a reappraisal of Renaissance theoretical references to the human body, and ultimately to the question of body image in architectural creation. Once again the "theory of winds" encompasses the theory of the four elements as a general discourse on the relationships between form and movement.

It is precisely in de l'Orme's time that the classical autonomy of Galenian humours was replaced by the notion of life as an exchange between the inside and the outside. The ancient theories of the soul as "breath" had to be re-established on new foundations. In Paracelsus'

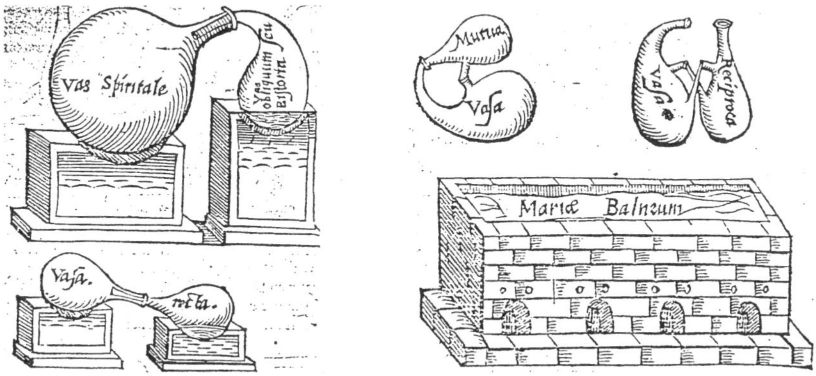

3.5 Four types of alchemical retorts along with the "vasa reciproca"; from Girolamo Cardano, *Les livres intitulez de la subtilité*, Paris, 1578, 397–8.

understanding of disease, for example, the ingestion of a foreign agent must find its counterpart in the expulsion of a similar entity. This concept is very close to the elemental theories articulated around the notions of reciprocity and reversibility. This is why, after quoting Hermes Trismegistus, de l'Orme can compare the world to a kingdom depending entirely on "the unity, conjunction, help, alliance and confederation of the seven parts or planets of this great and high kingdom called the Heavens, either by effect, participation, similitude, signification, or otherwise. In such a way that if one of the planets does not follow this, as was the case for our comparison with the parts of a building, the body and state of any kingdom will not have strength and will not last."[33]

It is perhaps not a coincidence that when architecture was disengaging from its medieval inclusion in the mechanical arts, alchemical medicine was revealing mysteries which would renew the architect's old thaumaturgic role.[34] As a dynamic messenger between the various counsellors who surrounded the architect's practice and ensured the accuracy of his graphic predictions, Hermes was stimulating and seductive for de l'Orme.

If one adopts an alchemical point of view, the two lions that protect the heading in book 4 of the *Premier tome*, one dark and the other luminous, symbolize respectively the opposition of fixity and volatility (see fig. 3.2). This is also suggested by the confrontation of the snakes which embrace the compasses and face the bird. All forms are composed of joints and geometrical angles, but in de l'Orme's imagination they are not isolated from the invisible movements that surround them and shape all the directions of his living perception of space. He summarizes: "This was very general, but more particularly to philosophize, and concerning the use of our architecture, it is not enough to know the already mentioned parts and angles of the world, but also the winds that come from them whether they are principal or cardinal, or even subprincipal and collateral (as they are called), that can help us or offend us, depending on their place and nature. Because they *alter* air, air and the humors of the body and the spirits within the blood, and therefore health – if this air is not corrected or stopped by its counterpart."[35]

Here, along with the notions of "winds" and "alteration," de l'Orme refers explicitly to the writings of Hippocrates.[36] Although the architect is suggesting that a good design can be this needed counterpart, a closer reading of Hippocrates' text is necessary to sharpen the analysis: "Wind in bodies is called breath, outside it is called air ... How air, then, is strong in the case of wholes this has been said; and for mortals too this is the cause of life, and the cause of disease in the sick ... Moreover, all other activities of man are intermittent, for life is full of changes, but breathing is continuous for all mortal creatures, inspiration and expiration being alternate."[37]

In the world Hippocrates described, any action becomes an alteration, a qualitative change, particularly in the design of places. De l'Orme often insists on this when speaking about the elements and he extols prudence as a fundamental virtue for the architect – a virtue which is more precisely a "practical wisdom." De l'Orme raises prudence to the level of guardian of architectural practice, because he sees matter as analogous to memory which as such demands to be manipulated with care and respect. Again, one must remember that the architect's work was still part of a living *physis* in which any action could induce a natural but frightening reaction. In fact, de l'Orme did not "introduce" prudence in architecture, as Blunt stated in his monograph,[38] but rather reminded his readers that the art of building was still under the power of Prudencia. His theory is very much rhetorical in this respect, for it deals with the ambiguous becoming of architectural building, in which action also means disruption. This resonates with Marco Frascari's description of the issue of architectural creation as the apparition of a "monster."[39]

De l'Orme's intuition about the special architectural role of the most immaterial of the four elements, air, needs further examination. As Mikhail Bakhtin showed in his celebrated work on Rabelais' world, physicians were familiar with the Hippocratic differences between *pneuma*, which inhabits bodies, and winds that move around them. For Bakhtin, this explains the grotesque image of the body, in which "its exterior aspect is not distinct from the inside, and the exchange between the body and the world is constantly emphasized."[40] In the Hippocratic tradition, air became the main element of the body. This is not, of course, the depersonalized air of the chemist, but an active participant that manifests its concreteness by *connecting* cosmic life to human life. Bakhtin also shows that such an understanding went as far as to connect the act of belching with the movement of the Sun![41]

A corollary of this prudent respect of *physis* is again the philosophy of alteration. Aristotle, in his *Physics*, had already introduced an analogy with architecture when dealing with movement. For him, the act of building is fully realized only when the materials can be said to participate – in other words, when they are in "motion." This movement, writes Aristotle, is an alteration: "Since any kind of being may be distinguished as either potential or completely realized, the functioning of what is potential as potential, that is 'being in movement': thus the functioning of the alterable as alterable is 'qualitative alteration.'" [42]

The notion of alteration enables us to pursue de l'Orme's allegory of the "prudent architect." De l'Orme wants the architect to be prudent because any action, being an alteration, is also a modification, the making of an otherness; the constructed place has become an "altered" place. But we should not understand this ethical attitude as an inhibition.The very title of his first treatise, *Les nouvelles inventions*, and his many encouragements to use creative geometrical artifice, as in the *Premier tome* , is evidence that de l'Orme's intention is to teach active prudence rather than to refrain action. Similarly, stating that prudence is action is not an aporia if we invoke the alchemical notion of *chaos*. In such a cosmological horizon, *physis* is by definition alive, in movement, and therefore always incomplete, never finished – porous and fissured, so to speak. Man is the agent who can intervene in this "in-between" world of unsatisfied potential. This last idea is crucial for understanding the dominant state of mind of most of Philibert's great contemporaries, from Rabelais to Paracelsus. Some commentators even go so far as to state that Rabelais' work, for example, is entirely articulated and sustained by the notion of alteration,[43] a notion which has to be understood parallel to de l'Orme's *thirst* for prudence.[44]

Rabelais was certainly a proponent of this philosophy of alteration. Throughout his works, Panurge is the one who always acts; he represents the dynamic aspect of being. His giant "companion" is obviously powerful, but needs Panurge in the same way that the macrocosm needs the microcosm. Rabelais writes that Pantagruel was *Pantagruelique* from his special birth: "And because Pantagruel was born on that very day, his father gave him the name he did: for *Panta*, in Greek, is equivalent to all, and *Gruel* in the Hagarene language (Arab) is as much as altéré: by this, meaning to infer that at the hour of the child's nativity, the world was all *changed* (altéré), and also seeing, in a spirit of prophecy, that one day his son would be ruler over the *thirsty* (altérés)."[45]

The interplay between the demiurge who creates a chaotic dissatisfaction and the one who operates in this space of desire is ironic in Rabelais' novel. With Gaster, who eats in order to create, and with the Pantagruelion, a magic herb regenerated in fire, Rabelais not only understood alteration as creation but he celebrated its embodied fertility. The entire human race is ruled by this *alterare,* this thirst for change and otherness. On the other hand, *désaltérer* (to satisfy a thirst) is to bring something or someone back to its original state, to an "un-change." The magic herb in Rabelais' third book, *Pantagruelion,* and de l'Orme's *Orme* are both vehicles for the same notion of *Festina lente.* For Edgar Wind, in his *Pagan Mysteries in the Renaissance,*[46] this philosophy of *hâte-toi lentement*, of hurrying slowly, is fundamental to Renaissance imagination. Ripening is an expression of vitality before representing a path toward death. The "man of the carnival," as Bakhtin calls medieval humanity, still knows that filth is a potential fertilizer. In fact, in the same way that the *Pantagruelion* allows for the most amazing magical inventions, de l'Orme's *Orme* can sustain the vine in its growth, for man cannot control ripening but only allow it to happen, and thus conform to it. In this sense, *Festina lente* is the deep secret of nature, the one explored by medieval alchemists and celebrated by Renaissance artists.

In de l'Orme's image of the "Good Architect" the elm tree is therefore doubly symbolic. Unlike the two trees behind the "Bad Architect," which seem to hamper each other's growth in an otherwise desolate landscape, the elm tree and the vine are meant to complement each other (see figs. 3.3 and 3.4). Jean Guillaume, referring to Virgil's *Bucolica,* was the first historian to identify this mirroring between the tree and the Good Architect.[47] This exegesis confirms the Dionysiac element of the architect's use of hermetism. J.R. Harris, in a rare study of the origins of the cult of Hermes that sheds some light on the metamorphosis of a myth which animated the Roman Empire, writes about the etymological scope of the word "Hermes": "From the similitude of *Hermas* we learn that in Rome in his day, it was the custom to train the Vine upon the Elm. *Hermes, then, is the Elm-tree.* When we make that equation, we see a gleam in the direction of philology: for *Herm*, as we shall see presently, is the same word as Elm. In Latin and the Roman languages, we find the forms: *Ulmus* in Latin, *Orme* in French, *Urmo* in Italian, by the side of English *Elm*."[48]

In a totally different context, Harris establishes archeological connections between Hermes and Dionysos. He shows not only that the elm-tree is the direct ancestor of the herm, the symbolic pillar of Roman crossroads, but that it also incarnates the traditional tutor of the vine. For instance, Praxiteles' *Hermes Carrying the Infant Bacchus* and *Silenus Carrying Dionysos* from the Vatican Museum are two clear aspects of the same sacralization of spiritual wine which, for obvious reasons, entered the Christian tradition.[49] This allows a deeper reappraisal of de l'Orme's treatises. The decisive feature of the Good Architect's tree is its explicit fertility and creativity, both in the text and in the plate. There is no doubt that de l'Orme came back from his Italian initiation with a fascination for Roman antiquity. What is more surprising is the fact that he also carried a secret respect for ancient cults that merged, even phonetically, with his name, his personality and his spiritual orientations – an embodied amalgam, so to speak!

THREE STAGES IN THE EDIFICATION OF AN ANALOGICAL TREATISE

Building a flying tower

"After considering what has been written above, and after listening to wise men, philosophers and physicians, who know the nature of places, Air, and Waters, as Hippocrates wrote in his book, then you will think of looking for an architect."[50] Yet, we may ask, why did it seem so crucial to choose an architect? What was the difference between the master mason, proud of his craft based on the secrets of stereotomy, and the learned architect who pretended to decipher the teachings of ancient texts in order to improve his drive to edify?

If the question is mainly one of virtuosity, we might as well think of a medieval *chef d'œuvre*, the proper *tour de force*, which decided whether or not the companion of a specific guild had acquired the proper knowledge of his craft. We have been told throughout the *Premier tome*, however, to think of architecture as a prudent gathering and beautiful assemblage of heavy stones, and it is perhaps hard to believe that de l'Orme's endeavour may be analogous to Rabelais' quest. If foundations can only be massive, then where is the spiritual lightness sought by de l'Orme? What is the analogy between both the means and effects of Rabelais' "good tasty and delicious wine" and de l'Orme's definition of architecture?

If the question is not only about virtuosity but also about the requirement for the architect to be virtuous, we should also consider carefully the tradition of the four cardinal virtues. The cardinal character of the practical virtues (prudence, fortitude, temperance, justice) certainly can be paralleled with the symbolism of the Cross as a major device for the everyday experience of the architect. Indeed, in the sixteenth century, the cardinal virtues do not yet refer to an abstract morality; they retain the concrete qualitative content encountered in the writings of Cicero and Macrobius. These four orientations of the incarnated soul certainly have ancient Roman origins, and their integration into Christianity was possible only by the addition of the three theological virtues (faith, hope, and charity). However, in pagan traditions the cardinal virtues played a fundamental role in the understanding of embodiment.[51] In medieval representations, Fortitude, for example, is often dressed in armour and holding a tower (the real "*tour de force*"), out of which she extirpates a gigantic dragon (see fig. 3.6). Yet de l'Orme's preference among the virtues is not Fortitude but rather Prudence, who abundantly displays her attributes, the compass and the serpent. The snake coils around the compass to illustrate the necessary awareness of the use of all the tools of geometry (see fig. 3.7). In other words, Prudence alone could serve to control the impetuosity so characteristic of Hermes, Prince of the Winds.

Symbolized in de l'Orme's blazon there is a tower along with the tree (the elm) and the rising moon (Diana)[52] (see fig. 3.2). If de l'Orme had remained the master mason he was in his youth, the symbol would simply be the *tour de force*. However, de l'Orme portrays himself in the "architect's dress," and as we have seen, thus with the precious knowledge of the winds. The tower on the blazon may also be analogous to

3.6 Fortitude with the *Tour de Force* in François II and Anne de Bretagne's tomb in Nantes (1502). From Fulcanelli, *Les demeures philosophales et le symbolisme hermétique dans ses rapports avec l'art sacré et l'ésotérisme du Grand Œuvre*, 2 volumes, Paris: J.-J. Pauvert 1966–1979, 2: 247.

the "Tower of the Winds." In book I, Vitruvius had already given a detailed description of a beautiful octogonal "Tower of the Winds" built in Athens by Andronicus of Cyrrhus. Such a tower qualified eight different types of winds and, of course, eight directions. Because of the mysterious qualities of a place, de l'Orme, as we know, recommends a great freedom in the use of winds. For him the architect is like a "bargee" who makes his way through the haze with his horn. This seems to

3.7 Left: The *Prudent Architect* coming out of his dark retreat; from de l'Orme, *Premier tome de l'architecture*, folio 51 v°.

3.8 Opposite: Prudent "alteration" of a Mediæval castle; from de l'Orme, *Premier tome de l'architecture*, folios 66, 67.

indicate that there were too many other winds taken into account by de l'Orme, for the tower to be this monument.

Here again we must underline the importance in his architecture of a "philosophy of alteration." That is to say the making of an otherness with what is already existing in place. Philibert de l'Orme's architectural projects certainly were inspired by a philosophy of alteration. His famous project for the transformation of an unfinished medieval castle through geometrical operations is described and eloquently entitled in book 3[53] (see fig. 3.8): "The artifice of geometry is useful when one wants to transform one or two badly started and imperfect houses into a beautiful and perfect house, accommodating all the parts and the members of the old building with the new."[54]

The original plan for Saint-Maur is another example of cardinal foundation, not so much because of the client's rank in the church's hierarchy as the Cardinal du Bellay, but rather due to the fact that the building was designed "in such a way that the four façades (faces) always looked at the four angles of the sky."[55] However, in these two cases, the artifice of geometry that gives architecture its real meaning is quite simple; it will become much more complex, subtle and, strictly speaking Hermetic, in the case of the *trompe du Château d'Anet*.

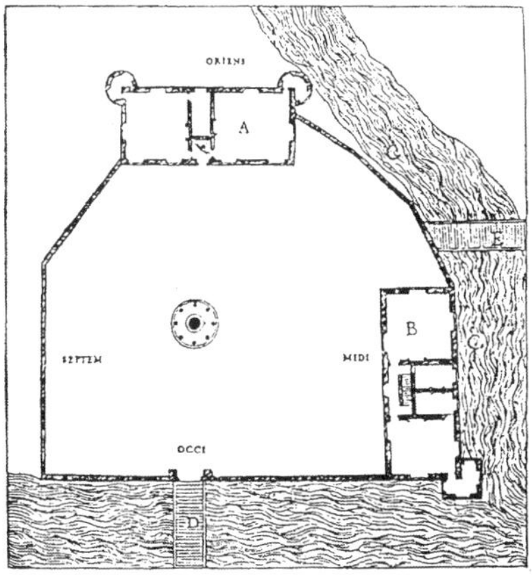

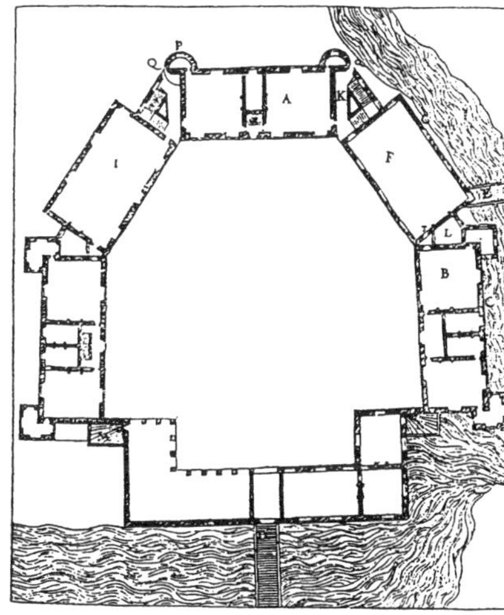

The case of the squinch is probably the best architectural example of de l'Orme's hermetic imagination. In his architecture, squinches are analogous to towers and hinges, allowing a synthesis of his Medieval heritage with Italian influences. In some cases, these architectural devices also reconcile contradictory programmatic requirements as in the paradigmatic *trompe* of Anet. The squinches are perfect symbols of *tours de force* that reveal the architect's skill in defying gravity. In describing the winds, de l'Orme attempted to qualify the meaningful horizon of place. In the design of the *trompes*, he confronts more precisely the vertical essence of architecture. Such acrobatic building devices are often described as feats of virtuosity: "Such a thing is proper to erect the suspended ones that we call squinches."[56] De l'Orme was literally spellbound by this capacity to confer lightness through geometric artifice (see fig. 3.9): "Many different kinds of vaults can be made in the shape of a squinch, and all suspended in the air, without having any foundation underneath, excepting for the sides, and all this is being done through the use of a drawing method."[57]

Aerial symbolism appears in all of de l'Orme discussions of squinches.[58] The Hermes Horn (*trompe* in French) is the double message given by the wind instruments, simultaneously the means and sign of a

3.9 Above: The unique and altered memory of the *Trompe du château d'Anet*; from de l'Orme, *Premier tome de l'architecture*, folio 89.

3.10 Opposite: Winged mask on a funerary altar/Venus in the heading in book 4; from de l'Orme, *Premier tome de l'architecture*, folio 147 / folio 86.

quest. As he writes, "Without blowing the horn, that is to say without asking for the advice of many wise and learned men,"[59] it is impossible to succeed in a complex task.[60] To get the full measure of this subtle mixture of poetic images, one could re-examine the frontispiece and its overlapping composition of stereotomical drawings of squinches with Hermetic devices. De l'Orme's text is, for once, sufficiently explicit, for he writes in folio 89v°: "But it is also true that some could ask what I mean and hear by this word *trompe*, since it is only used by craftsmen and therefore known by a few people and almost never by new workers. This is why I want to state, and tell the reader that it seems to me the term *trompe* came from, or has been derived from its similitude with the structure of the horn (*trompette*) called in many places *trompe*. For both of them being large in their front part, get narrower at the other end, in the shape of a vault."[61]

The *trompes* are analogous to the cardinal virtues necessary in becoming a good architect! It is ironic that the printer, in order to respect the margins, often used the old printing artifice replacing the "m" in a word with an accent on the preceding vowel; the word *trompe* then appears as *trôpe*. The original rhetorical motif, understood abundantly by Rabelais, is *tropos*, which meant "tower" and "manner" (*tour* in French). This trope *de force* requires a lot of prudence, otherwise one risks confusing the strange necklace of the Venus in the heading with a narrow beard, and thus seeing again an androgynous Hermes (see fig. 3.10)! Even more so if it looked like the winged mask adorning the funerary altar in folio 147. De l'Orme himself "s'y trompe," for he describes it as a Doric pedestal with a head of Mercury, before correcting it into a Medusa in the errata added to the *Premier Tome*.[62] This confirms the

numerous ambiguities we find in the analogical referents generated around the notions of macrocosm and microcosm. Indeed, as the Latin origin of "ambiguous" is *ambo*, it points to a special kind of polarity, a doubleness also typical of de l'Orme's astrological sign, Gemini.[63] The *trompe d'Anet,* the squinch, when considered as an architectural trope whose geometry is revealed by de l'Orme with the help of stereotomy, is an ultimate alteration. Indeed, it includes its own "error," its own "falsification," through an alteration of meaning (tropism), a rhetorical trick which greatly troubled the engraver when he had to reproduce it in folio 89. Ironically, it was to remain the only distorted memory of such a *tour de force* (see fig. 3.9).

Transforming "frozen words" into "windy thoughts"

> *Omnia tempus habent* (says the wise man) *tempus tacendi, et tempus loquendi.* Thus granting ourself, with this sentence, the freedom to speak at one time, and to remain silent at another.[64]

The prudent architect was considered by de l'Orme to be ruled by Hermes. Like the strange words delivered by the Holy Bottle in Rabelais' Fifth Book, de l'Orme's theoretical writings can offer only a cryptic message through a double movement of revealing and concealing. There is no real split between his theory and his practice because his architectural intentions are grounded on a spiritual understanding of materiality and a carnal approach to spirituality. This is perhaps best exemplified by de l'Orme's so-called invention of stereotomy. Too often is de l'Orme considered the first French architect: the one who drew his fame from the revelation of medieval secrets of stone cutting. Indeed, we can wonder what was the real need to display such complex geometrical figures to a larger public that would need considerable training to understand stereotomy. In fact, the geometric instruments revealed in the Fourth Book, in relation to stereotomy, appear to have little meaning without de l'Orme's ethical guidelines. It is clearly the *marriage* of prudence and geometry which prevented de l'Orme from abstract instrumentalism when he wrote his companions. Stereotomic traces correspond, by definition, to fine lines executed with a dry-point. This is essential to remember, for it emphasizes that stereotomy, whether responding to the movements of (elemental) matter or to ephemeral marks waiting to disappear in the cutting process, represented the invisible, the form, the idea. Stereotomic traces have an almost magic capacity to appear deeply embodied in a *virtuous* place and are thus quite different from the modern instrumental notion of a *virtual* space.

De l'Orme is far from associating geometric bodies with *frozen words,* which Pantagruel's friends discover in the midst of the ocean: words which cannot be understood, or rather "heard," in the language of the sixteenth century.[65] In fact, in de l'Orme's context, the stereotomic use of Platonic bodies is analogous to the highly meaningful *gestures of Nazdecabre,* a very erudite but silent person met by travellers on their quest. Rabelais tells us that he was particularly fond of the number 5, also called "nuptial" by the Pythagoreans.[66] The elaborate gesticulations used by the mute man to convey his message were as mysterious as they seemed accurate: "*Nazdecabre* looked at him curiously, then raised his left hand in the air, keeping all the fingers clenched like a bunch of nails, except the thumb and the indicating finger, keeping the two nails softly laid together."[67] Pantagruel concluded that Nazdecabre's gesture meant marriage. Similarly, de l'Orme's Platonic bodies allude less to a formal manipulation than to a conjunction of elements in the profound sense of the *marriage chymique.* It is the union of the elmtree and the vine in the background of the portrait of the Good Architect.[68]

In the Renaissance, the flesh of the world is shaped by the craftsman in a process which associated two types of creativity, Dionisian and Apollonian, without forming a mere dualism in a forest of distinctions. On the contrary, there is a necessary polarity. Bacchus and Apollo are inseparable because their tension is resolved (or coagulated) in Hermes.[69] In fact, imaginations mirroring Hermes are always eminently multiple and by nature heteronymous.[70] Hermes is above all the symbol of a heady multiplicity of things and beings, a demiurgic diversity which, like vegetal life, blooms in the spring and retreats into the dark in winter. Such a hermetism inhabited the symbolic powers of stereotomy and this is due to its capacity to invent relationships between forms and matter, rather than its technical and instrumental aspects. There is a major hermetic difference between the two directions of "windy actions." One can either *éventer,* that is, kill the chaos by revealing its structure, or *inventer* – perpetuate the dynamic potentials of matter through prudent alteration. In one case the secret is out, in the other the unknown still lies within.

Edification as analogy

De l'Orme did not define the architect as a demiurge who invents from nothing. The development of a dynamic awareness of materiality, which is an undeniable achievement of Hermetic symbolism, depends on the fact that its referents were always traced back to the everyday experience of the body. This is particularly clear in Rabelais' works, whose intentionality is openly thaumaturgic. A careful analysis of de l'Orme's text reveals the same ultimate intentions. So many features of his thought – the four elements conceived as emblems of movements; proportion understood in the sense of *analogia*; the microcosm-macrocosm interplay; and even the cardinal virtues – make little sense without being deeply connected to an embodied practical experience. This pragmatism, however, is not to be understood as an early version of materialism, for matter is never estranged from spirit in the sixteenth century.

For Rabelais, and de l'Orme, the body because of its reversibility and its reciprocal character is an ultimate analogical edification. Both believed that the body is not merely a substance which we must endure but rather a learning process, an apprenticeship: analogically speaking, an athanor. Through the disturbed voice of Panurge, who usually misunderstands the teaching of sacred texts, Rabelais criticizes those who do not "edify," in the full etymological sense of the word:

> As for your grand builders-up of dead stones, there is nothing written about them in my book of life. I only build up *live stones*, by which I mean men.[71]

Strangely, this echoed in de l'Orme's summary of his life:

> And instead of building up castles and houses I will learn to build up people.[72]

NOTES

1 Proclus, *Commentaire sur le timée*, 5 vols. (Paris 1967) III.27.20, 53–4; author's translation.

2 See André Chastel, *Renaissance méridionale – Italie 1460–1600* (Paris 1965), 49.

3 See the new edition directed by Jean-Marie Pérouse de Montclos, *Philibert de l'Orme's Traités d'architecture* (Paris: L. Laget 1988). For instance *Premier tome* (referred to as *P.T.* in the following pages), also the *Nouvelles*

inventions (referred to as *N.I.*), folio 282, and folio 79: "If some desire to know more, they can come to me, I will share my little knowledge and experience as much as possible." See also folio 99. Since there is still no English translation of de l'Orme's treatises I give my own.

4 This last word refers to Brian Vickers' definition in the editorial introduction to *Occult and Scientific Mentalities in the Renaissance* (Cambridge: Cambridge University Press 1986). See 6: "Yet although the issue was wrongly formulated by Frances Yates and her followers, it remains an important and challenging topic. The occult had a long and widely diffused influence, in parallel – as I see it – with the non-occult sciences, and it seems essential to anyone wanting to understand to try to evaluate what debts, if any, the two traditions owe to each other. The title of this book, in the word 'mentalities,' places the emphasis where I believe it should be put: on two traditions each having its own thought processes, its own mental categories, which determine its whole approach to life, mind and physical reality."

5 Pérouse de Montclos notes that Besson, Cousin, Mauclerc also emphasized the primacy of these two bodies for the same reason, but he tends to reduce de l'Orme's interest in the regular bodies to formal exercises of virtuosity. See "Présentation des traités" in *Philibert de l'Orme's Traités*, 13.

6 See Pérouse de Montclos, "Horoscope de Philibert de l'Orme," *Revue de l'art* (1986): 16–18.

7 See *P.T.*, folio 3 v°.

8 See Claude Gaignebet, *A plus hault sens: L'ésotérisme spirituel et charnel de Rabelais*, 2 vol. (Paris: Maisonneuve et Larose 1986), II, 333, no.91. Rabelais was trained at the Montpellier School of Medicine, was a centre devoted to vitalistic theories. This doctrine, which understood phenomena and natural objects as controlled only partly by mechanical forces and in some measure as being self-determined, did not refer explicitly to souls as did other animistic beliefs.

9 For this reason, I refer to the intermediary notion of *flesh* when talking about embodiment, essentially dynamic in its ambiguous implications. It is an aim of this paper to clarify our understanding of the *carnal* for de l'Orme, as inspired by Maurice Merleau-Ponty's use of the notion of flesh "as an element of being." See *The Visible and the Invisible* (Evanston, Ill.: Northwestern University Press 1968), 139.

10 On this question, see Albert Rivaud, "La première traduction française du Timée de Platon," *Revue du XVIe siècle* 9 (Paris 1922): 286–9.

11 Proclus, *Commentaires*, III, 51.17, 82.

12 See Fulcanelli, *Les demeures philosophales, et le symbolisme hermétique dans ses rapports avec l'art sacré et l'ésotérisme du Grand Œuvre,* 2 vols. (Paris: J.J. Pauvert 1966–79), II, 312: "Ce qui est en bas est comme ce qui est en haut et ce qui est en haut est comme ce qui est en bas: par ces choses se font les miracles d'une seule chose."

13 Proclus, *Commentaires*, III, 52.5, 82.

14 In such an understanding, imagination is very far from Jean-Paul Sartre's "folle du logis" for it was still an art of relationship in which "there are no absolute contradictions but necessary levels in-between which circulates the meaning of the literal and the one of the 'higher senses' and reciprocally. Following Roger Bacon's word it is necessary to speak spiritually of carnal things, and carnally of the spiritual." See Gaignebet, *A plus hault sens*, I, 26. See also Gilbert Durand: *L'imagination symbolique* (Paris: Presses universitaires de France 1989).

15 See Alberto Pérez-Gómez, *Architecture and the Crisis of Modern Science* (Cambridge, Mass.: MIT Press, 1983), particularly chapters 1, 2, and 9. On de l'Orme's understanding of stereotomy, see 227: "The plates illustrating the use of projections in de l'Orme's *Architecture* did not constitute a method: they did not derive from a general theory of geometry capable of generalizing specific solutions for specific problems."

16 See Rudolf Wittkower, *Architectural Principles in the Age of Humanism* (London: A. Tiranti 1967), 8: "The conviction that architecture is a science, and that each part of a building, inside as well as outside, has to be integrated into one and the same system of mathematical ratios, may be called the basic axiom of Renaissance architects." See also 102–21. When Wittkower explicitly studies the ratios from a mathematical standpoint, he does not work on the basis of analogical thinking about the world, which was nevertheless the vision shared by Humanists and Hermetists, whose ultimate keywords were not distinction and identity but amalgam and reciprocity.

17 See *P.T.*, II, ch. 7.

18 This is how we understand Henri Clouzot's mistrust about de l'Orme's strange "comparison of the world being composed of seven planets, as architecture is of seven parts." Henri Clouzot, *Philibert de l'Orme* (Paris 1910), 100.

19 See Pérouse de Montclos, "Horoscope." In fact the real starting point of this astrological hypothesis comes from the coincidental position of the astrological sign of Gemini on the armillary spheres of both the frontispiece and the head band. Furthermore, this sign is represented along with Mercury on a

carved beam from de l'Orme's house, as shown by the engraving in *N.I.*, folio 46.

20 *P.T.*, folio 51v°.

21 Ibid., folio 50v°.

22 Unfortunately, and as it is the case for his divine proportions, de l'Orme tells us that their description will occur in the forthcoming (but never published) *Second Tome*. Ibid., folio 47v°.

23 Ibid., folio 28v°. De l'Orme writes, "Il n'a gueres de nez, pour n'avoir sentiment des bonnes choses."

24 As was pointed out by Marco Frascari, Italian speak of an architecture *di grande respiro*, while the French expression is *un lieu qui respire*.

25 This is very close to the alchemical "récolte de la rosée," the solstice dew, which was supposed to possess a strong energy essentially helpful in the first stages of the Great Work.

26 In *The Planets Within* (Lewisburg: Bucknell University Press 1982), Thomas Moore considers that it is Mercury's special formal consciousness which makes him the confident of winds and clouds, and the mirror of dreams. See 151. In classical mythology, Hermes was the guide of souls.

27 *P.T.*, folio 16.

28 Ibid., folio 16v°.

29 In a remarkable study of the changes that occurred in medical mentalities in the early seventeenth century, Brian Vickers shows the importance of this paradigmatic notion of macrocosm in Hermetic practices and how it created the most profound metaphysical images. He insists that a disciple of Paracelsus such as Van Helmont tends toward a quest for identities, and thus will be forced to question the very existence of a link between the great and little worlds. In this process, it is the entire occult system, and not only that of Paracelsus, which will become useless and futile, the twelve signs of the zodiac becoming concepts waiting for a new rule! Brian Vickers, "Analogy versus Identity: the Rejection of Occult Symbolism, 1580–1680," *Occult and Scientific Mentalities in the Renaissance* (Cambridge: Cambridge University Press 1984) 95–163.

30 *P.T.*, folio 272v°.

31 De l'Orme and Mizauld probably read the French translation of 1556. I consulted a 1578 reprint of Cardano's *De Subtilitate* entitled *Les livres Intitulez de la Subtilité* (Paris 1578), 397–8.

32 M. Tuzet, *Le Cosmos et l'imagination* (Paris: Librairie Jose Corti 1965), 284.

33 *P.T.*, folio 2v°.

34 Rudolf Allers, "Macrocosmus – from Anaximandros to Paracelsus," *Tradition* (New York 1944), 2: 399. "Paracelsus defines man as an excerpt from the whole *machina mundi,* a microcosm: not in his shape and corporeal substance, but in his powers and virtues, he is like the big world." Allers insists that it is only after Paracelsus that some scientists categorized the notions of microcosm and macrocosm.

35 *P.T.*, folio 14. Emphasis mine.

36 Ibid., folio 15, 15v°, 16.

37 *Hippocrates* (London: Loeb Classical Library 1923), 2: ch. 3: "Breath," 229, 231, 233.

38 See Anthony Blunt, *Philibert de l'Orme* (London: A. Zwemmer 1958), 135.

39 On "teratology" and architecture, see Marco Frascari, *Monsters of Architecture – Anthropomorphism in Architectural Theory* (Savage, Md.: Rowman & Littlefield 1991). See, in particular, ch. 2; "Monsters and Semiotics; A Teratology."

40 Mikhail Bakhtin, *Rabelais and His World* (Bloomington: Indiana University Press 1984), 356.

41 Ibid., 356. See also Gaignebet, *A plus hault sens*, 227, who articulates his interpretation of Rabelais' animism from a passage in Macrobius' *Commentary on the Dream of Scipio* in which the soul is incorporated into a body after coming down through the Milky Way. In *A plus hault sens*, Gaignebet also shows the importance of the numerous "pneumatic games" combined by Rabelais' "maître contrepéteur." See tome 1, 410. A curious example is given page 12: "there is a motif that Rabelais knows very well: *le pet du mort, le dernier pet, mourir en pet.* He reactivates the old scatological tricks of the joyful carnavalesque brotherhoods… But in his deep crazy wisdom, he goes further: the anal breath is for him the specific form of the soul."

42 Aristotle, *Physics*, trans. R. Hope (Lincoln: University of Nebraska Press 1961) 3: 201a, 42.

43 See, for example, the most Hermetic of them all: Gaignebet shows in *A plus hault sens* that Panurge is another way of saying Hermes, since Panourgos means "the one who puts everything into work" (celui qui met tout en œuvre). Gaignebet also refers to other works, particularly to a German thesis by Ludwig Schrader, *Panurge und Hermes, zum Ursprung eines Charakters bei Rabelais* (Bonn: Romanisches Seminar der Universitat 1958).

44 "Altération" has two meanings: thirst and modification.

45 See François Rabelais, *Gargantua et Pantagruel* (Paris: SACELP 1980) 2: 2–3, 224. I used part of the English translation (Harmondsworth: Penguin

1976) by J.M. Cohen on page 176, but modified it where it fails to to take into consideration the dynamic ambiguity which makes the notion of "alterity" so unique.

46 Edgar Wind, *Pagan Mysteries in the Renaissance* (UK: Peregrin Books 1967), 6: "Ripeness Is All." Wind quotes Erasmus in his Adagia, 98.

47 See Jean Guillaume, "Philibert De l'Orme: un traité différent," *Les traités d'architecture de la Renaissance* (Paris: Picard 1988), 348. De l'Orme himself mentions the "rustic books" written by "Virgil and others."

48 James Rendel Harris, *The Origins of the Cult of Hermes* (Manchester: Manchester University Press 1929), 9. Emphasis mine.

49 Ibid., 52.

50 *P.T.*, folio 9 v°.

51 About the crucial role played by Macrobius in the medieval understanding of the Virtues, see Rosemund Tuve: "Notes on the Virtues and Vices, part one: Two fifteenth-century lines of dependence on the thirteenth and twelfth centuries," *The Journal of the Warburg and Courtauld Institutes* 26 (1963): 263–303.

52 Clouzot, in *Philibert de l'Orme,* mentions an intriguing early version of this blazon with two towers instead of one; see 63. On the alchemical role of the "Tour de Force," see the description of Fortitude given by Fulcanelli in the second tome of his *Demeures Philosophales,* 257–8: "On the other hand, the phonetic Cabala, which parallels the French word 'tour' with the Greek *Touos*, comes to complete the 'signification pantagruélique du tour de force.'"

53 *P.T.*, folio 66–7.

54 Ibid., folio 65.

55 In Ibid., folio 17 v°, Henri Clouzot describes this fully in "Saint-Maur, Paradis de Salubrité, Aménités ... et délices," *Études rabelaisiennes* 7 (1909): 259–84, and shows very well that de l'Orme had to face the other side of alterations when he was forced to modify the façade in order to please Catherine de Medici.

56 Ibid., folio 87.

57 Ibid., folio 89v°. Emphasis mine.

58 See, for instance, Ibid., folios 87, 87v°, 88v°, 89v°. In all these cases, the same terms recur: "Les trompes sont suspendues en l'air."

59 Ibid., folio 7.

60 See Ibid., folio 7v°. Mizauld adds that without the guidance of an architect, the art of building itself has no foundations (fondements).

61 Ibid., folio 89v°.

62 Pérouse de Montclos, "Présentation des traités," 39, shows de l'Orme's double mistake in giving the right answer: it is a Gorgon! Yves Pauwels, a collaborator of Pérouse de Montclos, recognized this altar on a plate in Cesariano's edition of *Vitruvius* (Côme 1521), folio LXV, v°.

63 This etymological "little wind" has been gracefully pointed out by Marco Frascari.

64 *P.T.*, folio 51. A translation could be: "There are all kinds of time: a time to stay silent and a time to speak."

65 See Rabelais, *Gargantua*, book 4, ch. 55, 729. In medieval French, "entendre" is synonymous with "comprendre," and the "entendement" is synonymous with intelligence.

66 Ibid., *book 3*, ch. 20, 442.

67 Ibid., ch. 20, 441. It is interesting to note that Cornelius Agrippa, in his *Occult Philosophy* (Rome: Edizioni Mediterranee 1978) indicates exactly the same gestures. See 2: XVI, 59–60.

68 *P.T.*, folio 283.

69 This was already true in Classical Antiquity, for Hermes was also Priapus.

70 This has been studied well by one of James Hillman's collaborators, W.G. Doty, who gathered an impressive documentation of the various terms that apply to Hermes. See Hillman, *Facing the Gods* (Dallas: Spring Publications 1988), 115–33.

71 Rabelais, *Gargantua* book 3, ch. 6, Cohen's translation, 303–4.

72 See "Instruction de Philibert de l'Orme," a manuscript kept in the Bibliothèque Nationale in Paris and reproduced in Blunt's biography in *Philibert de l'Orme*, Appendix C, 150.

The Angel and the Mirror: Reflections on the Architecture of the Amalgam[1]

Terrance Galvin

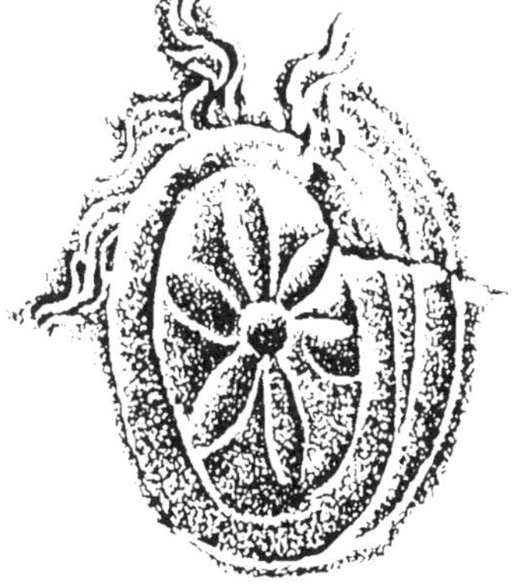

> The exact dwelling place of the angels is unknown, God did not see fit to tell us whether they dwell in the air, in the void, or in the other planets.
>
> (Voltaire, *Philosophical Dictionary*, 1764)

ARCHITECTURE HAS HISTORICALLY been a means of giving form to the invisible through the use of the faculty of the *imagination*. This essay will examine the symbolism of the angel as a manifestation of the invisible realm, specifically operating at the juncture of two realms, as evidenced by the marriage of the celestial firmament and the mirrored sea. In discussing the ontological meaning behind the symbolism of the angel, I will construct an argument supporting the angelic image as one that embodies a profound understanding of transformation and mediates the classical Cartesian separation of mind and body. The consequences of this construct as it pertains to making (*techné*) is essential for architecture, which continuously employs such poetic translation devices as allegory, analogy, metaphor, and metonymy in order to negotiate the act of creative transformation from the invisible to the material. This presencing of the invisible has been familiar territory to the architect, whose role has included mapping the celestial cosmos through sacred divination rituals related to the city and inventing "angelic" tectonic devices such as the hinge, the joint, and the gargoyle.

Our investigation of angelology acknowledges that mysterious aspect of the invisible which leads us toward the *Primum Mobile*. This desire to name the Unnamable has common roots; the monad of Leibniz, the concept of infinity, the alchemical union and cosmological myths depart from the ideal of tracing the origin of things to an invisible presence. Beginning with *City of God*, St Augustine describes the dwelling place of the celestial hierarchy, but ascribes the act of creation solely to God. The role of angels, he explains, is not the same as that of the Creator, but is to reflect divine light toward the mortals of the earth, acting as mediums or emissaries. Thus, the celestial hierarchy originates in the presence of the First Mover; angels have a nature midway between the Creator and man, while "man [has] a nature midway between angels and beasts, so that man, provided he should remain subject to his true Lord and Creator and dutifully obey his commandments, might pass into the company of the angels, without the intervention of death, thus to attain a blessed and eternal immortality."[2]

4.1 Disembodied Spirits – *Homer Invoking the Muse*; from John Flaxman, *The Iliad of Homer,* 1793.

Augustine's *City of God* is an ideal analogue for the "city of man." While the former is eternal, the latter is subject to physical time, thus distinguishing two entities, *terra firma* and firmament, which have mirrored each other since their inception. As Augustine states: "The distinguishing mark between time and eternity is that the former does not exist without some movement and change, while in the latter there is no change at all,"[3] identifying the duality between the ideal and the real. One could argue that following the initial cosmological division, the rest of recorded history has been an attempt to reconcile the duality of the fallen angel.

The same dual nature is evident in the form of "things." According to Aristotle, each *thing* has an outer material form and an inner form, which he calls the hidden nature, or soul, of that same body. While "the first kind of form we may attribute to any artificer ... the second, only to the Artificer, Creator and Maker who is God,"[4] illustrating that the "city of man" was made in the image of the "City of God," as man himself was created in God's image. The city of man continues to mirror the celestial other but, in remaining an image of the ideal, requires the presence of a symbol which intermediates these two concepts.

The purpose of the present study is to demonstrate that the Judaeo-Christian angel, the Greek figure Hermes, and his Roman counterpart Mercury each represent the principle of the *anima mundi,* or world spirit, which underlies all things and informs the making of architecture. This idea can be traced to the classical tradition, in which the poet attempted to invoke the Muse for inspiration during the creative process. The divine Muse was essentially an *angelos* – the poet could not produce works of significance without her assistance. As cosmological models of the Western world transformed, the concept of the Muse, or angelic guide, took many forms, but the essential idea of reconciling body and soul through an invocation of an entity outside the self has remained intact. In alchemical terms, the division of a unified principle, which subsequently seeks reconciliation, can be found expressed in many dualisms: body and soul, the self and the other, the male and female principles and the creative process itself. In each case, a symbolic messenger illuminates the process of reconciliation.

The capacity of the *angelos* to act as a hinge or joint between two mirrored realms gave rise to the concept of the angel as a being that inhabits an intermediary world. Belonging neither to heaven nor to earth, yet capable of fusing them together, angels form an *axis mundi,* or Jacob's Ladder, which permits material transcendence.[5] Throughout sacred history, the Judaeo-Christian *angelos* is represented most often as pure light, as a sign whose presence is not marked by a body but by the luminous transference of a message. In treatises on angels, we discover that they serve three sacred domains: acting as emissaries of the invisible; being responsible for the history of recorded time (since they mark eternity); and guiding the soul through the gateways of love (*eros*) and death (*thanatos*). Providing inspiration and transmitting *pneuma*, the *angelos* "is invisible because the angelic fire is too pure for one to see. When one sees the fire flaming up from the distance, one is seeing only the smoke that surrounds it."[6]

This description illustrates that angels are messengers of the divine light, acting as mirrors which repeatedly diffuse this light so that it finally reaches the earth in a form that will inspire and not consume humankind. According to Dionysius the Areopagite, this accounts for the nine orders of the celestial hierarchy,[7] collectively forming a spiritual ladder that

4.2 Disembodied Spirits – *Seraph Angel with two fiery Ophanim.* Bronze mirror, Aleppo, sixth century, from Peter Lamburn Wilson, *Angels: Messengers of the Gods* (London: Thames and Hudson 1980).

reflects messages from the sky to the earth through a series of mirror-like devices. One of the nine orders, the six-winged seraphim, has three pairs of wings: one to shield its face from God, another to hide its sex, and the third to fly.

Considered metaphorically, the role of angel wings is, first and foremost, to enable angels to traverse time and space, rustling between the earthly and celestial realms. Their wings also act as mirrors, whose angles of incidence and reflection guide divine light to another angel, who then continues this process of diffusion along the *axis mundi*. According to their place in the cosmos, the celestial hierarchy "moulds and perfects its participants in the holy image of God, like bright and spotless mirrors, which receive the ray of the Supreme Deity, which is the Source of Light."[8]

Having first delivered the message, the angel often completes the task of exegesis, so that the subject can determine between a dream of the unconscious and a vision of higher consciousness. Eleazer of Worms described the dual role of the angel as messenger and interpreter, where "the prophet tells the angel what he has seen and the angel explains the vision."[9] In the oneiric *Book of Enoch*[10] it is revealed that angels not only act as reflective mirrors but also as divine geometers, for the prophet

4.3 Intermediary Messengers – *Angelic Muse "Metaphysic" reflecting Light to Homer.* Giambattista Vico, *Scienza Nuova,* 1744.

Enoch "saw long cords given to those angels, and they acquired wings for themselves, and flew ... that they may measure."[11]

The *Book of Enoch* also introduces a now forgotten history where the prophet Enoch laments: "It happened, after the sons of men had multiplied in those days, that daughters were born to them, elegant and beautiful; and when the Angels, the sons of heaven, beheld them, they became enamoured of them."[12] Enoch is informed that certain angels, known as Watchers, disclosed celestial mysteries to these mortal women.

The angelic Watchers, totalling 133,306,668,[13] descended upon the first females and produced progeny known as giants.[14] The story concludes with the birth of Lamech's son, Noah, who was all white like a child of the angels of heaven. In turn, the angels helped Noah build the ark, and (in addition to being responsible for guiding the music of the spheres)[15] released the waters over the earth, orchestrating a great flood which finally purged the earth of the race of giants.

This history of the "fallen angels" may be interpreted as an allegory of the human conflict between Gnosis on the one hand and the angelic sin of turning their mirrored souls away from the divine light on the other. In response to the fallen angels' desire to mingle the incorporeal with the corporeal, God gathered together four of the seven archangels – Michael, Gabriel, Raphael, and Uriel – who then bound the angel Azazel by the hands and feet and threw him into eternal darkness at the centre of the earth, along with the other sinful Watchers. From that instant, the fallen angels were deprived of both speech and the power of the logos.[16]

The Judaeo-Christian *angelos* could not sustain corporeal hypostasis for theological reasons, whereas Greek gods could interact freely with mortals due to their capacity for metamorphosis and their ability to move between the realm of gods and the world of heroes. This distinction caused a major theological debate in the Judaeo-Christian world surrounding the manifestation of angels as embodied or disembodied spirits. If they could share corporeality, it would lead to questions concerning their gender, their form, and their substance. Finally, the accepted Judaeo-Christian view supported the argument that angels were disembodied spirits, not subject to human conditions of *gravity* and *light*, but capable of communion with both divine and human providence, acting truly as symbolic intermediary "joints."[17]

Struggling with the artificial distinction between body and soul that lies at the root of the Western philosophical tradition, the eighteenth-century mystic Emanuel Swedenborg identified the spirit, which animates the body and the soul, as the element which unites this duality and fulfils the role of the *angelos*. Swedenborg further differentiated the spirit from "the soul of man, which is held to be either pure thought, or some vital principle, the seat of which is sought for in the body; and yet the soul is nothing but the life of man, while the spirit is the man himself; and the earthly body which he carries about him in the world is merely

4.4 Disembodied Spirits – *Angelic Thrones, also called "Wheels"*; from A.N. Didron, *Christian Iconography*, 1886.

an agent whereby the spirit, which is the man himself, is enabled to act fitly in the natural world."[18]

To further trace the symbolic origins of the winged messenger as a "joint," let us refer to the Greek concept of soul. For Aristotle, the creation of the soul was a mirroring of the cosmos based on an analogy between the celestial *angelos* and the individual *anima*, from the moment that "the demiurge bent the straight line into a circle; this single circle he divided into two circles united at two common points; one of these he divided into seven circles. All this implies that the movements of the soul are identified with the local movements of the heavens."[19] In the *Timaeus*, Plato recounts the cosmological creation and conceives the world as a sphere that is imbued with a soul and intelligence akin to those of a living being. In Plato's schema, the world was comprised of the four elements working together in harmony and proportion. From this perfect sphere, the demiurge developed a complex set of relations, which generated the universe and established an analogy between the spherical "world body" and its subsequent division into the human body: "Now anything that has come to be must be corporeal, visible and tangible: but nothing can be visible without fire, nor tangible without solidity, and nothing can be solid without earth. So god, when he began to put together the body of the universe, made it of fire and earth. But it is not possible to combine two things properly without a third to act as a bond to hold them together."[20] Plato's concept of the symbolic triad in continual transformation is personified by the figures Hermes and Mercury, who we shall now investigate as further embodiments of the *angelos*.

HERMES AND THE TRIAD

In Greek mythology, the most celebrated intermediary between two realms is Hermes, whose character is revealed by his collection of hieroglyphs. Perhaps best known as the symbolic conductor of souls, *Hermes psychopompos*,[21] he is portrayed carrying a golden staff (*kerykeion*), which enables him to act as both shepherd and magician by placing his staff on the eyes of the sleeper and gently leading him across the threshold into the other world. Hermes' *caduceus* is made from a staff with two intertwining serpents, which Jung notes "is not straight, but snakelike, a path that unites opposites in the manner of the guiding caduceus, a path whose labyrinthine twists and turns are not lacking in terrors. It is on this *longissima via* that we meet with those experiences which are said to be 'inaccessible.'"[22] In alchemy, the serpent personifies the spirit of renewal by shedding its skin and becoming the *uroboros*,[23] completing the hermetic cycle and symbolizing the eternal return.

In the myth of Orpheus and Eurydice, the *angelos* Hermes guides the mortal Orpheus to the underworld of Hades and Persephone to plead that the gods return his wife, who was taken from him unjustly on their wedding day. Hermes' involvement with the archetypal poet Orpheus is strengthened through his invention of the lyre, the poet's musical instrument that profoundly stilled the creatures of Hades. When the winged god Hermes was a mere child, he had mastered human artifice, fashioning a lyre from the shell of a tortoise and the intestines of Apollo's cows. During the theft of Apollo's cows for the purpose above, Hermes displayed the art of the trickster[24] by making shoes which led Apollo to believe he had gone in the opposite direction, and by tricking the tortoise into entering his cave and then scooping out its contents for the use of its shell.

It is through Hermes' role as the guide of souls and the patron of mortal travellers that Orpheus succeeded in persuading the king and

4.5 Intermediary Messengers – *Orpheus, Eurydice, and Hermes*, bas relief; Museo Nazionale, Naples.

queen of the underworld to return his wife to him after her initial death. According to Karl Kerényi in *Hermes: Guide of Souls* (Zurich: Spring 1926), Hermes' dual role of guiding the journey and marking the way became twofold, portraying both fixity and motion. Hermes marks the point by the dolmen (*hermaï*) and the path by his movement – a duality represented by the symbol of the caduceus. Furthermore, through the phallic symbolism of the "herm," the pastoral god Hermes became associated with fertility, as personified in the etymologies of eros (*amor*) and thanatos (*mors*) – love and death. Each of these characteristics illuminates Hermes' archetypal role in the Orpheus myth, where he represents the union of opposites and completes the Orpheus, Hermes, Eurydice triad. The passage where Hermes guides the young poet Orpheus back to his lost bride[25] is expressed eloquently by Rilke:

> The god of faring and of distant message,
> the travelling hood over his shining eyes,
> the slender wand held out before his body,
> the wings around his ankles lightly beating,
> and in his left hand, as entrusted, *her*.[26]

THE SPIRIT MERCURIUS

Forged partly from celestial fire and partly from terrestrial earth, the *angelos* Hermes represents the embodied reunion of dualities, as does the alchemical spirit Mercurius, who is often portrayed uniting the paired opposites with his own caduceus. In his analysis of the alchemical figure in "The Spirit Mercurius," Jung outlines the multiple aspects of Mercurius, which we may relate to the Roman god Mercury and to his Greek counterpart Hermes, in constructing our image of the *angelos:*

1 Mercurius consists of all conceivable opposites. He is thus quite obviously a duality, but is named a unity in spite of the fact that his innumerable inner contradictions can dramatically fly apart into an equal number of disparate and apparently independent figures.
2 He is both material and spiritual.
3 He is the process by which the lower and material is transformed into the higher and spiritual, and vice versa.
4 He is the devil, a redeeming psycho pomp, an evasive trickster, and god's reflection in physical nature.
5 He is also the reflection of a mystical experience of the artifex that coincides with the *opus alchymicum*.
6 As such, he represents on the one hand the self, and on the other hand the individuation process, and, because of the limitless number of his names, also the collective unconscious (*mare nostrum*).[27]

According to Jung, the alchemist's pursuit of Mercurius was an attempt to transcend the duality of the conscious and the unconscious. In the seventeenth century, Mercury, also called quicksilver (*argentum vivum*), was portrayed as a symbol of the union of opposites "since body and soul, in spite of the artificial separation, are united in the mystery of life, the mercurial spirit."[28]

The transformation of the spirit Mercurius represents that aspect of the undivided self, a return to the ideal sphere described in the *Timaeus*. Jung notes that "the magic of his name enables him, in spite of his ambiguity and duplicity, to keep outside the split, for as an ancient pagan god he possesses a natural undividedness which is impervious to logical and moral contradictions."[29] It is evident that his Greek counterpart Hermes may be interpreted in the same ambivalent manner through the union of Hermes and Aphrodite, conceived of as a dualistic reunion of the male and female principles and manifested in their offspring *Hermaphroditus*. The androgynous Hermaphrodite is the fruit of a symbolic marriage between the Self and the Other, and as such, is a truly "monstrous" amalgam.[30]

From the sixteenth to the nineteenth centuries, alchemists valued mercury for its ability in forming an amalgam. Analogous to the alchemical union, the creation of mirrors was seen as the magical fusion of two substances, conjoined by the winged messenger Mercury in his form as quicksilver (*argentum vivum*). In order to establish a connection between Mercury, Hermes, and the *angelos* as symbolic "mirrors," an account of the actual process of mirror making, discovered by the Venetians and further developed through the invention of plate glass in seventeenth-century France, will reveal the importance of mercury's form as *argentum vivum*: "On an inclined table surrounded by gutters, a carefully cleaned sheet of tin is spread, on which the mercury is poured. Under a light and rapid hand, the glass, pushed straight forward, drives before it the surplus of the metal, and the mercury, shut in between the tin and the glass, spreads out, and amalgamates in a few minutes. But the glass has to dry for nearly eight days, under heavy weights, which completes the fixing of the tinfoil."[31]

By "quickening" the silver and forming a bond between two surfaces, through a process called "foiling," Mercury is responsible for bridging dualities by means of a third element, reaffirming the essential nature of the *angelos*. Following the notion that the angel symbolizes an interface

4.6 Intermediary Messengers – *Hermes/Mercury: The alchemical union of opposites*; Valentinus, Museum Hermeticum Reformaum et Amplificatum, 1678.

between opposites and manifests the invisible via the figures of Hermes and Mercury, Jung observes that "if one makes a synopsis of all the descriptions and alchemical pictures of Mercurius, they form a striking parallel to the symbols of the self derived from other sources. One can hardly escape the conclusion that Mercurius as the *lapis* is a symbolic expression for the psychological complex which I have defined as the self."[32] Thus, both Hermes and Mercury represent the archetype of the undivided self, through the process of becoming, as they amalgamate the duality posed by the Self and the Other.

The symbolic role of the angel has remained a pivotal concept, although its form has changed according to the prevailing world view. While philosophical and theological schemas for the visible and the invisible have transformed throughout recorded history, the essential idea of the *angelos* has remained part of the conceptual framework of the cosmos. The alchemical symbolism of the angel is as important today as it was for alchemists of the seventeenth century, although the contemporary view tends to reflect Rilke's realization that "every angel is terrible,"[33] rather than the disembodied luminous sphere worshipped in medieval theology. Since the very Being of the *angelos* deals with the continual process of transformation, let us now examine three angelic appearances in twentieth-century works of art.

THE TERRIFYING ANGEL

In contemporary angelology, we are invariably led to the works of Rainer Maria Rilke, whose two collections of poetry, *The Sonnets to Orpheus* and *Duino Elegies,* celebrate transcendental reflections derived from the world of "things." Rilke's search for individual meaning in the universe led him toward a phenomenology of the object that is at once beautiful and sublime. Following Edmund Burke, Rilke's modern concept of the beautiful[34] contains aspects of both the benevolent and malevolent, which are expressed in this invocation of the *angelos* by the angst-ridden poet:

> Who, if I cried, would hear me among the angelic
> orders? And even if one of them suddenly
> pressed me against his heart, I should fade in the strength of his
> stronger existence. For Beauty's nothing
> but beginning of Terror we're still just able to bear,
> and why we adore it so is because it serenely
> disdains to destroy us. Each single angel is terrible.[35]

Although Rilke's lament reflects a post-theocratic world, one can feel his struggle to find meaning within our contemporary situation – a struggle expressed in the process of becoming and in the relation of the Self to the Other. For Rilke, the "other" is symbolized externally by those outside the "self," and internally by the "other" half of the creative process:

> Lovers – were not the other present, always
> spoiling the view! – draw near to it and wonder …
> Behind the other, as though through oversight,
> the thing's revealed … But no one gets beyond
> the other, and so world returns once more.
> Always facing Creation, we perceive there
> only a mirroring of the free and open,
> dimmed by our breath.[36]

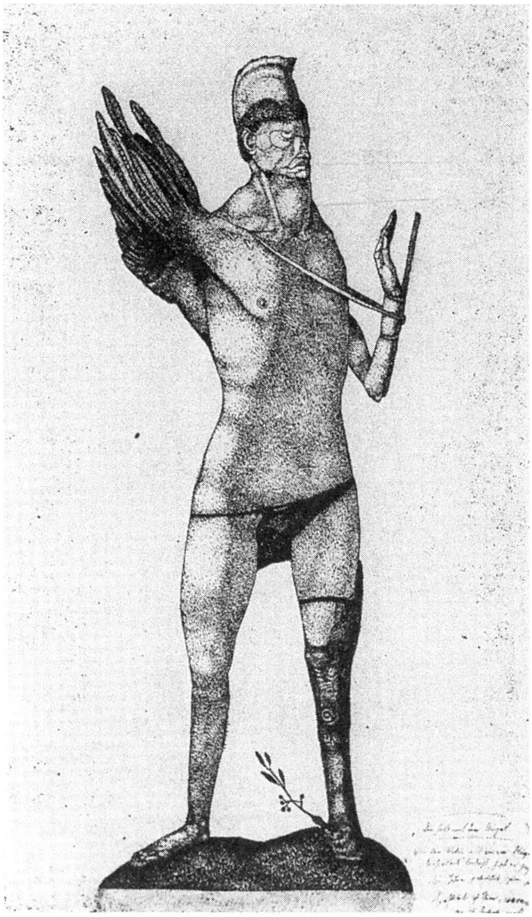

4.7 "Terrible" angel/monsters – *Hero with Wing*. Paul Klee, 1905; from Christian Geelhaar, *Paul Klee and the Bauhaus* (Greenwich: New York Graphic Society Ltd 1973), fig. 120.

In a similar manner, Rilke's contemporary Jean Cocteau wrote extensively about the modern angel as a mirroring of the self in an act of creative *mimesis*. For Cocteau, both the angel and the mirror were devices to reveal the invisible. Cocteau's *angelos* appears in an early poem entitled *L'ange Heurtebise*,[37] and is described as: "midway between the human and the inhuman. An angel is a brilliant young animal, full of vigour and charm, plunging from the seen to the unseen with the powerful gestures of a diver, and the thunder of a myriad wild pigeons wings. The radiant swiftness of its movements hides it from our view. Were it to slow down, doubtless we should perceive it. Now is the time for Jacob, that fine wrestler, to throw himself upon it. Death has no

4.8 Left: "Terrible" angel/monsters – Heurtebise as the angel/glazier Hermes, played by Cocteau, *Orphée*, 1932; from Arthur King Peters, *Jean Cocteau* (New York: The Vendôme Press 1986).

4.9 Opposite: "Terrible" angel/monsters – L'Ange Heurtebise. Jean Cocteau, *Le Sang d'un poète* (film), 1930; from Peters, *Jean Cocteau.*

meaning for this magnificent specimen of a sporting monster. It strangles mortals, and impassively tears out their souls. I imagine it to be something between a boxer and a sailing ship."[38]

Rilke's observation that "every angel is terrible" is evident in Cocteau's monstrous angel. The historical concept of the monster, like the angel, is an amalgam and is essential in understanding the literary metaphor of the angel/monster in both Cocteau's *Heurtebise* and Paul Klee's *Hero with Wing*.[39] Like the alchemical Hermaphrodite, Cocteau aptly refers to his angel as a *monstre-sacré*, in which the monster is a fusion of realms, like a minotaur or a dragon. In an early poem entitled *Dos d'ange*, written in 1922, Cocteau observes that the angel is a hunchback when seen from above, or at least appears to be a monster when his shadow is seen projected upon the wall of his room.[40] In Cocteau's sublime image, the angel Heurtebise departs from the realm of the invisible ideal and approaches an embodied duality by personifying angelic benevolence and daemonic malevolence.

The contemporary angel appears again in Cocteau's film *Le sang d'un*

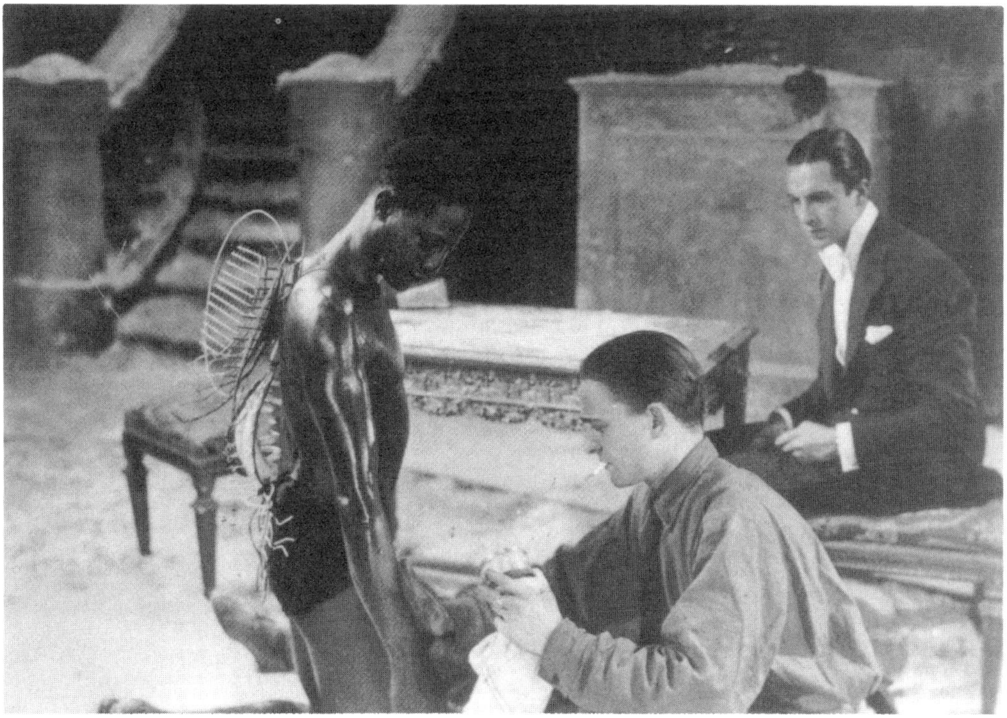

poète, in which a dark figure enters the scene and turns to reveal two racket-like "antenna-wings" attached to his back. Building his obsessive dark angel in the same way that Daedalus had built wings for his own son Icarus, Cocteau points the way for contemporary architects to consider artifice through the tectonic. Most important, in characterizing the artist's *métier* through the ludic process of *mimesis,* Cocteau once again invokes the Muses. This single image of the *angelos* is a potent metaphor of the angel incarnate.

Throughout this essay, I have followed the phenomenological concerns of thinkers whose transcendental understanding of embodiment has allowed us to discuss the perception of the invisible, and its projection into the invisible, material world as integrated. The prerequisite for this belief is that the contemporary angel remain an active, powerful mirror, symbolically bridging the subject and the object, the self and the world. When considered in this light, the image of the *angelos* in *Hero with Wing* discloses the modern potential of the architect as artificer, illuminated by the words of Rilke:

Consider the Hero continues,
even his fall
was a pretext for further existence,
An ultimate birth.[41]

Alas, in the spirit of Rilke, Klee, and Cocteau, we may interpret our collective sacred history and continue to forge our own meaningful Angels.[42]

NOTES

1 The amalgam is an alloy formed from marrying Mercury with another metal, and symbolizes the triad in this essay.
2 Augustine, *City of God,* trans. Gerald G. Walsh, Demetrins B. Zema, et al., ed. Vernon Bourke (New York: Image Books 1958), 262.
3 Ibid., 211.
4 Ibid., 264.
5 Transcendence is meant to be understood here in a phenomenological sense, which goes beyond the philosophical traditions of idealism and materialism. In Merleau-Ponty's terms, transcendence is coupled with immanence to arrive at a description of direct experience (existence).
6 Eleazer of Worms, *Three Tracts,* trans. Jack Hirschman and Alexander Altman (Berkeley: Tree Books 1975), 2. Eleazer was a thirteenth-century Kabbalist and mystical religious poet.
7 Dionysius the Areopagite, *Mystical Theology and the Celestial Hierarchies* (London: Garden City Press 1923). The nine orders are composed of three threefold choirs. Closest to God is the first choir: cherubim, seraphim, and thrones; the second choir: powers, virtues, and dominions; and the third choir: angels, archangels, and principalities. The nine orders represent nine archetypes in God and, together with the divine light, form nine concentric circles, accounting for the movement of the celestial spheres.
8 Dionysius the Areopagite, *Mystical Theology,* 29.
9 Eleazer of Worms, *Three Tracts,* 2.
10 Michael Knibb, *The Ethiopic Book of Enoch* (Oxford: Oxford University Press 1978), 148. This work traces the origin of the universe while Enoch sleeps and dreams.
11 If God is the creative Demiurge, it follows that his assistants, the angels, are the first surveyors. In recent history, architect John Hejduk expresses a

similar idea on page 155 of his book of architectural projects, *Vladivostok* (New York: Rizzoli, 1989):

> On the first note
> he sent out the angels
> they drew in outline
> with the tips of their wings
> the sphere of the earth.

12 Knibb, *The Ethiopic Book of Enoch*, 7: 2.

13 This figure represents the number of fallen angels, according to the Cardinal Bishop of Tusculum in the fifteenth century. Enoch speaks of some two hundred disobedient Watchers, who fell for nine celestial days into the dark abyss, accompanying Lucifer, the "morning star." For a complete glossary of angels, see Gustav Davidson, *A Dictionary of Angels* (New York: The Free Press 1967).

14 "Giant" is derived from *gaia*, the Greek word for "sons of earth," just as the angels are called the sons of heaven. According to Enoch, the race of giants were over 11,250 feet tall.

15 As mechanical models and empirical thought invented reasons to explain the "music of the spheres," the symbolic role of angels became increasingly unnecessary.

16 The theme of the incarnate fallen angel continues in the nineteenth-century Romantic poem by Thomas Moore entitled "Loves of the Angels." In his account, Moore expounds on the fate of three angels who leaked secrets to mortal women as symbols of their *amor*, only to be punished by unrequited love. The most relevant twentieth-century version of the angel incarnate is the film *Wings of Desire*, by Wim Wenders, whose main protagonist decides to exchange his spiritual enlightenment for carnal embodiment.

17 In architecture, this joint is often called a "reveal." It reveals the two elements and joins them at the same time, thus suggesting another form of amalgam. See n. 30 for further description.

18 Emanuel Swedenborg, *Heaven and Its Wonders and Hell, from things heard and seen* (New York: American Swedenborg Printing and Publishing Society 1900), 573. First published in 1758, Swedenborg's mystical theology opens with the statement that he had been in direct contact with angels who had informed him of the revelations held within his treatise.

19 Aristotle, "De Anima," in *Introduction to Aristotle,* ed. Richard McKeon

(New York: Random House 1947), 158. Aristotle is quoting from Plato's *Timaeus*.

20 Plato, *Timaeus*, trans. Desmond Lee (New York: Penguin Books 1971), 43–4.

21 For a comprehensive study of the Greek god Hermes, refer to Karl Kerényi, *Hermes: Guide of Souls*, trans. Murray Stein (Zurich: Spring Publications 1926).

22 Carl G. Jung, *Psychology and Alchemy*, trans. R.F.C. Hull (Princeton: Princeton University Press 1980), 6.

23 Both the *Uroboros* and the dragon are alchemical manifestations of Mercurius, or quicksilver. Mercurius is the symbol of the *prima materia* and the *lapis*, the beginning and the end.

24 The trickster is also an archetypal figure who discloses reality by transgressing conventional "boundaries."

25 To complete the hermetic cycle, Eurydice dies after being bitten by a snake.

26 Rainer Maria Rilke, "Orpheus. Eurydice. Hermes," in *Rilke Selected Poems*, trans. J.B. Leishman (England: Penguin Books 1964), 40.

27 Carl G. Jung, "The Spirit Mercurius," in *Aspects of the Masculine*, trans. R.F.C. Hull (Princeton: Princeton University Press 1989), 160.

28 Ibid., 162.

29 Ibid., 168.

30 For a further elaboration of this idea, see Marco Frascari, *Monsters of Architecture* (Baltimore: Rowman & Littlefield 1991), 51. The author states that "in Italian, *mostri sacri* originates in the Etruscan/Roman traditions of divination, which understood monsters as extraordinary events, celestial novelties, untouchable sacred signs of a possible future." Frascari argues convincingly that the monstrous aspect of architecture can be found particularly in the tectonics of the architectural detail.

31 Roger Francis and Alice Beard, *5000 Years of Glass* (New York: Frederick Stokes 1937), 201.

32 Carl G. Jung, *Alchemical Studies*, trans. R.F.C. Hull (London: Routledge & Kegan Paul 1968), 246. Also known as the philosopher's stone, the *lapis* was the supreme object of alchemy and a symbol for both Christ and Mercury. According to Jung, these two figures represent two aspects of the human psyche and stand for man and his shadow.

33 Rainer Maria Rilke, *Duino Elegies*, trans. C.F. MacIntyre (Berkeley: University of California Press 1961), 13.

34 See Edmund Burke's essay "A Philosophical Enquiry into the Origin of our Ideas of the Sublime and Beautiful," first published in 1757. This shift from

the classical definition of Beauty to the Sublime effect on the soul is extremely important in the formation of Romantic art and poetry, and is highly evident in the work of Piranesi, Turner, Baudelaire, and subsequent twentieth-century artists.

35 Rilke, *Duino Elegies*, 29.

36 Ibid., 69.

37 Jean Cocteau, "L'Ange Heurtebise" *Poèmes 1916–55* (Paris: Gallimard 1956). The poem "L'Ange Heurtebise" was written in 1925. I believe that Cocteau invented the name "Heurtebise" in an alchemical manner from two french verbs: *heurter* (to collide) and *biser* (to kiss), uniting the two concepts with a third. When Cocteau cast himself in the role of Heurtebise in the 1932 theatre production of *Orphée*, he portrayed Hermes (whom he renamed Heurtebise), as a glazier with glass "wings" attached to his back, confirming his belief in the angel/mirror analogy.

38 Cocteau, *Cocteau's World: An Anthology of Writings by Jean Cocteau*, trans. and ed. Margaret Crosland (New York: Dodd, Mead 1972), 359.

39 A similar fusion of the modern angel/hero is represented in Klee's etching entitled *Hero With Wing* (1905): a character in a state of metamorphosis, very much in the spirit of Ovid and Rilke. In diary entry (no. 585), Klee describes the dual image: "The man, born with only one wing, in contrast with divine creatures, makes incessant efforts to fly. In doing so, he breaks his arms and legs, but persists under the banner of his idea." From *Diaries of Paul Klee 1898–1918*, ed. by Felix Klee (Cologne 1957).

40 Jean Cocteau, *Poésie 1916–23* (Paris: Gallimard 1925). The original stanza reads:

> Que ce soit songe ou pas songe,
> En le voyant par dessus
> On découvre le mensonge
> Car les anges sont bossus.
>
> Du moins bossue est leur ombre
> Contre le mur de ma chambre.

41 Rilke, *Duino Elegies*, 23.

42 In this context, "forge" means to make or to invent. The root of the word is related to the Latin *fabricare*, to fabricate. In the act of making, two aspects of the human condition, *homo faber* and *homo ludens*, are equally at work.

In order to demonstrate the "invention" of angels, the following is a select angelography from Gustav Davidson's *A Dictionary of Angels* (New York: Free Press 1967):

Abaddon: Hebrew for "angel of the bottomless pit," he was responsible for binding Satan for 1,000 years.

Azrael: The traditional angel of death, whose name means "whom God helps." Since Azrael provided seven handfuls of earth for the creation of Adam, he was appointed to separate body from soul, and was said to have 4,000 wings and 70,000 feet. Azrael was forever writing in a large book: writing the names of man upon birth with one hand and erasing the names of man upon death with the other.

Liwet: The angel of love and invention in Mandaean lore, and one of the seven planetary spirits.

Penemue: Taught mankind "the art of writing with ink and paper" and, as a result, became one of the fallen angels according to Enoch.

Pi-Hermes: In hermetics, Pi-Hermes is the genius of Mercury, and head of the order of archangels.

Raphael: The angel of healing, whose name means "God has healed," Raphael is one of the seven archangels, according to Enoch, along with Michael, Uriel, Raguel, Seraqael, Gabriel and Haniel.

Satan: Once chief of the Seraphim, Satan is said to have been created on the sixth day of creation. The Hebrew name meaning "adversary," Satan symbolizes the prince of evil and enemy of Perfection.

And so on ...

Lessons of a Dream

Karsten Harries

Chora

AS JOSEPH RYKWERT has so convincingly shown, architectural theory cannot dispense with dreams or stories about an ideal architecture. Thoughts of the Heavenly Jerusalem once gave expression to such an ideal. So did Laugier's reconstruction of the primitive hut. So do speculations *On Adam's House in Paradise*.[1] The following remarks examine another such dream: Heidegger's description of a Black Forest farm house. The frequency with which Heidegger and more especially this questionable image of genuine building and dwelling have been invoked by recent architectural theorizing, calls for such an examination.

> The nature of building is letting dwell. Building accomplishes its nature in the raising of places by the joining of their spaces. *Only if we are capable of dwelling, only then can we build.* Let us think for a while of a farmhouse in the Black Forest, which was built some two hundred years ago by the dwelling of peasants. Here the self-sufficiency of the power to let earth and sky, divinities and mortals enter *in simple oneness* into things ordered the house. It placed the farm on the wind-sheltered mountainslope looking south, among the meadows close to the spring. It gave it the wide overhanging shingle roof whose proper slope bears up under the burden of snow, and which, reaching deep down, shields the chambers against the storms of the long winter nights. It did not forget the altar corner behind the community table; it made room in its chamber for the hallowed places of childbed and the "tree of the dead" – for that is what they call a coffin there: the *Totenbaum* – and in this way it designed for the different generations under one roof the character of their journey through time. A craft which, itself sprung from dwelling, still uses its tools and frames as things, built the farmhouse. (160)[2]

Heidegger chooses an example removed from our modern world. To be sure, many such farmhouses have survived and continue to shape the popular image of the Black Forest region. But they have survived as relics from another world, jutting into our own, inviting us to measure our way of life by one not yet shaped by technology. Heidegger himself emphasizes the temporal distance that separates us from the farmhouse, underscores that distance with his own archaizing style, a two-fold distance that may lead the reader to dismiss his example as irrelevant, even as it invites rethinking of what is often taken for granted.

The example is part of the conclusion of "Building Dwelling Thinking," a lecture first delivered on Sunday morning, 5 August 1951, to an audience of mostly architects, as part of a Darmstädter Gespräch, which that year focused on the theme "Man and Space." The lecture begins by stating what would seem to be obvious: the nature of building is letting dwell. To be sure, "Not every building is a dwelling" (145). In the lecture Heidegger mentions a number of such "buildings," including bridges and hangars, stadiums and power stations, highways and dams, factories and market halls. In their different ways all these serve our way of life, but we would not call them dwellings. To work in a factory, to shop in a store is not to dwell; we do not reside there. But just this equation of dwelling and residing is called into question by Heidegger's suggestion that even many residential buildings, "well planned, easy to keep, attractively cheap, open to air, light, and sun" though they may be, hold no "guarantee that *dwelling* occurs in them" (146). Of course not, we may want to agree: no more than a hammer can guarantee that it will be used as a hammer can a house guarantee that people will actually reside in it. But such easy agreement would miss Heidegger's point: to distinguish dwelling from mere residing, from merely inhabiting a structure or finding shelter. What then does Heidegger mean by "dwelling"?

Building is said to accomplish its nature, that is, to allow for dwelling, "in the raising of places by the joining of their spaces." The builders of Heidegger's farmhouse did so by placing it on its hillside, orienting the part of the house in which the farmer and his family ate, cooked, rested, and slept toward the valley, leaving the farmhouse's larger back half to cows, horses, and goats. To choose a site is already to establish a place: here I am going to dwell. Such establishing, to be sure, is not yet building. Building is not only an imaginative, but an actual establishing of space, requiring work.

All this seems obvious enough and hardly worth saying. And yet Heidegger warns us not to settle for what is so readily taken for granted: "As long as this is all we have in mind, we take dwelling and building as two separate activities, an idea that has something correct in it. Yet at the same time by the means-end schema we block our view of the essential relations. For building is not merely a means and a way toward dwelling – to build is in itself already to dwell" (146).

To be sure, the farmhouse serves a quite specific kind of dwelling, fitted to a particular landscape. The climate helped dictate that animals and humans share the same roof, while comfort demanded the separation of their quarters, joined only by a narrow walkway. One could thus discuss the farmhouse as a machine for living, although "tool" might

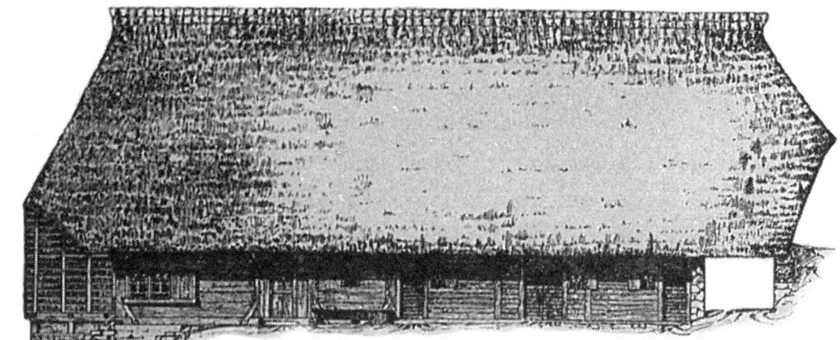

Abb. 1. Vordere Ansicht.

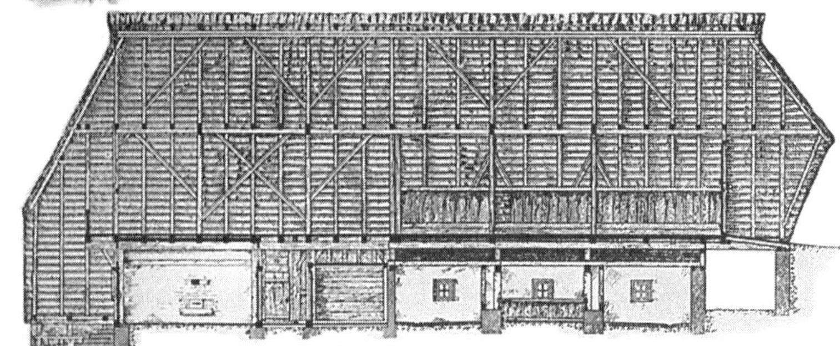

Abb. 2. Längenschnitt.

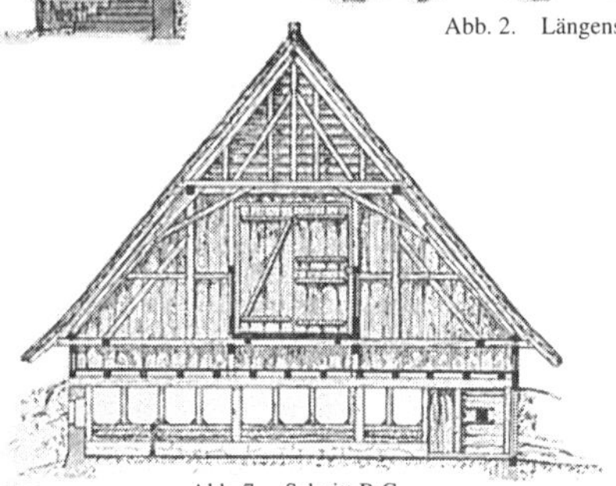

Abb. 7. Schnitt B C.

Abb. 8. Ansicht gegen das Thal.

seem to fit better. But, Heidegger insists, talk of building serving dwelling fails to consider "the real meaning of the verb *bauen*, namely, to dwell" (146). To support his claim that building and dwelling are inseparably joined, Heidegger appeals to Old English and High German: the now lost, but nevertheless real meaning, of the verb *bauen,* to build, is said to be "to dwell," and "to dwell" in turn originally meant "to be." Dwelling thus names "the basic character of human being" (148), which is not to be understood first of all as a being cast into boundless space, but as always already a dwelling, a being at home in the world, placed in an always already bounded space. This is to claim also that the world

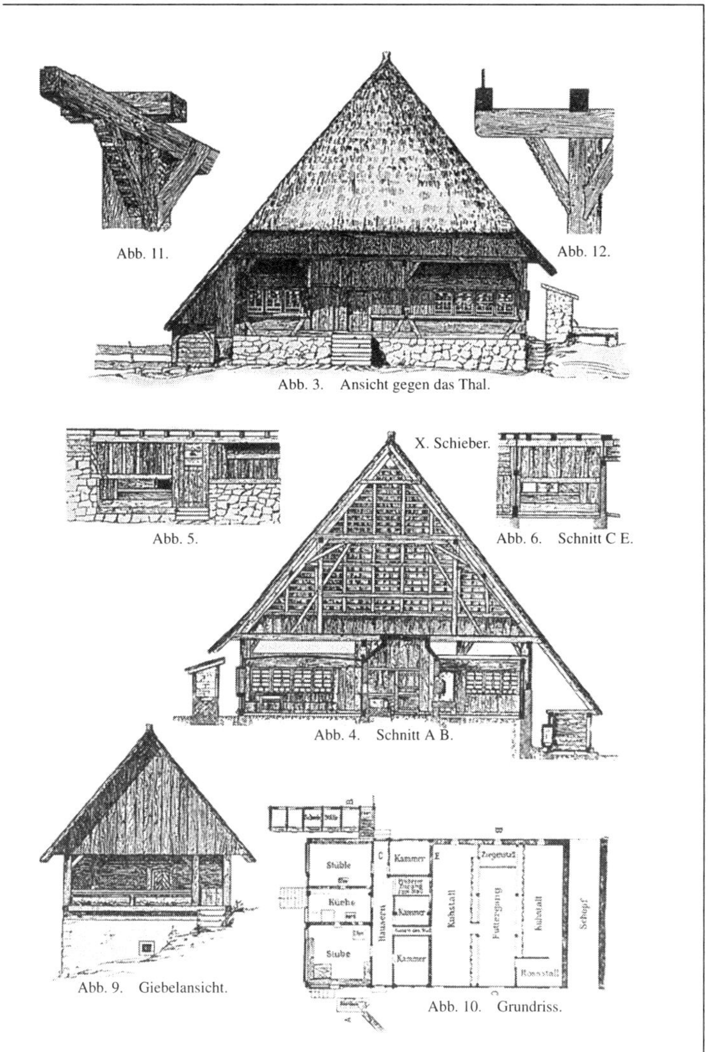

5.1 Black Forest Farm House; from *Das Bauernhaus im Deutschen Reiche und seinen Grenzgebieten* (Dresden: Küthmann 1906).

is experienced first of all as rather like a building. "The relationship between man and space is none other than dwelling, strictly thought and spoken" (157).

If "building is letting dwell," and "building accomplishes its nature in the rising of places," and if, further, "dwelling names the basic character of human being," this must mean that space is experienced fundamentally not as a homogeneous manifold in which things are then located, not as a Cartesian *res extensa*, but as a space of joined places, each with its own character. The bridge that spans the Neckar in Heidelberg is such a place: "The place is not already there before the bridge is. Before the bridge stands, there are of course many spots along the stream that can be occupied by something. One of them proves to be a place, and does so *because of the bridge*. Thus the bridge does not first come to a place to stand in it; rather, a place comes into existence only by virtue of the bridge" (154).

Itself a place, the bridge also opens up places: the river, the river banks, the city. It is in terms of such places that we experience space. Instead of thinking place in terms of space, Heidegger would thus have us invert that order. "What the word for space, *Raum*, *Rum*, designates is said by its ancient meaning. *Raum* means a place cleared or freed for settlement and lodging. A space is something that has been made room for, something that is cleared and free, namely within a boundary, Greek *peras*" (154). So understood, space is first of all bounded. Such bounding is inseparable from our experience of things, which we always experience as placed in one way or other: the fork on the table, the car on the road, Venus in the evening sky. Inseparable from our encounter with things is the experience of different spaces: table, road, evening sky. "That for which room is made is always granted and hence is joined, that is, gathered, by virtue of a place, that is, by such a thing as the bridge. *Accordingly, spaces receive their being from places and not from 'space'*" (154).

Already in *Being and Time* Heidegger had insisted that our experience of space is intimately linked to the activities in which we are engaged. The body, more especially the moving body, mediates our experience of space: the street is to be walked down, the mountain to be climbed, the bridge to be crossed. To be sure, we can locate the bridge by measuring how far it is from other things: "Thus nearness and remoteness between men and things can become mere distance, mere intervals of intervening space" (155). But just as this is an abstracted understanding of distance, so the understanding of space as the three-dimensional manifold rests on a reduction from a richer understanding of space. Think of the different ways in which we experience rooms, buildings, neighbourhoods, cities, landscapes. We have to agree with Heidegger: our experience of space is first of all an experience of spaces, mediated by our encounter with things and their places, and as such, is regional: this office is a region with boundaries that mark it off from other regions; so is a kitchen. Regions assign to persons and things their proper places; were it not for this, we could not consider certain things out of place.

In the case of this room, the region in question is bounded by floor, ceiling, and walls. But regions need not be bounded in that fashion. A forest clearing is a region; so is a valley. Regions are generally nested within regions: this room in my house, the house in its neighbourhood, the neighbourhood in the city, and so on. The region of all regions is the world, understood now not as the totality of all things but as the context of contexts that assigns everything its place.

Aristotelian space, which assigns to the four elements and thus to all things their proper places, is closer to this regional, everyday understanding of space than the space of geometry or the space presupposed by modern science. The space we inhabit is not the homogeneous space of Euclid. We live in a heterogeneous space. Furthermore, that heterogeneity is charged with meaning. Take a shopping plaza on a hot summer day; or a Maine beach on a cold February morning.

It is in terms of activities that we understand proximity and distance: that is to say, in terms of the moving body. As humanist architecture recognized, the human body furnishes something like a natural measure of space. Bound up with that measure is the qualitative difference of the directions of the space we inhabit: up and down, front and back, right and left, for example, carry different meanings, as becomes clear as soon as we begin to reflect on the metaphorical use of these terms: "I am down," "He is sinister looking," "He went behind my back." If building is the construction of boundaries in space, this space cannot be understood as a homogeneous given. Space has always already been separated into regions, of which sky and earth are only the most basic. This allows Heidegger to say that human being is essentially a dwelling on the earth and under the sky. And if dwelling expresses the relationship between man and space, this means that space is always already charged with meanings. Space is not mute; space speaks to us, and only because it speaks, do buildings speak to us.

"Only if we are capable of dwelling, only then can we build." But if "the nature of building is letting dwell," must we not also hold on to the reverse: dwelling presupposes building? If the particular dwelling made possible by the Black Forest farmhouse can be said to presuppose that more primordial dwelling that is nothing other than the human way of existing, must it not also presuppose a more primordial building? How are we to understand this building? The answer is found in what was just said: if "dwelling" names "the relationship between man and space," this primordial "building" must mean space, but space understood as a sort of room, as a bounded whole, joining regions and granting things their separate places.

The traditional analogy between human building and divine creation comes to mind. God has often been described as the archetypal architect, who fashioned the world as a perfectly ordered whole, the fit dwelling place for human beings. The Middle Ages thus understood the church as a representation of the cosmos. Mircea Eliade similarly appeals to construction rites to suggest that in primitive societies the building of every house is "an imitation, hence reactualization of the cosmogony."[3] The primordial building that provides human building with its ground and measure would then be the cosmos, where "cosmos" names precisely the world into which we have been cast, experienced as a meaningful order. The later Heidegger makes such an experience constitutive of human being: "It is not that there are men, and over and above them *space*; for when I say 'a man,' and in saying this word think of a being who exists in a human manner – that is, who dwells – then by the name 'man' I already name the stay within the fourfold among things"(156).

But this equation of human being, dwelling, and staying within the fourfold of earth and sky, divinities and mortals, such staying understood as a preserving of "the fourfold in its essential being, its presencing," (150) must be questioned. What sense does it make to claim both: that human being is essentially dwelling and that dwelling is a staying within and preserving of the fourfold? Something like the distance that separates us from the Black Forest farmhouse also would seem to separate us from Heidegger's fourfold. If genuine dwelling must indeed be understood as a staying within the fourfold, would this not mean that we moderns are no longer able to dwell in Heidegger's sense? But what forces us to say that? Why not distinguish instead between dwelling understood just as being in the world and dwelling understood as "staying within the fourfold"? And why privilege the latter? Such questioning returns us to Heidegger's understanding of the fourfold.

Three of the terms would appear to pose little difficulty although they do raise questions:

By "earth" Heidegger means the ground that supports us, literally, and in the sense that it sustains us with its gifts of food and water: "Earth is the serving bearer, blossoming and fruiting, spreading out in rock and water, rising up into plant and animal" (149). Human being is essentially a being on the earth, and it remains so, despite space flights and dreams of colonizing other planets. More problematic is the suggestion that dwelling requires recognition of our dependence on the earth and its gifts, requires "saving" the earth in Heidegger's special sense: "To save the earth is more than to exploit it or even wear it out. Saving the earth does not master the earth and does not subjugate it, which is merely one step from spoliation" (150). That human beings often fail to save the earth in this sense requires no comment. A more genuine dwelling is opposed here to the way we exist first of all and most of the time, to the way we deal with persons and things. And if Heideggerian dwelling is equated with being human, such being human can be understood only as an essence or ideal, at a distance from our world, calling us beyond it.

By "sky," too, Heidegger means pretty much what we usually mean by the word: "The sky is the vaulting path of the sun, the course of the changing moon, the wandering glitter of the stars, the year's seasons and their changes, the light and dusk of day, the gloom and glow of night, the clemency and inclemency of the weather, the drifting clouds and blue depth of the ether" (149). But again, what seems obvious at first soon becomes questionable. Dwelling is said to require an openness to the sky as sky. Those who dwell "leave to the sun and the moon their journey, to the stars their courses, to the seasons their blessing and their inclemency; they do not turn night into day nor day into a harassed unrest" (150). The challenge to our modern way of living – just think of our dependence on artificial light – is evident, inviting the reader not just to question this way of life, but also the assumptions behind Heidegger's delineation: would Heidegger have us live in a pre-technological world? What special lesson does his Black Forest farmhouse and the presupposed way of dwelling hold for us today? Why not choose some more familiar building, say a house in some American suburb with its television sets, VCRs, telephones, radios, and light bulbs? Can we not say of it, too, that it was built by "a craft which, itself sprung from dwelling, still uses tools and frames as things," although, uncomfortable with such stilted talk, we may just want to say that the suburban home, too, both makes possible and presupposes an established and generally taken for granted way of life. The distance that separates such language from Heidegger's invites us to reflect on the distance that separates our modern "dwelling" from the dwelling that built the farmhouse. Is it also the distance that separates us moderns from genuine building?

The third term once again seems unproblematic at first: Heidegger's "mortals" are of course we human beings. To speak of "mortals" is to emphasize the precariousness and finitude of our existence. In *Being and Time* Heidegger had shown being-unto-death to be constitutive of being human and linked authenticity to a resolute appropriation and affirmation of our essential mortality. And with good reason: as the possibility that means the end of all my possibilities, as this final possibility, death circumscribes my life and gathers it together, giving weight to every one of my actions. To be open to this possibility is to acknowledge how inescapably my life is my own. All self-assertion is thus shadowed by nothingness. Just because of this, human beings tend to cover up their essential mortality and with it their own essence, flee to the world, to different roles and activities. The resolute anticipation of death rescues us from such dispersal, makes us whole, heals in that sense.

But do we have to speak here of flight? Can we turn the matter around and interpret the link that *Being and Time* establishes between authenticity and the resolute anticipation of death as a running away from life? We have to grant that death is constitutive of individuality. But human beings not only exist as solitary selves, but also belong to larger wholes, stand in the tension between both, experience the claims of both. That Heidegger himself came to recognize the incompleteness of the analysis of authentic being-unto-death offered in *Being and Time* is suggested by his subsequent analysis of genuine dwelling as a staying within the fourfold.

This returns us to the last and most difficult of its four constituents. How are we to understand Heidegger's "divinities"? Heidegger calls them "the beckoning messengers of the godhead" (150). This is how angels have traditionally been understood and following the poet Hölderlin, instead of speaking of "divinities" or "gods," Heidegger at times also speaks of "angels." Whatever content we can give to the divinities, this much seems certain: by making these messengers of the godhead constitutive of dwelling, Heidegger distances himself from all views that would make human beings the authors of what finally gives direction to their lives. Genuine dwelling is tied to a sense of vocation or calling. Talk of divinities or messengers of the godhead points to the inevitably mediated nature of that call.

But is not God, for Heidegger as for Nietzsche, a poetic fiction that, unmasked as such, has lost its authority? Heidegger knows that the godhead and its messengers are not present to us as is the earth, that we cannot receive them as we can the sky. The divinities, he tells us, we can only await: "Mortals dwell in that they await the divinities as divinities. In hope they hold up to the divinities what is unhoped for. They wait for intimations of their coming and do not mistake the signs of their absence. They do not make their gods for themselves and do not worship idols. In the very depth of misfortune they wait for the weal that has been withdrawn" (150).

Heidegger asks us to dwell in the knowledge of the absence of the godhead's messengers, attentive to intimations of their coming. In another essay he invites us to look for such intimations to the things that surround us, to "everything that shimmers and blossoms in the sky and thus under the sky and thus on earth, everything that sounds and is fragrant, rises and comes – but also everything that goes and stumbles, moans and falls silent, pales and darkens. Into this, which is intimate to man but alien to the god, the unknown imparts himself, in order to remain guarded within it as the unknown."[4]

To be called by something in the world in such a way that life is given a direction is to receive the godhead's message, where depending on the message received we may name the messenger Aphrodite or Hera, Dionysus or Apollo – or Christ. But because any attempt to name the gods and God in order thus to take the measure of human being and to allow them to dwell is always a violation of the unknown essence of divinity, it is in danger of obscuring divinity with some golden calf. Heidegger therefore warned his audience to resist the temptation to dance around some golden calf, to substitute idols for angels, measures we have created for measures gained by precariously interpreting the messages of the godhead's messengers.

But if Heidegger rejects idolatry, how, in the absence of divinities, is our modern dwelling to find measure and direction? His suggestion, that we wait for what has been withdrawn, hardly provides the content necessary to give guidance to our dwelling and building.

What can such perhaps suggestive, but disturbingly vague talk, freighted with Christian, and in Heidegger's case, more specifically Hölderlinian associations, still mean to us? I pointed out that Heidegger's lecture was delivered in 1951, at a time when Germany was suffering from a severe housing shortage in the wake of the Second World War, and the *Wohnungsfrage*, the question of dwelling, was thought of first of all in terms of the need for physical shelter. But that need, the assembled architects were told, was not at all the real problem: "However hard and bitter, however hampering and threatening the lack of houses remains, the *real plight of dwelling* does not lie merely in a lack of houses. The real plight of dwelling is indeed older than the world wars with their destruction, older also than the increase of the earth's population and the condition of the industrial workers. The real dwelling plight lies is this, that mortals ever search anew for the nature of dwelling, that they *must ever learn to dwell.* What if man's homelessness consisted in this, that man still does not even think of the *real* plight of dwelling as *the* plight?" (161). Heidegger's invites his audience to consider the essence of dwelling. Even though generally unrecognized and unthought, that essence confronts us moderns as *the* task.

Did Heidegger's discussion of the fourfold and the concluding example of the Black Forest farmhouse intersect with the problems faced by his listeners, who heard him in respectful silence? Where was he pointing? Heidegger certainly did not mean to suggest that the Germans ought to build as their backward forebears built two hundred years ago. "Our reference to the Black Forest farm in no way means that we should or could go back to building such houses; rather, it illustrates by a dwelling that *has been* how *it* was able to build" (160). But just what are we to learn then from this illustration? The dwelling that built the farmhouse did not know what Heidegger calls the misfortune of the withdrawal of the godhead's beckoning messengers. It had its measure in a sacred order. Like Heidegger's audience, we no longer know such a measure. Is it then still possible for us to dwell in anything like Heidegger's sense? Are we condemned to fail to live up to what the essence of dwelling demands? I am too much of a modernist to be able to take such suggestions very seriously. Should we then dismiss Heidegger's example as hopelessly, perhaps even dangerously anachronistic? The Black Forest farmhouse belonged to a world not yet touched by the Enlightenment, not yet shaped by technology, to a premodern world. And if the Black Forest farmhouse should indeed lie irrecoverably beyond and behind us, can we deplore this? Who of us would want to change places with Heidegger's Black Forest farmer? Only if we are able to substitute for the kind of dwelling that built this farmhouse one genuinely of our age, will we be able to arrive at a notion of building that is not anachronistic. But does Heidegger's understanding of the essence of dwelling even allow us to delineate a dwelling genuinely of this age? What would it be like?

Recall once more Heidegger's problematic gloss on what it means to "receive the sky as sky": *not* to turn night into day. Is artificial light incompatible with Heideggerian dwelling? Or think of the revolution in communications and the way it has shaped the world we live in, especially our sense of space, and consider the freedom gained by this revolution. For Heidegger's Black Forest farmer the particular place into which he happened to have been born tended to become a destiny from which he could not escape, limiting the possibilities available to him in a way we would find intolerable. Place circumscribed vocation and community. Inseparable from such a strong sense of place is a lack of freedom. The rootedness of his existence was bought at a price few of us would and should be willing to pay. However we might want to reappropriate Heidegger's remarks on dwelling, such reappropriation would have to recognize technology's ability to liberate human beings and thus to allow them to become more truly themselves.

But just this promise of liberation is called into question by Heidegger's juxtaposition of dwelling as a staying within the fourfold and residing in a world ruled by the essence of technology. Technology, Heidegger insists, is not just a means to an end, an instrument we use as we might use a hammer. In its essence technology is a way of understanding the being of what is, a way marked by Descartes' famous promise of "a practical philosophy by means of which, knowing the force and the action of fire, water, air, the stars, heavens, and all other bodies that environ us, as distinctly as we know the different crafts of our artisans, we can in the same way employ them in all those uses to which they are adapted, and thus render ourselves the masters and possessors of nature."[5] Nature comes to be understood increasingly as available material, to be used and to be disposed of when no longer of use. That includes human beings. We cannot simply shrug off Heidegger's claim that the technological spirit presiding over the modern world threatens to reduce human beings to material, subject to calculation and planning as just another resource. Think of traffic engineering; or of modern medicine; or of modern war – Heidegger would have us add Hitler's final solution to such examples.

Heidegger, too, understood the extermination camps as factories of death, buildings built to reduce human beings to human material, built to betray the essence of building because built to betray what is a condition of genuine dwelling: staying within the fourfold, and that means also preserving the possibility of really dying. "Do they die?" Heidegger asks of those who perish in the extermination camps. "Hardly noticed," they are *umgelegt*, "cut down," "liquidated." Such perishing is not dying in Heidegger's sense. "Only those, able to die, become mortals in the full sense of this word. A mass of misery, of countless, dreadfully undied deaths everywhere – and all the same, the essence of death remains blocked. Not yet are human beings mortals."[6] Heidegger would have us understand the concentration camps as an extreme example of what in "Building Dwelling Thinking" is called "the plight of dwelling." Their "architecture" is indeed the horrifying realization of the counter-ideal buried in the essence of technology: the anti-type to Adam's house in paradise.[7]

Despite the pressing housing shortage, few of those hearing Heidegger could have disputed that "the real plight of dwelling does not lie merely in a lack of houses," that "the real plight" is rather this, "that mortals ever search anew for the nature of dwelling, that they *must ever learn to dwell.*" Such learning, Heidegger had told his audience, requires strength to resist the temptation to make gods for ourselves and to worship idols. This must have touched those who heard him: had the Germans not fallen into idolatry when they substituted a house built by Hitler for that primordial building whose outlines haunt and elude us? And had Heidegger himself not participated in their dance around the golden calf? Convinced that with the death of God the edifice of our culture had lost founder and foundation and lay in ruins, Heidegger had hoped to recover the archaic truth of pre-Socratic Greece for the modern age. That hope let him be receptive to the Nazis' promise of a new order raised on blood and soil. Those who seek inspiration and a sense of direction in the much cited temple passage in "The Origin of the Work of Art"[8] should remember that it was written at a time when Nazi Germany sought to reappropriate the Greek paradigm, which has played such a fateful part in German history, giving it architectural expression in its own brand of Neo-Classicism. Postmodern architects and theorists have shown increasing appreciation for both Heidegger's reflections and the Nazis' sublime perversion of Athenian architecture. To them especially I would recommend Robert Jan van Pelt's "Apocalyptic Abjection," which begins with a discussion of Heidegger's failed attempt to serve a distinctly German reappropriation of the greatness of our culture's Greek beginning, passes on to a discussion of Nazi architecture as a repetition of the architecture of Athens, of Hitler's attempt to make Berlin "into a mondial acropolis," Nuremberg into a national agora, Munich into a German necropolis, and concludes with an interpretation of Auschwitz as the topsy-turvy city Hitler built.[9] It should be obligatory reading for all who seek to appropriate Heidegger's thought for architectural theory, indeed for all who dream of recovering the greatness of its Greek beginning, but also the seductive simplicity of his Black Forest farmhouse for our modern culture.[10]

Still, the threat of falling into idolatry – I prefer to speak of the threat of Kitsch – should not lead us to lose sight of the problem with which Heidegger and his audience were wrestling: the plight of our dwelling. The evening preceding the lecture the well-known architect Rudolf Schwarz had prepared the audience for what Heidegger had to say by challenging the prevailing understanding of building as a compromise of functional and aesthetic considerations: "Many of you who like to travel and to look at works of art will not like to hear me say this: that unfortunately you do not really understand these works. But that is a fact. If you really want to understand a Baroque cathedral, you have to reenact it spiritually so to speak. Here all those beautiful books and words are of little help. You have to join in the great celebration of the community before the eternal, so that you carry yourself into this work and in this manner understand it, not only with your all too clever eye, but with body and soul."[11]

To understand a Baroque church as an aesthetic object, with our clever eye, is not really to understand it. For what is thus understood is not the church. To really understand a church we must join in the communal celebration of the mass that the church building serves. Generalizing, Heidegger might have said, to really understand a building we have to participate in the dwelling that built it. But let me continue with the Schwarz quotation: "It does not help at all to draw pretty houses. There are modern architects who are especially clever at that sort of thing, they take away whole walls and then they replace them with display windows, and the front lawn is brought right into the living room and other such pretty things. All this is good and well, but such tricks will never lead us to a house. Rather to an often highly admirable aesthetic construction of houselike character."[12]

How then do we build a house? Schwarz's answer may seem even more old-fashioned and anachronistic than the example of a Black Forest farmhouse Heidegger was to offer the same audience the following morning: "I am terribly sorry to have to say this, but you only get a house by marrying and by devoting yourself unconditionally to that great law. That may well be much more demanding than designing a house with wonderfully large windows. But I don't think we can arrive at a house in any other way. And this should be the first step towards establishing a decent house, then a village, then a city."[13]

The emphasis on marriage must have seemed embarrassingly conservative even when the lecture was given. But Schwarz's main points deserve to be taken seriously. Schwarz too ties the problem of architecture to a lost or at least threatened ability to dwell. This loss or threat again is tied to an inability on the part of the individuals to commit themselves to something larger than their own mortal selves. The problem of architecture for Schwarz is thus a problem of ethics, inseparable from the exaggerated individualism – if you wish, narcissism – that so many have understood as at the heart of modernity's malaise. As the individual is made the highest court of appeal, self-gratification becomes central, as it must when human beings understand themselves as self-sufficient wholes. To existing as an individual Schwarz opposes existing as a part, where as a Christian builder of churches he dreamed of a Christian socialism. Those of us who, like Heidegger, lack such faith, are given a pointer by Schopenhauer's account of the human being as not only a mortal, but also a sexual being. Sex, Schopenhauer insists, preparing the way for Freud, is misunderstood when it is reduced to an instrument which we use to amuse ourselves and others. It would be more correct to call the individual an instrument of the species, which through sex strives for immortality. As this instrument, the human being belongs to a larger ongoing order. Given such an interpretation, the individual who takes his own death to be the end that circumscribes all others would exist inauthentically precisely because he has refused to acknowledge the tragic tension between individual and species in human being. The human species should not be understood here in a narrowly biological fashion. The human being is, after all, the *animal rationale*, *zoon logon echon*. Species therefore means also an ongoing community; community in turn depends on communication; and to understand the possibility of communication we have to open our understanding of species to the *logos* presiding over it. For Heidegger's messengers of the godhead I would like to substitute the uncertain call of that *logos*.

This revision of Heidegger's understanding of dwelling calls for building responsively, not just to our mortality, but to a love that lets us experience ourselves as essentially incomplete, in need of others, in need of community. Such building would provide interpretations of our place in an ongoing historical context. Heidegger recognizes the need for such interpretation when he says of the Black Forest farmhouse that "it designed for the different generations under one roof the character of their journey through time." This then is a house built not for an individual, but for the different generations. Temporal reality is established as a historical order in which the individual stands, an order that assigns us our place and charges us with responsibility. This is to say, just as buildings establish regions, wrest place from space, so they establish temporal situations, place the individual in time, and not just in time, but in a communally shared time, in history. Such establishment constitutes the highest vocation of architecture. Temple and church can serve as paradigms.

Schwarz raises the obvious question: "Of course there will be those clever people who ask: are we today still capable of this? I don't know whether we are capable of this, but the architect has to make this demand. If there is and if there is supposed to be real architecture, then one has to go this bitter road. I can't help it."[14]

It is of course possible to object that what Schwarz here calls "real architecture" is indeed a thing of the past, that it belongs in a museum, just as the kind of commitment that is here demanded may be felt to belong in a museum. Is Schwarz not terribly old-fashioned with his emphasis on marriage and a communal dwelling? But we have to accept Schwarz's basic point: "real architecture" has always had its measure in, and been an interpretation of, some communal ideal. That was recognized by those medieval builders who built their churches as imitations of the Heavenly Jerusalem, placing them as illuminating figures on the ground of everyday buildings.

There is an obvious objection to this concept of "real architecture": does such emphasis on community not shortchange the individual and his rights and creativity? But the answer to this challenge is not difficult to give: our interpretations of an ideal dwelling must recognize not only the community, but also the individual, and the inevitable tension between the two, just as it must recognize the inevitable tension between public architecture giving voice to the values presiding over the community and more modest comparatively private building. Building that serves the requirements of dwelling must preserve and represent the tensions between private and public domains, house and temple, building and architecture, building and nature. So understood, Heidegger is right when he insists that we "must ever learn to dwell" and inevitably such learning includes dreams of an ideal architecture.

NOTES

1 Joseph Rykwert, *On Adam's House in Paradise* (New York: Museum of Modern Art 1972).

2 Martin Heidegger, "Bauen Wohnen Denken," first published in *Darmstädter Gespräch Mensch und Raum* (Darmstadt: Neue Darmstädter Verlagsanstalt 1952), 72–84. Translation by A. Hofstadter: "Building Dwelling Thinking," *Poetry, Language, Thought* (New York: Harper and Row 1971). Page references in the text are to this translation. I have substituted "sky" for "heaven" as a translation of *Himmel*, and "place" for "location" as a translation of *Ort*.

3 Mircea Eliade, *Cosmos and History. The Myth of the Eternal Return* (New York: Harper Torchbooks 1959), 76–7.

4 Heidegger, " ... Poetically Man Dwells ... " *Poetry, Language, Thought*, 225.

5 René Descartes, *Discourse on Method* VI, in *The Philosophical Works of Descartes*, trans. Elizabeth S. Haldane and G.R.T. Ross (New York: Dover 1955), I: 119.

6 "Die Gefahr," *Bremer und Freiburger Vorträge, Gesamtausgabe*, vol. 79 (Frankfurt am Main: Klostermann 1994), 56.

7 See Robert Jan van Pelt, "Apocalyptic Abjection," in Robert Jan van Pelt and Carroll William Westfall, *Architectural Principles in the Age of Historicism* (New Haven and London: Yale University Press 1991), 317–81.

8 Heidegger, "The Origin of the Work of Art," *Poetry, Language, Thought*, 41–2.

9 van Pelt, "Apocalyptic Abjection," 335.

10 Ibid., 417.

11 Rudolf Schwarz, "Das Anliegen der Baukunst," *Mensch und Raum*, 67.

12 Ibid.

13 Ibid., 67.

14 Ibid., 68.

Architecture as Site of Reception. Part II: Sea-Food and Vampires[1]

Donald Kunze

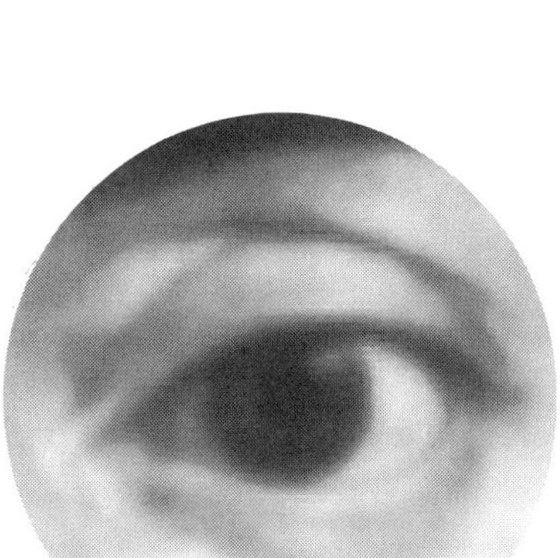

There are three Fine Arts – Sculpture, Painting, and Ornamental Pastry-making – of which Architecture is a Branch.

Pierre-Simon Fournier

ANAMNETIC BROTH (AQUACOTTA)[2]

1 Stir up the memories of a past, using anecdotal pasts as substitutes if necessary.
2 Skim off the extreme bottom and top; discard.
3 Stir the remainder until transformed into something vaguely familiar.

THE NOW SOMEWHAT INFAMOUS futurist impresario Filippo Tommaso Marinetti recognized that a public numbed by the over-intellectualized debates of artists, historians, and critics could be refreshed by shifting the venue to issues of cuisine. The "point" of *The Futurist Cookbook* (1932) may have been a serious joke about the culinary conservatism of the twentieth century, but it displayed a showman's wit in its willingness to translate aesthetic issues into a readily recognizable language – or, rather, to split the language of art into two parts, one that seemed to speak of recipes for nourishment, another that considered "food as a raw material for art."[3] Both these languages have come upon hard times at the end of the century, which has considered Marinetti's vocabulary and syntax unacceptably xenophobic, sexist, fascist, militaristic, and racist. The recipes bore names such as "Manandwomanatmidnight," "Fisticuff Stuff," "Ultravirile," "Steel Chicken," "The Excited Pig," and "Elasticake." There were also descriptions of actual and proposed dinners, such as the "Declaration of Love Dinner":

A shy lover yearns to express his feelings to a beautiful and intelligent woman. The following Declaration of Love Dinner served on the terrace of a grand hotel in the twinkling night of the city will help him to achieve this aim.

I Desire You: antipasto composed of a myriad selection of exquisite tid-bits, which the waiter will only let them admire, while She contents herself with bread and butter.

Flesh Adored: A big plate made from a shining mirror. In the centre, chicken slices perfumed with amber and covered with a thin layer of cherry jam. She, while eating, will admire her reflection in the plate.

This Is How I'll Love You: Little tubes of pastry filled with many different flavours, one of sweet rice, etc. She, without batting an eyelid, will eat them all.

Super Passion: A very compact cake of sweet pastry with small cavities on the top filled with anise, glacier mints, rum, juniper and Amaro.

Tonight With Me: A very ripe orange enclosed in a large hollowed-out sweet pepper, embedded in a thick zabaglione flavoured with juniper and salted with little bits of oyster and drops of sea water.[4]

The shallow side of this analogy is occupied with translating the element concealed in food terms into hidden meanings, at first sexual and subsequently artistic, an exercise that holds the attention of those for whom art is the raw material for hermeneutics.[5] Marinetti's provocative recipes do not establish a truly serious commitment to considering art from the point of view of cuisine. His propaganda employed the favourite tool of morality tales, allegory. The allegorical interpretation transposes the whole text into a code that, viewed from afar, is both a joke and a tongue-in-cheek commentary.

In allegory, we are not surprised when animals speak or angels visit. They do so to fill symbolic roles in the story, to point us toward meaning hidden behind the veil of poetic invention. The value of the "vehicle" of hidden meaning is zero. We don't *care* whether the message is delivered by an angel or a parking-lot attendant. However, in part 1 of this article, "Cuisine, Frontality, and the Infra-Thin,"[6] we discovered that there is a deep end to this pool: an essential web of relationships binding cuisine to matters of dimensionality, frontality, anamorphosis, and time. The *uncanniness* of food's relation to art resides in the possibility that food, hunger, and eating actually embody artistic truths. The "uncanny" view finds itself amidst a conflation of topics where art *is* food and food *is* art. But, the uncanny suffers from the critical limitation that the uncanny is just that. Our response to the unknown is simple wonder or fear. As with allegory, a neutralization takes place. The work of art produces a response we can experience easily enough without art. Allegory breeds a passive indifference to the medium it employs, but the audience of the uncanny is, typically, reduced to an adrenalin factory. Contamination of meaning is the norm. It is the night in which, as Hegel put it, all cows are black.

What is the middle ground between these opposed choices? I would assess this as the *central* question of architectural criticism: the choice between a total conflation of categories on one hand and a process of restrictive characterization on the other. Defining the literary genre of the fantastic, Tvestan Todorov constructed a linear model that is appropriate here.[7] For the fantastic to work, he argued, the reader must pause between an "uncanny" interpretation of events and an "allegorical" one. The fantastic is more interesting than either of these interpretive poles because it is about both fear and the neutralization of fear by the rational consciousness; and it is about the *moment of hesitation* between the two. In the uncanny, we are in the middle of a nightmare. In the allegory, we are allowed to dream while fully awake. In the fantastic, we wake up but we suspect we are in another dream, more potent and more confounding. While inhabiting this infra-thin space of doubt, we are in possession of a concretely universal situation, an atom shared by all humans and all cultures, and out of this immediacy flower forms elaborating the possibilities before us.

It is necessary, however, to move from the literary genre of the fantastic to a more general model of imagination relevant to the critic's task: a move from "the fantastic" to *fantasia*. First, it is necessary to identify in fantastic literature those elements that have relevance for the discursive formations characteristic of criticism's fundamentally "empirical-argumentative" mode. Second, one must make clear that elements shared by poetry and criticism are shared on the basis of their *effectiveness* in establishing the conditions for art, on one hand, and thought, on the other. The fantastic/*fantasia* axis is not constructed to facilitate indiscriminate snitching out of poetry's larder, but as a basis for showing that poetry, too, must work hard at what it does. Both the fantastic and critical *fantasia* aspire to topical "openness," the ability to get from one mental point to any other through a poetically lateral, angular movement as opposed to Cartesian thought's vertical ascent along a chain of particulars suspended from universals.

Like Sanchez, the sixteenth-century skeptic who identified three kinds of "objects of cognition,"[8] Todorov contrasts the external world of allegory to the internal and internalizing world of the subject. Where the concept dominates the former, the metaphor rules the latter. A forensic investigation now would turn its suspicions to metonymy, the trope that structuralists allied with "realistic" discourse. Metonymy, a strategy for displacing meanings from one realm to another (cause to effect, whole to part, act to agent), traditionally focuses on detail. As the clinical hallmark of semblance aphasia, metonymy understands the world in terms of sequential connections, deductions, and contiguities.[9] Metonymy in art, allied with exaggerated materialism, does seem to steer a course between the romantic images of "pure" metaphor, which can be reduced easily to allegorical motives and meanings, and the "conceptually real," which thematizes all phenomena according to abstract principles. Metonymy offers the only means of leaving the question of meaning open and, hence, unstable. Immune to conversion into conceptual system on one hand and allegorical system on the other, metonymy meets Diogenes' criteria of *physis* (truth) by virtue of denying *nomos* (convention). Metonymy seems to favour, in this regard, narrative over image, detail over geometry. In its "zero state," metonymy is ironic. When it "flowers," it converts itself to synecdoche, the part for the whole. One is tempted to say that metonymy is the essence of displacement.

I would argue that metonymy's capacity to "hesitate" constitutes art's means for precise action. Jorge Luis Borges once described the themes in the literature of the fantastic fueled by this hesitation: (1) the double – Jekyll-Hyde, the evil twin, etc., (2) the story-within-the-story, (3) travel through time, and (4) the contamination of reality by the dream or fictional story.[10] Behind these themes is the single logic presupposed by the artistic work itself, the fact that art constitutes another world, Nabokov would call it, in *Ada*, an "Anti-Terra." Here, we must pass over a boundary whose conditions we must swallow before tasting. Synecdochally, we take the part for the whole, the work of art as a world whose temporary reality competes with that of the world we left behind. Who are "we" in that world? What is our status as *body*, as *living or dead*, as *hunter or hunted*? What is the nature and quality of our motion, our space, our time? The condition of our entry is the simple hesitation between fear and interpretation, but the consequences are much more complicated.

Aspic Marinière Disparu (in Ring-Mold)

1

2

3 (repeat)

There is a famous anecdote about the contest between the two famous painters of ancient Greece, Zeuxis and Parrhasios. For their talent duel, the painters worked on murals on adjacent walls. When Zeuxis pulled back the curtain covering his work, a *trompe-l'œil* bowl of fruit, a bird convinced of the illusion flew into the wall, breaking its neck. Confident of victory, Zeuxis strode over to Parrhasios's wall and asked that the curtain be pulled back. Parrhasios wryly divulged that the curtain *was* his painting. Parrhasios trumped Zeuxis because, whereas the latter had fooled a bird, the former fooled a man, and an expert at that. Lacan has noted that the story illustrates the following principle: to trap a human, one need present only the *possibility* that something is concealed.[11] For architects, whose palettes are well supplied with potential concealment devices such as walls, portals, thresholds, and the like, this is a definite professional advantage.

Concealment is different from camouflage in animals, which either get eaten or survive. Human concealment brings about the reality of a virtual world that is not seen or directly experienced. Concealment is the job of boundaries. If we follow Husserl's expansion of the term "horizon" to cover all sorts of boundaries that mark the edge of our sensual penetration of the universe, then some "virtual reality" is hidden behind every simple edge or profile. These virtual realities share a causality created out of our *ignorance*, which assumes a common logic behind multiple unknown phenomena. The space and time beyond our reach contains all things valuable. The passive privation of our senses is understood as an active prohibition: what we cannot reach has been *placed out of our reach*. The exiles of this common edict, the inhabitants of this virtual realm, are conflated; they are made to share a common origin and physics. Thus, human boundaries are different from the boundaries that animals experience. A human boundary comes into being as soon as we are capable of desiring what is invisible and unreachable. The meaning of the threshold is inseparable from the notion of human desire.

To my mind, the best anecdotal example of this phenomenon is Okeanos, or "Ocean," the ring of sea surrounding the earth that is a poetic mixture of death, outer space, dreams, and pure elsewhere. It is a Homeric *Ur*-boundary, and its poetic geometry is instructive. The ancient Mediterranean peoples thought of Ocean in religious terms. It was the bound of the boundable, but itself was not boundable (*a-peiron*); that is, unlike the classic images of a circular river surrounding the fetal

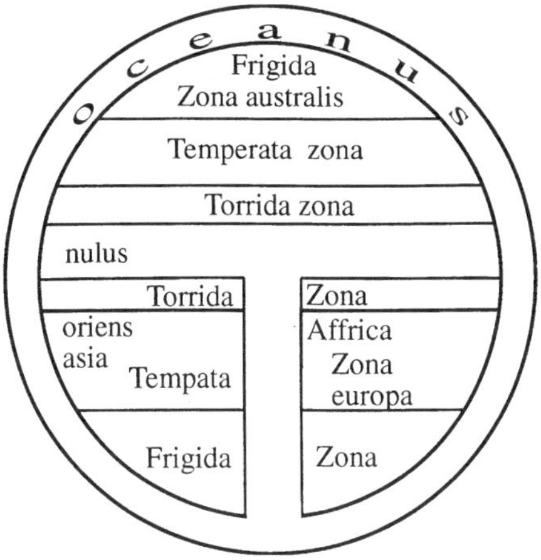

6.1 Above left: *Ocean as a River.* Honorius Augustodunensis, *Imago Mundi*; from Visconde de Santarem, *Atlas* I (Paris: 1845); redrawn by author.

6.2 Above right: The Uroboros, design on a brass shield, Benin, Nigeria; from Leo Frobenius, *Kulturgeschichte Afrikas*, (Zurich: 1993); redrawn by author.

land-masses of Europe, Asia, and Africa, Ocean had no outer edge. It was "self-consuming," as was its image in many cultures, a serpent eating its own tail. Once one was admitted "to it" – the geometry of entry is not geographical but, rather, poetic and liminal, via the death experience or the heroic quest – one entered a dimension that allowed a super-mobility and super-mentality.

One should note that, traditionally, this primary realm of displacement was compulsively dedicated to mensuration. While there is no distinct here or now, ordinary spatial and temporal measure was replaced by something infinitely more exact. As in Dante's *Inferno*, the foot measured not only spiral depth but moral distance and temporal proximity to the origin of things. The bound was simultaneously spatial and temporal; also heroic, theological, and gnostic.

This concept was so potent that the gods themselves took their oaths astride a poetic "branch" of Ocean, the River Styx, whose coldness froze them lest they tell the truth. This ability to function as a lie detector probably derived from the belief that water was the first material, the essence of primordial chaos. In Homer, only when the Ocean invited the gods to dine did the world begin; that is, only when the abstract fires of the remote planets achieved a bodily form by nourishing themselves in Ocean could thought and life begin.

Anamorphic Appetizers "Delminio"
1 Fold in topics gently with a spatula,
without deflating, until mixture is blank.
2 Spice dubiously. Correct seasonings.
3 Insert laughing gas using fourth-dimensional
pneumatic lardons, penetrating all layers.
Tie off with an old (Duchampian) string.

Giulio Camillo, inventor of a famous sixteenth-century device that was rumoured to have existed in the court of Francis I, made special use of the imagery of primordial ocean by locating, on the first level of his "memory theatre," all the gods except one, which he displaced to the second row. This missing piece, all the more prominent because it was in the front row centre of Camillo's auditorium-turned-stage, was labeled, alluringly, "Banquet." The objects stored in its closet were related to either the matters of ratio or quests: a pyramid; a golden bough for passing through forbidden lands; and Pan, who portrayed the cosmos from his starry head to earthen hooves. Also in this compartment was an image of a girl with hair streaming upward. The iconography of the times used wild hair or headlessness, as in the image of *Justizia* with her head in the clouds, to indicate direct contact with the divine. Modern versions emphasize the aperture of passage rather than the organs of perception, such as Borges' short story about "The Aleph," a small, shining object through which one could see beyond three-dimensional space into a timeless beyond.

Camillo's use of Ocean was similar to Borges' use of the Aleph. Ocean stood for a particular form of knowledge whereby topics, restricted by logic and appearance earth-side, stand in their revealed interrelationships within Ocean's transformative depths. Shakespeare captured this in the image of Ferdinand's father lying "full fathom five," with pearls for eyes and coral bones. Similarly, Hegel's image of Golgotha was echoed in the final pages of the *Phenomenology* by a gallery containing the full wealth of human wisdom – how like Camillo's memory theatre![12] As Botticelli featured in his painting of Venus, Ocean was nourishing because it was the source of the *ros-marinus* – sea-dew whose herbal form was regarded as an anti-toxin and aphrodisiac. In this light, it is easy to see why the seventeenth and eighteenth centuries regarded the cabinet as the best container of the souvenirs of universal knowledge, and how Flaubert

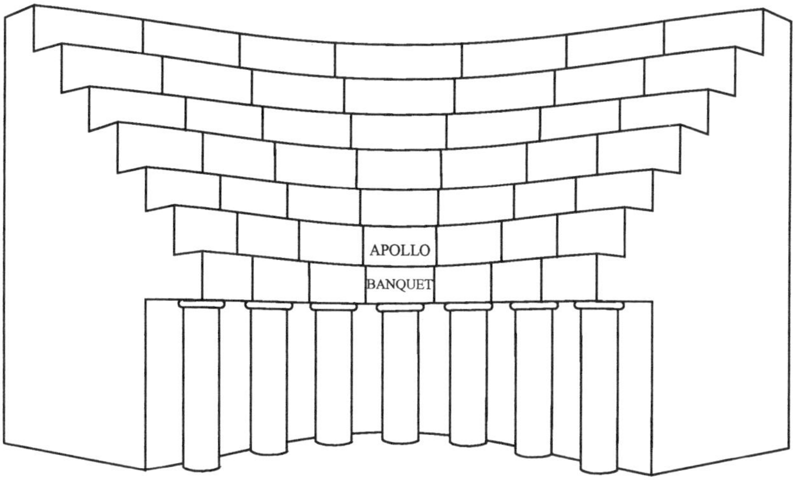

6.3 Giulio Camillo's "Theater of Memory"; from Lu Beery Wenneker, *An Examination of "l'Idea del Theatro" of Giulio Camillo...* (dissertation), University of Pittsburgh, 1970, 446; redrawn by author.

could attack this universal knowledge simply by parodying the home museum of the tragi-comic pair, Bouvard and Pécuchet.

In this first oceanic meal of the universe, we must note the presence of two specifically architectural themes, frontality and anamorphosis. Frontality is evident from Ocean's common stone version, the labyrinth. The labyrinth is the essence of the edge, boundary put into its purest logical form, a building whose void is on the verge of collapsing into pure *poché*. Frontality has to do with the fact that the labyrinth is a meander, not a maze. There is no way to turn off the path. In the act of penetration, one is always "facing" centre no matter how many times one turns. Why, then, is the labyrinth equated with a puzzle? The answer lies in the fact that it takes a long time to get to the centre. If one pauses somewhere for a brief rest, it is easy to forget whether one is going in or out. Imagine a series of such pauses, especially annoying because the last few sections contain some of the straightest stretches. The labyrinth distills horror by making it transparent and weightless in a context of opacity and massiveness. There is no *reason* to be afraid, yet fear is the inevitable result.

Anamorphosis is Ocean's way of telling you you're dead. The theme of *katabasis* (descent), adopted by heroes visiting the underworld from the eschatology of the soul underground, was a visit inside the impossible, digestive geometry of self-canceling spirals (Aeneas, Dante),

6.4 Left: *Herakles voyaging through Okeanos*, from base of an Attic vase, ca. fifth century B.C.E., Etruscan Museum, the Vatican; redrawn by author.

6.5 Opposite: Hans Holbein, the Younger, "The Ambassadors" (1533); courtesy of the Trustees, the National Gallery, London.

whale bodies (Jonah), serpent stomachs (Odysseus), or impenetrable wildernesses. By reducing spatiality to the geometry of conditional passage, Ocean and its masonry twin show how anamorphosis is tied up with the extra-, non-, or ultra-dimensionality of the horizon. Duchamp coined the term "infra-thin," which stands for any delay between a conventional meaning and a further-on meaning – Duchamp's most potent example is the case of the warm toilet seat in the public lavatory. Anamorphosis, however, involves a change or disguise of form that is the monogram of concealment – as we see in many of Picasso's paintings, where a literal or anamorphic skull image destabilizes the representational and formal meanings of the literal images. Lying between the range of two-dimensional representations and three-dimensional "reality," anamorphosis *is* the fourth dimension.

I might also claim that anamorphosis is synonymous with the genres of the grotesque and the fantastic. As in Holbein's famous painting, *The Ambassadors*, the anamorphic skull demands that we kneel before the lower left corner of the painting. At this point, we are involved in a "proof of the body." We place ourselves in a position where we demonstrate a truth unrealizable through intellect alone. Like the gods swearing an oath astride the River Styx, we are frozen by the zero-value of the

boundary, which in this case is the frame of the portrait which almost hits us in the head. Curiously, the Ambassadors are still looking at us. The anamorphic point of "entry" is frontal in two directions, a seeming contradiction. The "fourth" dimension of space is probably not fourth at all, but number two-and-a-half. Interposed between dimensions two and three, it is muscular, corporeal, and associated with trickery – specifically the trickery of Hermes, the god of boundaries. The "anamorphic fourth" is, in fact, Ocean.

An example: in Réne Daumal's *Mount Analogue,* a group of intrepid Frenchmen in search of the fourth dimension, where truth might be found, sail to an island in the South Pacific whose space must be entered through a precise series of nautical manœuvres. After the ship stealthily penetrates the fourth-dimensional space of the island, the crew join in a search for the mysterious invisible crystals, "the paradam, the standard of all value," to be found on the island through a combination of exercises of imagination and the searcher's purity of soul. In the 1930s jargon of the fourth dimension, Daumal describes the mythic inhabitants of Mount Analogue, the Hollow-Men:

> [The Hollow-Men] have houses in the rock whose walls are made of emptiness, and tents in the ice whose fabric is of bubbles. During the day they stay in the stone, and at night they wander through the ice and dance during the full moon. But they never see the sun, or else they would burst.
>
> They eat only the void, such as the form of corpses; they get drunk on empty words and all the meaningless expressions we utter.
>
> Some people say they have always existed and will exist forever. Others say they are dead. And others say that as a sword has its scabbard or foot its imprint, every living man has in the mountain his Hollow-Man, and in death they are reunited.[13]

In our roles as the sites of the reception of architecture we are the Hollow-Men.

Kaiserhartenußbrötchen und Hoffmansnebeneinanderürsteinblockfest

1 Slice thinly.
2 Arrange slices on rectangular white plates.
or
2a Make a pile of confectioner's stone.
3 Spruce the splices for spaces and black
the blocks for blicks.
4 Serve in crystal.

In a project undertaken by Christopher Kaiser at Cranbrook Academy

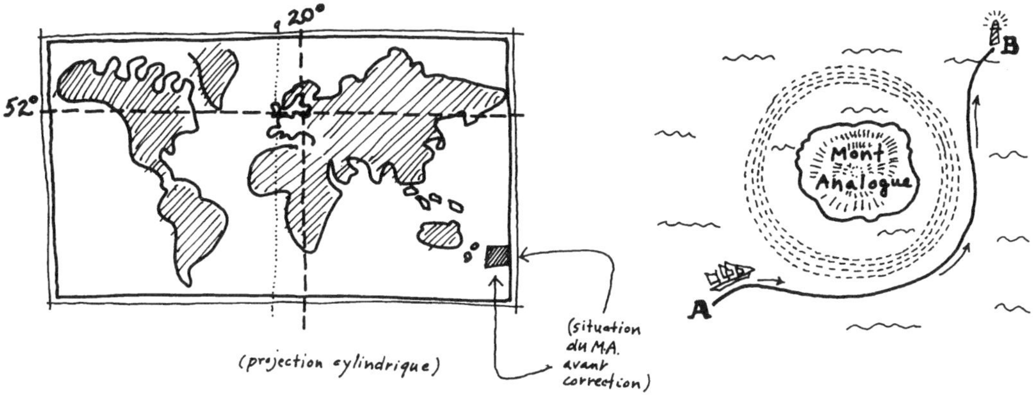

6.6a and 6.6b Passage to the infra-thin; from René Daumal, *Mount Analogue*, trans. Roger Shattuck (New York: Penguin Books 1974), 65, 69; redrawn by author.

of Art, a 35mm camera was mounted on a special track that allowed it to move incrementally above objects placed on the table or floor.[14] The photographs were collated by assembling small slices of each that corresponded to the order of the step-wise path about the object. The first print yielded, in some cases, the bottom-most slice, with consecutive slices completing the image through a collation of views, each from a slightly different camera position. Kaiser's objects included a cello clef, power saw, and typewriter – wry analogues of the very process used to represent them through micro-interval cuts.

The series of experimental collages is deceptively simple. Unlike the similar photo-collages of David Hockney, Kaiser focused on the mechanism that positioned the camera at each point. In Hockney's "walks" through landscapes, a familiar world emerges. In Kaiser's surgical displacements, an anatomical dissection takes place. It looks as if Kaiser, like Jirí Kolár, perversely tried to restore order after demonically deconstructing all normal optical means to it, as if in fact we returned to Mary Shelley's *Frankenstein*, without the neck-mount electrodes of the movie version, a *handsome* simulacrum of a normal human being whose artificiality surprises us by being so subtle. We pause momentarily in the infra-thin moment/space between an allogorical interpretation of the photograph as artistic composition and a response to it as purely uncanny. As Borges might have predicted, we sense the realm of contamination, of competitive identities. The photographs show *themselves* by

6.7 Left: Christopher Kaiser's "veg-o-matic" photograph of a double-bass clef; photograph by artist.

6.8 Opposite above: Daniel Hoffman, "Sisyphian Wall"; photograph by artist.

6.9 Opposite below: Daniel Hoffman, "Sisyphian Wall," detail; photograph by artist.

revealing the secret of their movement over (within?) the object. We forensically recover the original moment of production.

Kaiser's photographs demonstrate that measure and shadow are tied up together. We are reminded of the practice, related by Sir James Frazer, of Romanian builders who, lacking the stomach for on-site sacrifice, would measure the shadow of an innocent passerby with a string, bury the string in the foundations, and thereby capture the soul of the victim who reportedly would die within the year.[15] The shadow here is the anamorphic capture of process through dismemberment and reassembly. Because we receive the *measure* of the work before we realize it intellectually, the term *collation* is doubly suitable: first, as a description of the literal process of assembly; second, as a term signifying a *meal*.[16]

Kaiser's idea, not suprisingly, is pitched in the same key as Dan Hoffman's dry-laid concrete masonry wall, constructed following a

meditation on the Greek myth of Sisyphus. Each block displayed a photograph of that particular block being set in place. This is what I would call a "virtuous" work. First of all, it constitutes a paradigm exemplar of the "proof of the body" described philosophically by Diogenes, Sanchez, and Vico. It reduces the nomothetic value of construction process – its relation to a practical or semantic function – to zero.

The work's "projectability," its physical presence as an artifact that can be photographed and measured in other ways, is canceled in the mirror-logic of the wall as representation of itself, being a representation of itself to begin with. The work is virtuous: it achieves an architecture in the worst of circumstances. Sisyphian futility is revisited as essence, as *physis* in Diogenes' terms. The wall makes one think of the painting duel between Zeuxis and Parrhasios. Like the winner of that contest, Hoffman manages to construct a man-trap by devising a wall that "eats itself" like the mythic world-encircling Uroboros. Although the wall is in the ordinary sense straight and plumb, its effective geometry is that of the labyrinth. It achieves frontality through absurdity and anamorphosis through the physical (dis)placement of its documents. It is important to understand how Kaiser's veg-o-matic photos, Hoffman's photo-op wall, and Ocean are essentially the same, and how all constitute the idea of "banquet" as conceived by Camillo.

Self-Consuming Arts-t'y-Faits "Kristevian"
1 Collect left-overs into a medium-sized bowl (approx. 2 pp.); sprinkle with *poivres grecques*.
2 Place Cartesian metaphors sideways near the bottom.
3 Follow the recipe for "blood pudding" (see appendix D).

"Self-consumption" can be considered from a number of angles. In the liminal dimensionality of Ocean, self-consumption refers to the means by which a topologically transformative structure may, without any real extrinsic properties,[17] satisfy multiple imagistic needs. Ocean is thus the source of imagery for the folkloric theme of the descent (*katabasis*), for the classical image of the labyrinth, for the concealment of the victim within the sacrificial building, for the Enlightenment model of compartmented knowledge, for counter-Enlightenment projects of anamorphosis, and for the twentieth-century projects exploiting "fourth-dimensionality." Self-consumption also refers to the way in which a spatial phenomenon reveals its true essence as temporality, a traditional component of Ocean.

For those readers who enjoy finding within the "literal" level of phenomena a full range of analogous meanings, self-consumption can refer just as profitably to the acts of cannibalism reputed to have taken place at the margins of the settled world – first, those reported by Herodotus and others, where the boundary between known and unknown was personified by the *topos* of "the monstrous race"; second, the accounts of native American peoples brought back by sixteenth- and seventeenth-century travelers; and, third, the legends of various marginal peoples that developed into popular images such as that of the vampire.

Self-consumption may be considered *primarily* as an ingestive metaphor. The culinary practices of the margin, apocryphal or actual, demonstrate that ingestion is both accident, condition, and cause of the marginal condition. It is thus necessary to review ingestion itself in light of the marginality so commonly associated with it, and to consider extending to cuisine in general a liminal logic that is so fundamentally architectural in its involvement of frontality, anamorphosis, and temporality that we can hardly think of food without involving architecture. Both are about a science of margins.

Ocean is about self-consumption in the immediate sense that Kristeva described.[18] The young girl who had been deprived of her mother's affections was existentially hungry. Out of her hunger, she posited a dog who wished to eat her. To postpone this possibility, she filled her own mouth with an overabundance of words. Let us first imagine that this dog is finitely present but concealed, and further, then define the horizon as *that device which* permits both conditions. In these terms, to approach the Oceanic horizon is to confront *our* lack displaced, generically, "beyond" our immediate domain. Thus, as Montaigne discovers, we find in the cannibal something revolting but also something especially attractive.

Architecture may constitute another of those devices which permit special conditions denied elsewhere. Just as Kristeva's young girl sought survival in an exchange of words for space and space for loss, architecture lives on building and is "nourished" through a parasitic relationship that postpones a direct meeting of the realms of building and art, allowing both to achieve a certain symbiosis. With the goal of surviving in mind, architecture requires a zone of indifference. It must avoid, at all costs, codes that would subject it to the editorial influence of convention and taste. No doubt, it must frequently lend its name to the concerns of building and style, but it risks none of its essence. Architecture always remains, from the point of view of building, "senseless."

The symbiosis of architecture and building is not a Ruskinian, but an ecological concept: a food relationship. It is demonstrable by treating both building and architecture as terms in a regression equation where two variables have a perfect negative relationship. As the value of building nears zero (as when Romulus plowed a furrow for a wall, or when a building falls into ruin) the value of architecture – the potential for open-ended meaning – shoots upward. In the former example, a cosmic order is specified with minimal material supports and, in the latter, an order of history is revealed after its specific concerns have been silenced.

The other end of this regression line, when building is strong but architecture is weak, maps the well-known territory of the shopping mall, where continuity of shelter has been bought at the expense of fragmenting architecture into thin, terse, and ironic signs. So, clearly, although architecture and building depend on each other for their mutual survival, they are neither rivals for resources like cats nor the adversaries of a deadly hunt. Nourishment flows quietly from one to the other, although it is not clear who is the parasite, who the host.

To resolve the issue of whether architecture eats building or building eats architecture, I resort to the realm of popular culture anecdotes about vampirism. This is based on a personal principle, that it is always important to invite the fool to dine with the philosophers, and fools are a species within the larger *genus* of monsters. In this case, the fool may dine *off* the philosophers. Before seating *Dracula* beside Derrida, however, some preparation is required.

Architecture Roumaine "Palingénésienne"

1 Execute the steps of the first recipe in reverse order.
2 Revisit favourite old recipes, altering quantities and adjusting flavours.

The vampire is at least as ancient as ancient Greece, probably older. Its famous representatives have been the legendary Bulgarian, "Wlad, the Impaler," and Bram Stoker's classic, *Dracula*. The vampire is a combination of cannibal and parasite. He lives in the margins of the world, defined geographically or sciagraphically, in terms of shadows. The vampire is *about* the frame and boundary, if about anything; and in the vampire we can see the workings of conflation, where issues of life-and-death, visibility-invisibility, reflection and frontality, blood-based cuisine, skull and bones, and anamorphosis are all thoroughly blended and – if such an expression might be permitted – congealed.

Bram Stoker's story may be read forward, as a morality tale imagined by English people at the height of their nineteenth-century xenophobia, or one may perversely read it, vampire fashion, backward.[19] Dr Alucard would be amused to hear his story inverted to tell of art's relation to the normative life for which it is, like Dracula, a kind of inverse shadow. Living as vampires do at the boundary, the most they can hope for is a bite here and there, a few converts, and a gift box of ancestral earth. Their sensuality is displaced from copulation to collation, and I think that just a little play on that word will indicate the importance in art of order, especially inverted, or "pied," order.

There is an amusing tale told by Robert Graves about the writing down of Genesis by Hebrew scribes.[20] Working from Sumerian tablets engraved with icons depicting the origins of the universe, Mesopotamia style, the scribes, in their scribe-like devotion to custom, read every line of the tablets right to left. The trouble with this method was that the tablets were arranged according to a "boustrophadon," an order derived from the way in which a field is plowed by a team of oxen. Amusingly (although not for theologians), every other line was read backwards, and the connections between the lines were always off. Of course there was much invention to begin with in the translation between images and words, but in the process of miscollating, a quite impressive document got off the ground in the publishing world, and an equally influential religion established its official beginnings.

Architecture and its relation to building is much like this: a system set up for errors that have an ultimately theological value. In the backward version of *Dracula*, the vampires are the good guys, the Van Helsings of the world are the experts who never had a studio experience, the supply-side critics who are used to justify architectural innovation. The blood running warm in the veins of the victims is in truth the capacity for the reception that never quite disappears, no matter how jaded an age's public might become. Art is, after all, about eternal life, albeit life as a parasite.

Is architecture dead? Dracula certainly hopes so. To advance this case, it is appropriate to introduce a few architectural "Draculas," which are not usually thought of as such. Despite the over-dramatization inherent in the image of the vampire, I would eventually wish to separate the sheer "uncanniness" of vampirism from what architecture achieves through vampirism: delay, a temporality that is also a spatiality involving the fourth dimension. The paradigm exemplar is the Japanese tea room that imposes an anamorphic obligation on all who enter it through a "crawling-in" entry; or the famous temple, also in Japan, whose spectacular view of the sea is prohibited to all premature glimpses until the pilgrim crawling up the steep path at last reaches the door and bends down to bathe in the stone basin. Such items are mechanisms, wound up by desire and set into motion by the precise mechanisms only an artist can provide.

In *A Scientific Autobiography,* Rossi describes the inside-out experience of entering the hollow statue of San Carlone, a smaller version of the Statue of Liberty. "As with the Homeric horse, the pilgrim enters the body of the saint as he would a tower or wagon steered by a knowing technician. After he mounts the exterior stair of the pedestal, the steep ascent through the interior of the body reveals the structure of the work and the welded seams of the huge pieces of sheet metal. Finally, he arrives at the interior-exterior of the head; from the eyes of the saint, the view of the lake acquires infinite contours, as if one were gazing from a celestial observatory."[21]

We are familiar with this genre of experience, so familiar in fact that it is easy to overlook the process of entering into a mechanical giant as ingestive, the journey to the top as a flesh-reducing mortification, or the extrusion at the top as a form of decapitation. Were it not for the upward verticality of such experiences, we would immediately realize that they are descents. They diagram our epistemological fall from the empirical world of shadows into a gallery classified by cardinal directions, palingenesis, and ideal temple form.

Tourists who ascend to the top of Europe's famous ecclesiastical domes face some version of the following. The path at first is broad and well defined. Gradually the steps take their toll on the cardio-vascular system. If the same route is used as an exit, one secretly scorns those descending, robust, relaxed faces. Near the base of the dome, the passage narrows drastically. The sweat of bodies mixes with the tomb-like exhalations of the stone. Occasional oval windows only add to the sense of claustrophobia. Toward the end of this upward spiral, the path turns almost sideways. The body is being chewed up by the dome. At the door to the cupola, the ecstasy of release is met with the horror of vertigo and turned into a quite inexplicable emotion suitable (if one observes one's fellow travelers) to kissing, to running recklessly, to acts of recollecting points of the scene below. Cameras and binoculars conceal eyes glazed by excess. It is difficult to distinguish between smiles and grimaces. One has just experienced a labyrinth-in-reverse, with the result that the Minotaur

6.10 Architectural ingestion, *à la Tour Eiffel*; photograph by author.

is discovered to be one's own self-image, lower half timidly clinging to the tiles, upper half beastially drunk with sky.

This extraordinary experience does not seem very important, for there are many diluted, scaled down copies. Almost every town has some point from which visitors and residents have walked to gaze out on their home domain. Even towns lacking promontories have their "gateway" images, the graphic signatures used for post-cards. But, what really happens at these special points from which the landscape is served up on a visual plate to the literally detached observer?

Jorge Silvetti's project, the Tower for Leonforte, condenses the causal features of the tower into a hieroglyph of the dome experience.[22] On one hand this project can be seen as a clever manipulation of the visitor's viewing experience. On the other hand, there is the *needless* resemblance

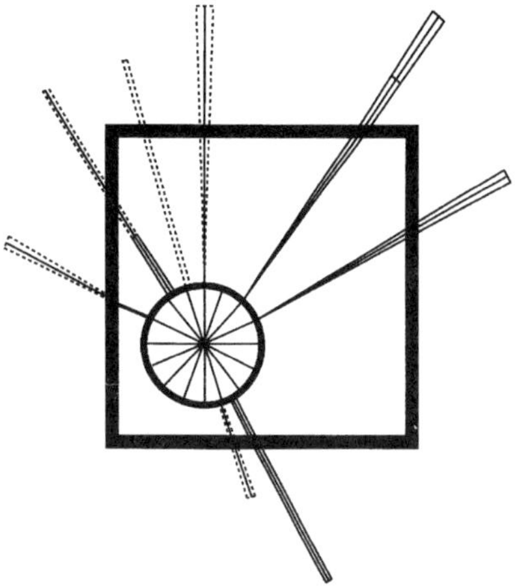

6.11 Above: Jorge Silvetti, Tower for Leonforte, Italy (plan); from Jorge Silvetti, in Judith Wolin, "The Rhetorical Question," in *Architecture and Literature*, *VIA* 8 (New York: Rizzoli 1986) 30; redrawn by author.

6.12 Left: Roof-top view, *vers le centre Pompidou* from la Samaritaine department store, Paris; photograph by author.

between the telescopes and javelins, or between the tower itself and a body tortured by darts like some architectural St Sebastian. Add to this resemblance the dart-like quality of some of the views, which point to sites of political violence, murder, and torture as well as to the points of usual civic pride.

Paris's *Tour Eiffel* and rooftop café at the famous department store, *La Samaritaine*, convey something of this sense in the relaxed surroundings typical of international tourism. After coffee at *La Samaritaine*, one is treated to a tour of Parisian roof tops aided by views painted into the widened railing. A few newcomers have not yet been added, most famously *Le centre Pompidou*. The decapitating experience of dome visits is, quite unexpectedly, present in the warning on the parapet stair to "Let Down Your Head," an excellent translation for our purposes. We should take this seriously. Octavio Paz connected Duchamp's *Large Glass* with Indian mythologies of decapitation.[23] In a more ambiguous fashion, sixteenth-century emblems mixed decapitation with transcendent discovery, as in the image of Justizia, whose head in contact with the divine *primum mobile* appears to be missing.[24] The head is the vampire's object of desire, the tap into the fourth dimension.

The head has a two-fold significance, according to these anecdotes. The first is as a mark of knowledge's ultimate status as self-knowledge, the Socratic "know thyself" as the theology of epistemology. The second

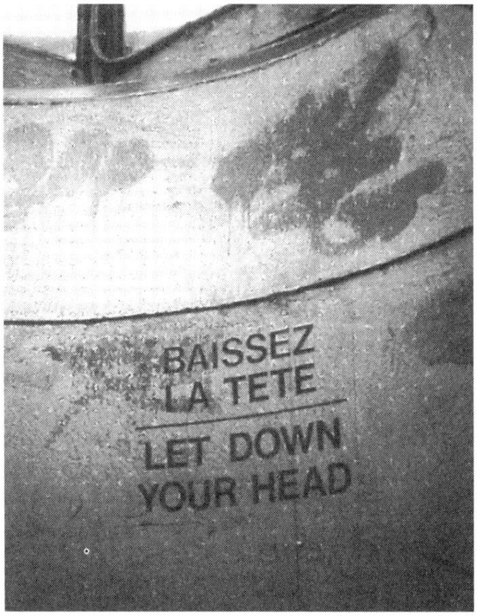

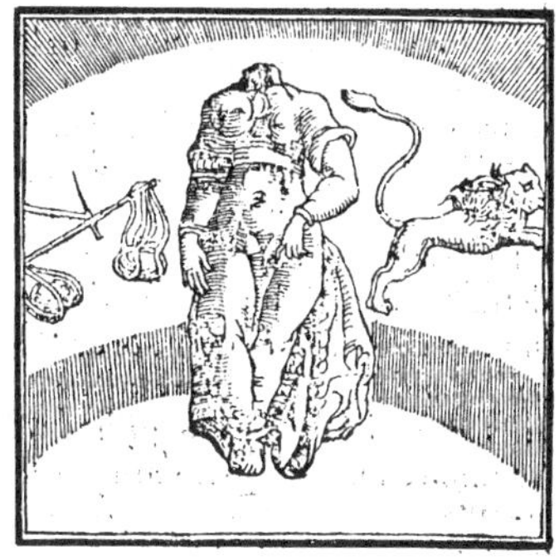

6.13 Left: Stair to the rooftop observatory, la Samaritaine; photograph by author.

6.14 Above: Justizia, emblem from Curione; from Pierio Valeriano, *Les Hieroglyphiques* (Lyon 1615).

is related to the use of the skull as icon for *memento mori*, "reminder of death." Even without Freud, we might come to the conclusion based on architecture alone that the ultimate hunger – and the ultimately *inexplicable* hunger – is the hunger for death. The vampire displaces this into the taste for blood, the cannibal into a taste for flesh disguised beneath the *chiles* of southern cuisine, the lover into silent communication within exchanges of sensations. We are in the realm of *déjà vu*, where the mind presents to itself a perceptual stream in the form of memory. This is Frascari's "knowledge which does not know."[25] In the skull, one's face is presented to oneself from the side of death's realm. This identity becomes a "knowledge which does not know" by revealing that the realm of death is in truth a self-production, the infinite repository of privation. In human perception, privation, the limit of the senses, is read as prohibition. The mythic mind forms this prohibition into a theology of gods and interior demonic presences that rule from their invisible station. Minds more skeptical and modern gloss the theological into the forensic forms of puzzle, problem, or conspiracy. The anecdote of Zeuxis and Parrhasios teaches us about the simplicity, and thus stability, of prohibition's logic within the turbulence of signs. The immanence of our body (one might as well say, simply, "body") is pure limitation. Our presence in the world is spatially and temporally belated; we cannot see beyond the horizon, we cannot embrace more than a passing instant. To transform this belatedness into prohibition and, thus, theology is to see within the term "denial" the necessity for an act precipitated by an *agent*, for our willingness to be listed as victims.

The mechanism of this exchange reveals that the exchange is pure mechanism. In the statue of San Carlone, one gives one's eyes to the saint. Frontality, as in the painting literally and in all works of art operationally, is the parallelism and exchange of the body outside art for the body within: the logic of the vampire. *The resurrection of the body and life everlasting* of the Nicene Creed is more appropriate as an aesthetic principle: knowledge without knowing. The *déjà vu* quality is the monogram of Kaiser's and Hoffman's projects, where memory is bound tightly within a monad of uselessness that defeats all extrinsic projection. Memory is equally the theme of architectural vampires that penetrate the ozone in search of head-ward perspectives. Camillo's theatre shrink-wraps the viewer on the stage with a head-size auditorium that turns into a supplement to the cone of vision. The same prosthesis is supplied to patrons of *La Samaritaine*, who are advised to "let down their heads." Face to face with the world remembered, the world ingested, the world already seen, we receive and possess a knowledge of identities. This knowledge "does not know" because it is a mechanism of concealments. The knowledge of Ocean, that thin broth, is both anamnetic and forgetful, like the Lethe from which souls were ordered to drink to disguise their knowledge of eternity. The Camillan theatre is the darkness that we carry with us to plant in the light that we see, the transparency of the world.

NOTES

1 See part 1 of this article in *Chora 1: Intervals in the Philosophy of Architecture* (Montréal: McGill-Queen's University Press 1994).

2 Apologies in advance to the creators and consumers of fine cuisine whom the section headings of this paper malign. My abused sources are: Giuliano Bugialli, *The Fine Art of Italian Cooking* (New York: Times Books 1989); Louis P. De Gouy, *The Gold Cook Book* (New York: Greenberg 1947); and Charles H. Baker, Jr, *The South American Gentleman's Companion* (New York: Crown Publishers 1951).

3 Lesley Chamberlain, "Introduction," in Filippo Tommaso Marinetti, *The Futurist Cookbook*, trans. Suzanne Brill, ed. Lesley Chamberlain (London: Trefoil Publications; San Francisco: Bedford Arts, Publishers 1989), 7.

4 Marinetti, *Futurist Cookbook*, 134.

5 Allegorical transpositions are the subject of the essays contained in *Cooking, Eating, Thinking: Transformative Philosophies of Food*, ed. Deane W. Curtin and Lisa M. Heldke (Bloomington: Indiana University Press 1992). Food here is placed within the moral contexts of personal hygiene, feminism, Zen meditation, vegetarianism, animal rights, and world hunger. Within each of these post-modern categories of concern, food is reduced so far from its Rabelaisian potential that artistic issues are out of reach. In fact, Rabelais is not once mentioned in the forty-four selections. Neither, of course, is the bad boy, Marinetti.

6 See part 1 of this article, *Chora 1*.

7 Tvestan Todorov, *The Fantastic, A Structural Approach to a Literary Genre*, trans. Richard Howard (Ithaca: Cornell University 1975).

8 See part 1 of this article, *Chora 1*.

9 Kurt Goldstein, *Language and Language Disturbances, Aphasic Symptom Complexes and Their Significance for Medical Theory of Language* (New York: Grune and Stratton 1948); Roman Jakobson, *Studies in Child Language and Aphasia* (The Hague: Mouton 1971).

10 James E. Irby, "Introduction," in Jorge Luis Borges, *Labyrinths: Selected Stories & Other Writings*, ed. Donald A. Yates and James E. Irby (New York: New Directions 1964), xviii.

11 Jacques Lacan, *The Four Fundamental Concepts of Psycho-Analysis*, ed. Jacques-Alain Miller, trans. Alan Sheridan (New York: Norton 1981), 111–12.

12 This exceptional gallery scene may be found on the last two pages of Hegel's *Phenomenology*. For Hegel's use of skulls and faces, see Alisdair McIntyre, "Hegel on Faces and Skulls," in Alisdair McIntyre, ed., *Hegel: A Collection of Critical Essays* (Notre Dame: University of Notre Dame Press 1976), 225. For more discussion, read Donald Phillip Verene's chapter on phrenology in his *Hegel's Recollection, A Study of Images in the Phenomenology of Spirit* (Albany: State University of New York Press 1985), 80–91.

13 René Daumal, *Mount Analogue, A Novel of Symbolically Authentic Non-Euclidean Adventures in Mountain Climbing*, trans. Roger Shattuck (Middlesex, England: Penguin 1974), 83.

14 Christopher Kaiser's work took place during the fall of 1990. He is currently engaged in architecture internship in New York City.

15 I discovered this account when working on an article, "Skiagraphy and the *Ipsum* of Architecture," *Architecture and Shadow*, VIA, vol. 11, ed. David

Murray (New York: Rizzoli 1990): 62–75. The bizarre part is that there were, allegedly, "shadow traders" who, like manufacturers' representatives, would go from architect to architect with cases of shadows suitable for securing the foundations of buildings. One wonders if there were different shadows for different building types. Sir James George Frazer, *Taboo and the Perils of the Soul,* part 2, *The Golden Bough: A Study in Myth and Religion*, 3rd ed. (New York: St Martin's Press 1955), 89–90.

16 *Oxford* defines "collation" as a "light meal ... often at exceptional time," such as a fast-day. It is also a comparison of one copy of a text with another, as well as an assembly of a text or other materials *in order.*

17 Ocean can be dismissed as a representable margin of a bounded surface, but when that surface is defined as both closed and curved, Ocean can undertake the role of the paradox, impeding direct simultaneous intuition of this condition. Thus, as J. J. Callahan writes in "The Curvature of Space in a Finite Universe," *Cosmology + 1* (San Francisco: W. H. Freeman and Company 1977), 20–30, Ocean can be transposed to the case of a closed, curved *space* of three dimensions, which can be mapped but not intuited directly. This is because a closed curved space has no *extrinsic properties* that allow us to reduce its dimensionality for the purpose of symbolic graphic projection. When Wallace Stevens writes that when the blackbird flew "out of sight," it marked the edge of "one of many circles," he is being scientifically as well as poetically precise.

18 See part 1 of this article, *Chora 1*.

19 Bram Stoker, *Dracula* (Westminster, England: A. Constable 1897).

20 Robert Graves, *Adam's Rib, and Other Anomalous Elements in the Hebrew Creation Myth, A New View* (New York: T. Yoseloff 1958).

21 Aldo Rossi, *A Scientific Autobiography* (Cambridge: MIT Press, 1981), 3.

22 See Jodith Wolin's lucid review of this work, "The Rhetorical Question," in *Architecture and Literature*, VIA, vol. 8 (1986): 29–30.

23 Octavio Paz, *Marcel Duchamp, Appearance Stripped Bare*, trans. Rachel Phillips and Donald Gardner (New York: Seaver Books, 1981).

24 Donald Kunze, "Skiagraphy and the *Ipsum* of Architecture," *Architecture and Shadow,* VIA, vol. 11 (1990): 62–75.

25 Marco Frascari, "Semiotica *Ab Edendo,* Taste in Architecture," *Journal of Architectural Education* 40 (Fall 1986): 6. Also, see part 1 of this article, *Chora 1*.

Concrete Blonde: A Probe into Negative Space where Mysteries are Created[1]

Joanna Merwood

7.1 Rachel Whiteread, *House* (1993), sculpture, East London; from *Architectural Review* 1163 (January 1994).

THE PHOTOGRAPH SHOWS A SERIES of similarly sized monolithic concrete cubes stacked on top of one another. The grey surfaces are rough, stained, and marked with many small geometric indentations and protuberances. Inscribed in each cube and standing out in relief are modular rectangles, some divided into four parts. Between each pair of the cubes is a thinnish layer of crusty brick and timber.

House is the concrete cast of the inside of a nineteenth-century house in Hackney, East London, the last of a row of terrace houses demolished to make way for a park. The work, a sculpture by English artist Rachel Whiteread, was constructed and demolished within a few months in late 1993.

The purpose of this essay is not to review

House or to provide a critical interpretation of it as an art work, but to discuss the nature of architectural representation by considering *House* as an alternate strategy for the representation of built space.

A MONOLOGUE FROM THE MARGINS

In her essay "Sculpture in the Expanded Field," Rosalind Krauss describes the efforts made by some sculptors since the 1960s to expand the boundaries of sculpture.[2] While retaining the autonomy of the discipline, they began to define sculpture in terms of architecture and landscape, rather than as a field of operation completely removed from all others.

I knocked on the door with my knuckles, loudly. There was no answering sound. I pushed the door open and went in. The sound of water came from the sink. I looked in the sink.

House is a site-specific construction in the same tradition as works by the artists Robert Irwin and Richard Serra. Krauss describes these works as explorations of the possibilities between "architecture" and "not-architecture," in that they are "a process of mapping the axiomatic features of the architectural experience – the abstract conditions of openness and closure – onto the reality of a given space."[3]

House operates at the scale of a building. However, it addresses the representation of interior space in quite a different way than conventional architectural representation, with its inherent assumptions about the nature of space. These assumptions are: that space is continuous; that it can be divided into three homogeneous dimensions; that what matters is not the space itself, but its boundaries; and that it is experienced in a linear manner, with respect to time. *House* reveals and questions some of these assumptions, by representing space not as a conceptual abstraction, but as a synaesthetic experience.

Under a thin stream of water running from one of the faucets lay a carving knife with nearly a foot of keen blade. The knife was clean, but the back of the porcelain sink – where water had splashed with only small, scattered drops – was freckled with red brown spots. I scraped one of them with a fingernail – dried blood.

THE MEANING OF THESE THINGS CONTINUED TO ELUDE HIM

The use of the word "representation" is contentious. In discussing the problem of representation in the modern era,[4] Michel Foucault says, "Representation is in the process of losing its power to define the mode of being common to things and to knowledge. The very being of that which is represented is now going to fall outside representation itself."[5]

Except for the sink, I could see nothing out of order in the kitchen. I opened a pantry door. Everything seemed all right there. Across the room another door led to the front of the house. I opened the door and went into a passageway. Not enough light came from the kitchen to illuminate the passageway. I fumbled in the dusk for the light-button that I knew should be there. I stepped on something soft.

Expressing a similar idea, Dan Hoffman states, "It is evident that both representation[6] and simulation evolve from a way of thinking that sees the 'real' in the reconstruction (mathematical or technological) of the world."[7]

Foucault claims that the modern era is characterized by the impossibility of knowing the world through representation, that representation has become entirely self-referential, with its own history and laws, and is not related to the world we experience at all. By considering how *House* represents architectural space I shall propose that a meaningful[8] form of representation is still possible – a representation that is critical in questioning accepted assumptions, and imaginative in suggesting alternate possibilities.

PERPETUAL ALLUSIONS TO SECRET ATTITUDES

ii

Darkness settled. The old man turned on a light in a tall lamp that threw a soft yellow circle upon us, and left the rest of the room dim.

iii

The rustle of gently falling rain came from an open window that I couldn't see.

In making *House*, Whiteread took as her starting point an existing Edwardian house. A ten-centimetre shell of concrete was sprayed onto the inside of every wall. The concrete was left to harden and the walls of the original house stripped away. Through this process of transformation a new object was created, one that has the shape and form of its original but is at the same time alien to it.

Modern houses are no longer individually crafted artifacts but modular assemblages of factory-produced components. In casting these components – window-panes, door knobs, and electrical outlets, which pockmark the surface like clumsy hieroglyphs – Whiteread emphasizes the technological production of modern housing, making it strange and unfamiliar. Walter Benjamin said, "To live means to leave traces."[9] We inhabit the world by marking it. *House* is the literal cast of our imprints on the world. It casts both the house that was purposely made – the rooms, the doorways, the windows – and marks that were made inadvertently – the scratches, the dents, the peeling wallpaper, the sagging floor joists. Whiteread said of one of her previous works, a cast of the space around a bathtub, "Plaster is a dead material, but the surface is very sensitive ... It picks up details – stains and cobwebs – and embalms them, leaving mummified space and a sense of silence."[10] In objectifying space, its quirky and perverted nature is uncovered.

House inverts the traditional precedence of a house's exterior face over its interior body. The exterior container is stripped away, and the space inside literally is made concrete. In an article about the work, *Architectural Review* states, "With the function of shelter denied, the house becomes sculpture."[11] However it is not only the utilitarian function of the house that is denied, but the function of the modern house as the built representation of an idea. This house was one of a series of twenty row houses, themselves a subgroup of countless others in England and around the world. The row house was one of many nineteenth-century architectural types that defined what a house for a particular person or family should be. The type was a normative paradigm, an ideal that could be applied in any situation. In *House* the skin that once described and dictated the social and economic class of the inhabitants, what they believed, and how they behaved, is dissolved. The house, in becoming a tool, a machine for the production of *House*, is usurped as the representation of an ideology.

iv

He spoke in an undertone, with a furtive glance at the ceiling, above which soft steps padded back and forth.

v

"No, I'm not a killer," he said, very softly; and he smiled the first smile I had seen on his face. It wasn't a pleasant smile: and there was something in it that made you want to shudder. "But I am other things, perhaps, of which you haven't thought. But this talking is to no purpose. Elvira!"

The girl came obediently forward.

"You will find sheets in one of the bureau drawers," he told her. "Tear one or two of them into strips strong enough to tie up our friend securely."

The girl went to the bureau. I wrinkled my head, trying to find a not too disagreeable answer to the question in my mind. The answer that came first wasn't nice: *torture*.

"MYSELF" NEVER COINCIDES WITH MY IMAGE

While the viewer of *House* is a voyeur in the sense that the surface of the interior is starkly, even nakedly, revealed, the space itself maintains its mystery. In creating a work that is purposefully unknowable, Whiteread reinforces the essentially private nature of domestic interior space. Beatriz Colomina has drawn attention to Le Corbusier's photographic representations of the interior of the Villa Savoye, in which a woman appears as part of the space-making apparatus.[12] In one photograph she gazes out of a distant window, drawing the viewer's eye from the interior of the room toward that window. In another, she ascends a staircase, lending a sense of direction to the space. No inhabitant can be similarly objectified in *House*, because it is by nature uninhabitable. Since the space cannot be occupied physically, no one can be objectified or categorized as part of the space.

THE RITUAL OF MASS

In conventional architectural space, the interior is defined by its edge, usually a wall. It takes effort to cross this boundary – opening a door, climbing up a step, projecting one's body through an opening – in order to reach the outside. In thickening the "wall" so that it fills up the entire interior space, *House* becomes the ultimate boundary – one that is not only difficult to cross, but impossible. *House* destroys the wall, and in eliminating the "in-between" or middle ground of this threshold, exterior and interior are collapsed together in direct confrontation. It is impossible to project oneself mentally into the work. To do so would be to become entombed. The "overstuffed, suffocating bourgeois interior"[13] Benjamin described has become entirely filled. The tea sets, fire screens, and stags at bay have become solidified into an impenetrable mass. One's only real access to the work is through its pitted and flaky skin, in "pure, untranslatable, sensuous immediacy."[14] The dimension of depth is intensified and becomes radically different from width and height. It is unreachable and unknowable. In being simultaneously precise and immeasurable, the work has the qualities Sergei Eisenstein finds in a certain Piranesi etching: "In *Carcere oscura* the concreteness is retained while the means of representation 'fly apart' ... the flatness of form, softened by light, flows into space, the preciseness of facets is absorbed in the fluid contours of form."[15]

vi

The room into which he had led me resembled an auctioneer's establishment just before the sale – or maybe one of those alley tea rooms. Fat blue vases, crooked red vases, vases of various shapes and colours; marble statuettes, ebony statuettes, statuettes of any material; lanterns, lamps, and candlesticks; draperies, hangings, and rugs of all sorts; odds and ends of furniture that were all somehow queerly designed; peculiar pictures hung here and there in unexpected places. A hard room to feel comfortable in.

THE MEANS OF INDUCING TRANCES

In his article, "The Function of Fiction in Shaping Reality," Paul Ricoeur describes the tension created by a metaphor through the simultaneous compatibility and incompatibility of the phenomena that it brings together. He says, "Remoteness persists in closeness. To see similarity is to see likeness in spite of the difference."[16] *House* operates at the scale of a building, but it cannot be used as a building. By mapping the house so closely and precisely that it becomes *almost* knowable, the desire to enter it is strong. Because it is both close to and distant from its original, *House* operates as a *reverse* metaphor in which we see difference in spite of likeness. Thus, a vital characteristic of this representation is the difference between

vii

The street door closed and I was alone in the house for a while.

viii

The carpet was thick. I went down on my face, with the heavy chair atop me, all doubled up, but my right arm was free of the tangle and my right arm grasped the gun.

ix

I avoided the window by going the long way around the room.

x

I was in a hole! Alone in a strange house that would presently hold two who were hunting me – and that one of them was a woman didn't soothe me any – she was none the less deadly on that account.

For a moment I was tempted to make a dash for it; the thought of being out in the street again was pleasant; but I put the idea away. That would be foolishness, and plenty of it.

I slipped out of my triangular shadow and went up the stairs. Thanks to the street lights, the upstairs rooms were not too dark for me to move around. Around and around I went through the rooms, hunting for a place to hide.

the world and its reconstruction, between the object and its illumination.

Ricoeur makes a distinction between image and fiction. Images, he says, always refer to something that is absent, while fictions have no real referent. He goes on to claim that "only the image which does not already have its referent in reality is able to display a world."[17]

I would argue that *House* is fictional in the way that Ricoeur defines the term, because it does not refer in a *reproductive* way to something that is absent, rather it *re-presents* the thing, showing something about it that was previously unknown or undiscovered. *House* is a creative rendering of the architectural space of a house, one that attempts to "remake" it by revealing the rich corporeality of the interior previously veiled by the proper paper clothing of the facade.

AN EXPERIMENTAL DEMONSTRATION

Although Whiteread represents private space, *House* is not a private work. Her re-making is a communicative activity. The site-specificity of *House* abandons the gallery in favour of a more public realm. The piece, financed by the local council and the Artangel Trust, whose purpose is to fund art in unorthodox places, was highly visible, both physically and through the media. Its very presence excited and enraged people, not only art critics and art "consumers," but a wider audience including local residents and politicians. It received extensive coverage in the local and international press. While the work was not always treated seriously in the media, in representing private space as monstrously large and visible, dense, and impenetrable, it communicated a sense of strangeness and unfamiliarity that was universally understood. Writing in *Architectural Review*, Miranda Chitty says of *House*, "It is frustratingly impenetrable with doors that lead nowhere and windows that reveal nothing. Circling round the outside is like trying to talk to the body of a friend."[18] "*House* delivers the shock of the not-new," claimed *The Independent on Sunday*, "the eerie half-recognition of known objects made strange."[19]

The unknowable density of *House* has the quality Roland Barthes describes as the "punctum,"[20] something that is at once familiar and strange. It is subversive not because it frightens or repels, but because it is vaguely unsettling. As Susan Sontag writes, "Real art has the capacity to make us nervous."[21] Ultimately mysterious, *House* is simultaneously present and distant from us. A certain tension exists. The work is not resolved into "the quietness of the concept."[22] *House* represents the interior space of a house synaesthetically, rather than conceptually. Its content need not be read or intellectually constructed by the viewer because it is already present in the form.

THE IMAGE VANISHES AS YOU ARE MAKING IT

House is an attempt to capture something other than the objective, measurable dimensions of interior space. Its perceptual dimensions cannot be described by the conventions of architectural

xi

Toward the street door, the hall was lighted with the glow that filtered through the glass from the street lights.

xii

The luminous patches on the watch burnt my eyes. I couldn't afford to blink. A foot could pass the dial while I was blinking. I couldn't afford to blink, but I had to blink. I blinked. I could have sworn something had gone between me and the watch.

xiii

Suddenly a window rattled, as if from a draught created by the opening of an outside door somewhere.

drawing – a system of representation that has become abstracted into a language with its own laws and conventions to such a degree that it has become yet another object, rather than a way of knowing. When a drawing is valued for itself, as a repository of architectural reality, its potential exploratory properties are neglected. If the representation and what it represents are seen as the same thing, the possibilities of both are lost.

It is futile to represent *House* using the conventions of plan, section, and elevation. To do so would reveal nothing of its quality. Such drawings represent the positive of line (the wall or the boundary), never the positive of space, which is always considered as a negative. Since Whiteread worked with a team of architects and engineers to make *House*, it is highly likely that drawings of the work do exist, but they would be no more than a technical description of *a series of operations.* The opacity of *House* cannot be described through such conceptual abstraction.

TIME FLIES LIKE AN ARROW;
FRUIT FLIES LIKE A BANANA

An authentic representation of architecture should also include time, as space is never inhabited in discrete and autonomous moments. Conventional architectural representation implies a sequential perception of space – a convention based on the idea of circulation from one "unit" of space to the next. However, this supposed linearity is disrupted by the acts of pausing, remembering, returning, and seeing for

xiv

Gunpowder burned at my face.

the first time, to such a degree that montage or collage may be equally valid models of spatial perception.

The impenetrability of *House* is a critique of this conventional view of the relationship between space and time in architecture. It cannot be passed through physically – the assumption of homogeneous, continuous, linear movement is disallowed completely. In its place is the "continuous presence"[23] of the space in one's imagination.

PERHAPS YOU WILL SAY, "ARE YOU SURE YOUR STORY IS THE REAL ONE?"

To conclude, I shall return to the question of whether, in the context of architecture, it is possible for representation to be a meaningful form of knowledge, for it to relate to the world as we experience it. The argument cited above declared that the "real" world and the representative constructed world have become confused to the point at which representation has as much authenticity, perhaps even more, claim to truth than the substantial, experienced world, and that we can thus no longer have access to the world through representation. In suggesting that the real and the representational have become collapsed, Foucault and Hoffman imply that a conscious construction of reality can have the same status as our embodied perception of the world. Although it is impossible for there to be a total and direct correspondence between the two, it may be, as Gianni Vattimo points out, that there has been a "weakening" of the notion of reality – that it has become more "fluid," as our experiences come to lack

xv

My arms had him. I twisted around, kicking his face. Loosened one arm. Caught one of his. His other hand gouged at my face. That told me the bag was in the one I held. Clawing fingers tore my mouth. I put my teeth in them and kept them there. One of my knees was on his face. I put my weight on it. My teeth still held his hand. Both of my hands were free to get the bag.

Not nice, this work, but effective.

His fingernails dug into my thumb. I had to open my mouth – let his hand escape. One of my hands found the bag. He wouldn't let go. I screwed his thumb. He cried out. I had the bag.

I tried to leave him then. He grabbed my legs. I kicked at him – missed. He shuddered twice – and stopped moving. A flying bullet had hit him. I took it. Rolling over to the floor, snuggling close to him, I ran a hand over him. A hard bulge came under my hand. I put my hand in his pocket and took back my gun.

xvi

Then a faint sound brought us all into tense motionlessness.

The room we were in had two doors: one leading into the hall, the other into another bedroom. It was through the hall door that the faint sound had come – the sound of creeping feet.

xvii

The girl spun back across the room – hammered back by the bullets that tore through her chest. Her back hit the wall. She pitched forward to the floor.

xviii

They had started off by double crossing each other.

xix

As she was being led away, she stopped and asked if she might speak privately with me.

We went together to a far corner of the room.

She put her mouth close to my ear so that her breath was warm against my cheek, as it had been once before, and whispered the vilest epithet of which the English language is capable.

Then she walked out to her cell.

The End.[26]

fixed reference points.[24] However, this does not negate the possibility of representation's being meaningful with regard to the world. It is possible for representation to reflect this ambiguity inherent in modern experience. The kind of representation embodied by *House* refers to the real, but it is not paradigmatic; it does not attempt to represent a single "truth." This kind of representation is interpretive rather than productive, constitutive rather than resolvable. Its abstraction is not reductive but imaginative in that it refers not to a single definable reality, but to many possibilities. This is representation that does not attempt to *be* real, but makes us rethink our ideas about the real. Vattimo, talking about Heidegger's theory of "disorientation" in art, says, "The encounter with the work of art is like an encounter with someone whose view of the world is a challenge to our own interpretation."[25]

By suspending the familiarity of the world, the distance between the world and the work is preserved. *House* does not represent the accepted conceptual space of a house, in which all is known; instead it represents a more eloquent, alien quality. More than a signifier, *House* is a built fiction that transforms reality, both in revealing the gap between the house as a type and its built representation, and in communicating a totally new reality – the reality of *House*, as opposed to house.

NOTES

1 Dan Hoffman, *2 447 328* (Bloomfield Hills, MI: Cranbrook Academy of Art 1990), 1.

2 Rosalind Krauss, "Sculpture in the Expanded Field," in *The Anti-Aesthetic: Essays in Postmodern Culture*, ed. Hal Foster (Seattle: Bay Press 1983), 31–42.

3 Krauss, "Sculpture in the Expanded Field," 41.
4 Foucault defines the modern era as dating from the end of the eighteenth century.
5 Michel Foucault, *The Order of Things* (New York: Vintage Books 1973), 240.
6 In the context of his discussion on architecture, Hoffman defines representation as "a means of referencing in the form of a deliberate construction."
7 Dan Hoffman, "Representation in the Age of Simulation," in *Architecture, Ethics and Technology*, eds. Alberto Pérez-Gómez and Louise Pelletier (Montreal: McGill-Queen's University Press 1994), 131.
8 In this context I define meaning not as "absolute truth" but as something that refers to our own subjective experience and understanding.
9 Walter Benjamin, "Paris: Capital of the 19th Century," in *Reflections* (New York: Schocken Books 1986), 155.
10 Robert Tapin, "Rachel Whiteread at Luhring Augustine," *Art in America* 80 (Sept 1992): 124.
11 Miranda Chitty, "House," *Architectural Review* 1163 (Jan. 1994): 13.
12 Beatriz Colomina, "The Split Wall: Domestic Voyeurism" in *Sexuality and Space* (New York: Princeton Architectural Press 1992), 73–128.
13 Benjamin, "Paris: Capital of the 19th Century," 156.
14 Susan Sontag, *Against Interpretation* (New York: Anchor Books 1990), 9.
15 Sergei Eisenstein, "Piranesi, Or the Fluidity of Form," *Oppositions* 11 (Winter 1977): 94.
16 Paul Ricoeur, "The Function of Fiction in Shaping Reality," *Man and World* 12 (1979): 129–41.
17 Ibid., 135.
18 Chitty, "House," 13.
19 Jan Dalley, "The World Turned Inside Out," *The Independent on Sunday* (24 October 1993): 52.
20 Roland Barthes, *Camera Lucida* (New York: Hill and Wang 1981), 26.
21 Sontag, *Against Interpretation*, 8.
22 Ricoeur, "The Function of Fiction in Shaping Reality," 131.
23 Mary Alice Dixon-Hinson, "Vico's Discovery," *Volumezero* 1 (1985–6): 8.
24 Gianni Vattimo, *The Transparent Society* (Baltimore: Polity Press 1992), 59.
25 Ibid., 50.
26 All quotations in the margins are from *The Continental Op* (New York: Vintage Books 1989), a collection of short stories by Dashiell Hammett.

Surrealist Paris: The Non-Perspectival Space of the Lived City

Dagmar Motycka Weston

> La rue, que je croyais capable de livrer à ma vie ses surprenants détours, la rue avec ses inquiétudes et ses regards, était mon véritable élément: j'y prenais comme nulle part ailleurs le vent de l'éventuel.
>
> André Breton[1]

> Arrachez-moi le cœur vous y verrez Paris.
>
> Louis Aragon[2]

SURREALISM IS OF GREAT IMPORTANCE to twentieth-century culture because of its fruitful efforts both to restore poetic wholeness to a daily reality which had been fragmented and impoverished by nineteenth-century positivistic and instrumental attitudes and to reinstate the imagination as the distinctive attribute of human existence.[3] The surrealists' quest to reconcile the seemingly contradictory states of "reality" and "dream" in a poetic state of *surreality*[4] is powerfully embodied by their urban texts, epitomized by André Breton's *Nadja* and *L'amour fou*, and Louis Aragon's *Le paysan de Paris*.[5] These writings are of great interest to anyone thinking about the nature of architectural representation, because in them the authors draw particularly on their own situatedness in the fertile context of the city of Paris.[6] This vivid evocation is very different from most conventional writing about architecture, with its emphasis on the comparative analysis of the formal aspects of de-situated objects.[7] In the exploration of the ontological nature of human existence, the surrealist texts reveal a non-perspectival space which is conducive to the evocation of their poetic world. It is the structure of this space which this paper will examine.

The surrealist rejection of rational control as a means toward the release of the fecundating powers of the imagination, and the desire to evoke the multivalent essence of live, embodied experience is reflected in a corresponding subversion of perspectival space. The mathematical space of linear perspective is a drastic reduction of direct experience, yet since its codification in the Renaissance, it had increasingly become accepted as the "true" space of human habitation. In the artificial model of perspective, space is conceived as a universal, geometric structure: homogeneous and isotropic. It is a neutral, empty container in which objects are located, their position precisely measurable by their spatial co-ordinates. The perspectival system also implies the illusory possibility

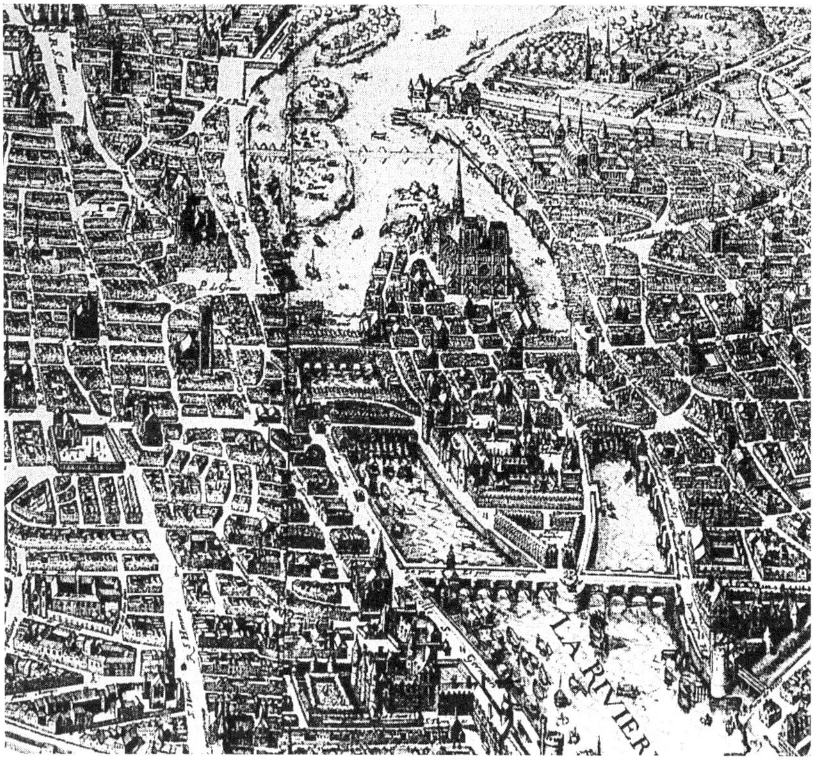

8.1 Bird's-eye view of central Paris, 1615; from Merian, in Leonardo Benevolo, *The Architecture of the Renaissance* (London: Routledge & Kegan Paul 1978), 2: 700–1.

of a fixed, disembodied spectator who observes the constructed reality from a point of detachment. While such a conception is largely arbitrary and a caricature of direct experience, it gained dominance (in a culture increasingly enthralled by the promise of certainty offered by the mathematical sciences) through its power to rationalize the untidy diversity of phenomena into a comprehensive, intelligible system, well suited to the efficient manipulation of reality. It is these instrumental aspects of mathematical space which have precipitated the poverty of so much of modern architectural practice.[8]

The surrealists rejected ossified literary conventions analogous to the conceptualizations of perspective illusionism (such as the use of indiscriminate, objectifying descriptions of settings as if they possessed equal meaning). Interested in evoking the experiential truth of phenomena, Breton sometimes deployed a deliberately non-literary, quasi-documentary form using, as he claimed, real people and events without substantial alteration[9] and in which, as in the heterogeneity of direct experience, the significance of events is inherently variable. He distinguishes between "the most decisive episodes of my life"[10] – events pregnant with meaning which are worthy of recording and those other *moments nuls* – unremarkable mundane activities which, as in the daily flow of experience, go largely unnoted. This principle extends to the evocation of spatial settings; those which support memorable situations rise crisply into relief, while others remain part of an implicit, amorphous background.[11] This heterogeneity of perceptual space is analogous to the spatial experience of mythical consciousness. In this primordial mode of being, sacred space was perceived as structured, real, and meaningful, while the profane remained unformed.[12] The poetic evocation of the marvelous, residing in primary states including that of mythical consciousness, was one of surrealism's stated aims.

Breton starts *Nadja* with the question "Who am I?" announcing the theme of self-discovery and of striving after the revelation of life's meaning which, disclosed through his urban journeys and his encounters with the clairvoyant heroine, is to permeate the whole work. Breton's little book consists of a series of reflections triggered by various marvelous episodes which occur during the course of his daily life in the streets of Paris. One day, while browsing in the Rue Lafayette, he has his first encounter with the enigmatic Nadja, the phantom-like guide of his journey and his allegorical opposite and complement. She is to be the means toward complete self-knowledge and a desired dissolution of all contradictions. The theme of the reconciliation of opposites and the resulting reconstitution of the primordial unity of the cosmos (reclaiming immortality and wisdom) is the subtext of much of Breton's work and is evoked here through an alchemical allegory.[13] In alchemy the combining of the fundamental elements sulfur and mercury is understood as the marriage of the opposing male and female (or solar and lunar) principles. The main prototype of this union is brother-sister incest. In the novel, the brother-sister pair (limited reason and the liberating irrational) is represented by the not-yet-transfigured Breton and by Nadja. Their union corresponds to the archetypal reconciliation of the anima (female principle in man) and animus (male principle in woman),[14] and symbolizes the return to a primordial completeness. The result of this union is a new bisexual being who harmoniously combines the attributes of both,

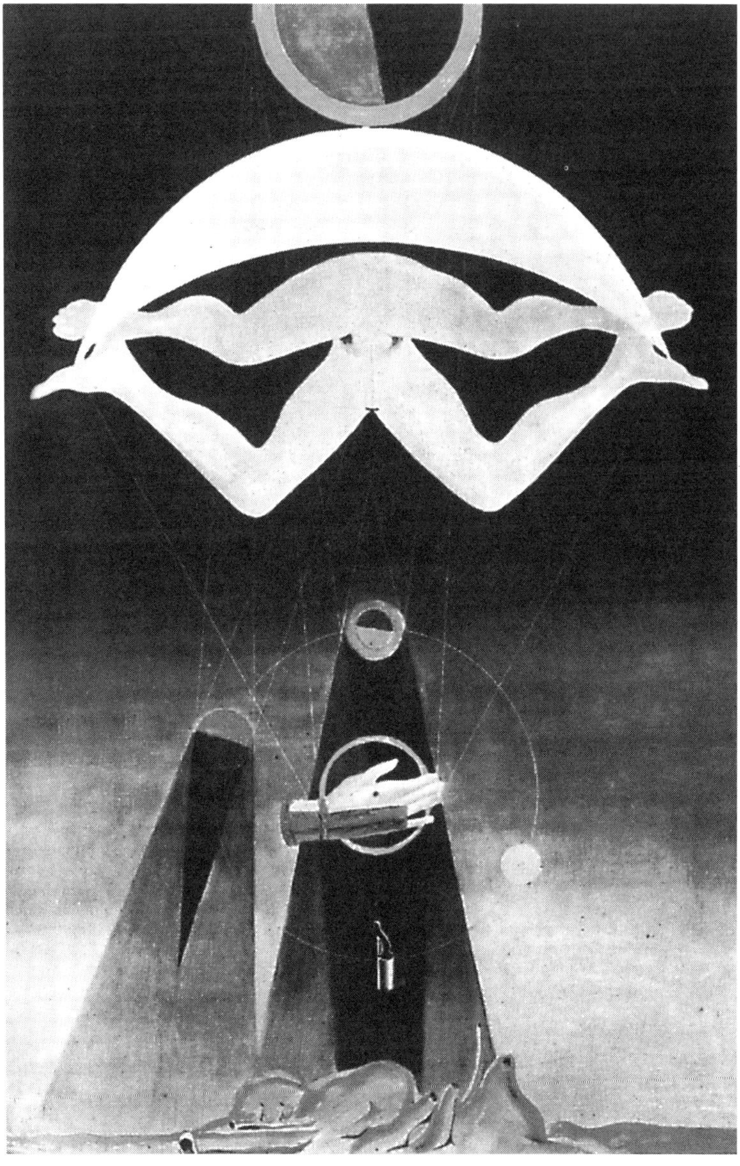

8.2 Max Ernst, *Men Shall Know Nothing of This* (1923); Tate Gallery, London.

and is thus complete and perfect, and consequently immortal.[15] The original androgyne is the *Rebis* (the double thing) or philosopher's stone, the goal of the alchemical and surrealist quests. By restoring primordial androgyny (or, in surrealist terms, by reconstituting the full richness of existence in surreality), man attains a deeper, poetic mode of being.[16] The rest of *Nadja* is dominated by descriptions of the couple's subsequent urban journeys together. Increasingly under his magnetic power, Nadja tells Breton about her life, and it becomes apparent that she has visionary powers which elude rational explanation. Breton's story is a metaphor for a number of archetypal journeys, from the medieval pilgrimage toward a sacred shrine to the hero's initiatic journey (guided by a mysterious female guide) through places of peril and chaos,[17] toward light and a higher state of consciousness.

The urban setting of the novel thus acts simultaneously on many different levels, providing a real and memorable setting for the story, mirroring and shaping the characters' inner world and – through a metaphorical structure – evoking the text's mythical undercurrents. For example, Breton's fateful encounter with Nadja is situated in a temporal and spatial setting which endows it with symbolic meaning. The time is the end of a gloomy October afternoon (suggesting death, which is the necessary beginning of the cycle of regeneration). Having just bought a work by Trotsky in the Humanité bookshop in the nineteenth-century area of Paris near the Opéra, Breton watches people surging past him from the emptying buildings with a sense of despondency and unfulfilled promise: "No, it was not yet these who would be ready to create the Revolution."[18] By Revolution, Breton means not merely an economic revolution, but primarily what for him it will engender: the liberation of human consciousness from various kinds of present oppression (including the tyranny of what he liked to call "bourgeois reason"), and the achievement of a reconciliatory mode of being.[19]

Into this desolate landscape suddenly materializes the woman whose name announces her symbolic role as the catalyst for this transformation: "Nadja, because in Russian it's the beginning of the word hope, and because it's only the beginning."[20] Through her other-worldly attributes and expression, Breton immediately recognizes her as unique among the crowd.[21] The significance of this encounter in Breton's quest for surreality is reflected in the spatial setting. He first sees Nadja having "just crossed an intersection whose name I don't know, in front of a church."[22] There is a sense of Breton's aimlessness and disorientation to this point, followed in the image of the church by a suggestion of death but also of some imminent auspicious event. The state of primordial chaos is an appropriate start of the cycle of death and regeneration, and it parallels

8.3 Photograph of the *Humanité* bookshop in Rue Lafayette; photograph by J.A. Boiffard.

the early stages of the alchemical *Opus*.[23] A particular place is thus conjured up out of the unremarked continuum of the city, a place which is a setting for this significant encounter. In contrast to a formal conception, the setting is configured situationally, in response to the event which takes place there and from which it gains its meaning. Reciprocally, the meaning of the event is inseparable from its spatial and temporal emplacement.[24] This again corresponds to the reciprocity between place and content which characterizes mythical space.[25]

Later on in their peregrinations, Breton and Nadja progress southward toward the most ancient, primordial realms of the city. The day is fading. Nadja, who has been in a state of great agitation, has them driven in a taxi which, instead of to the Ile Saint-Louis, mysteriously takes them to the western tip of the Ile de la Cité, to the Place Dauphine. In Breton's writing this island, the site of the most ancient settlement, figures as the archetypal centre and origin of Paris.[26] His evocation of the Place Dau-

8.4 Place Dauphine in the 1930s; photograph by Roger-Viollet, from M.C. Bancquart, *Paris des surréalistes* (Paris: Seghers 1972), facing 160.

phine, in this central region surrounded by water, maps out its multivalent meaning as a setting for a significant initiatic ordeal: "The Place Dauphine is certainly one of the most profoundly secluded places I know of, one of the worst wastelands in Paris. Whenever I happen to be there, I feel the desire to go somewhere else gradually ebbing out of me, I have to struggle against myself to get free from a gentle, over-insistent, and finally crushing embrace."[27]

The triangular shape of the Place Dauphine (which Breton does not describe but of which he assumes that the reader is aware) is important in the symbolic reading, both for the triangle's sinister connotations in the occult tradition and also for its role in the alchemical work.[28] The form of this setting also endows it with latent sexual meaning. The somewhat isolated triangle bisected by a double row of trees was associated in the surrealists' imagination with the female pudendum.[29] This corresponds to the ancient affiliation of the triangle with woman and

8.5 Giorgio de Chirico, *An Agonizing Journey (The Enigma of Fatality)* (1914); Emanuel Hoffmann Foundation, Kunstmuseum, Basel.

universal fertility.[30] There are also connections between the uterine imagery of the Place Dauphine and the sealed alchemical vessel or philosophic egg,[31] in which the dissolution of opposites in the *nigredo* phase of the *Opus* is enacted. The surrealist vision of Paris as a female body again recalls aspects of the structuring of mythical space, where the order of the body, itself a microcosm of the greater whole, is recognized in the orientation of space and carries cosmological significance.[32] Breton's text thus invites the reader's imaginative participation in interpreting and completing the meaning. The light is fading, suggesting death and threat (but also preparation for the main alchemical operation, which requires darkness). Breton and Nadja sit down to dine in the square. The sense of threat and menace is accentuated by the presence of a persistent prowling drunkard shouting obscenities and "lugubriously ... cracking jokes."[33] At the end of the meal, Nadja becomes aware of an underground tunnel passing below them. She is disturbed by the thought of the suffering and death evoked by this place and seems to see a crowd of the dead. This passage can also be interpreted as quite an explicit reference to the pair's descent (conducted by the spectral ferryman/taxi) into the underworld.

The imagery associated with the Place Dauphine alludes to the *axis mundi*, the place where communication with the transcendent or between cosmic strata (the world and the underworld) occurs. This is the most perilous part of the couple's initiatic journey. The evocations of the suffering and death linked to the real Palais de Justice (of which Nadja has had personal experience) further allude to themes of the last judgment and the descent into the underworld (with the implicit possibility of salvation). The setting thus has a strong ethical dimension.[34] This part of their journey also corresponds, as we have seen, to the so-called *nigredo* phase of the alchemical *Opus*, in which the first union of opposite principles undergoes a "death" or putrefaction. It is interesting to note how Breton's evocation of the familiar sinister character of a real place is used to convey something of the characters' anxious state of mind and can in fact be seen as a reflection of that state. The reference to the underground tunnel is an evocation of the dark, potentially regenerative (and essentially feminine) powers of the chthonic,[35] and of the labyrinth of the subconscious. This dark tunnel, Breton suggests, will take the pair from the realm of death toward the light.[36] The couple's stay in this nether region is marked by fear and the threat of death,[37] as the surrounding gloom is gradually transformed into colours.[38] They leave the Place Dauphine past the law courts, emerging from the realm of death. This moment of transition marks an important step in the quest.[39] They cross the river onto solid land and walk along the north bank toward the Louvre (an image of castle),[40] Nadja still upset. The imagery now signals the completion of the first union of the opposing principles of fire and water (and of the couple themselves) as their gazes unite on the surface of the Seine, ablaze with lights.[41] Toward midnight they reach the Tuileries, where they sit in the darkness watching the jet of the fountain, comparing its spurts to their now and hence forward united thoughts.[42] The theme of this psychic union is further reiterated in Nadja's knowledge of what Breton is thinking. In the amorphous paradisal setting of the midnight garden, the first alchemical stage of the union of opposites has been accomplished.[43] (The initial union will be

8.6 *Below the Pont Neuf*; photograph by André Kertész, from *J'aime Paris* (New York: Grossman Publishers 1974), 13.

followed for Breton by a complete and all-consuming marriage. This is prefigured in the final pages' paean to an anonymous new lover, but realized only some years later in *L'amour fou*.) The elemental and marvelous world of the garden setting simultaneously evokes the mental landscape of the characters. At such moments, enveloped in primordial darkness and the theatre of nature (when space perception becomes almost wholly a matter of pre-reflective faculties), the psyche is most free of the shackles of social convention and perspectival vision, and most able to surrender to the primitive force of the night.[44] The Place Dauphine and Tuileries sequence illustrates how places – the spatial and temporal settings of events in the phenomenal world – partake of archetypal meaning, acting as the concrete embodiment of certain primordial images or paradigmatic situations,[45] and enabling us thus to recognize some basic truth about our own place in the cosmic whole. The recognition which situations engender is our primary way of participating in our culture. This is essential in understanding the fundamental role of cities in the continuation of our cultural tradition.[46]

The continuity in experience between the concrete outer world and the inner psychic world of man is a pervasive surrealist theme.[47] One of the characteristics which makes the undirected urban walk such a powerful metaphor for the explorations of consciousness is the involuntary flow of places and events which it engenders, resembling the flow of images in a dream. It is thus the embodied equivalent of the surrealist techniques of objective chance and automatism. As in automatic writing and drawing, in which a few existing fragments were used to release a stream of images from the subconscious, the urban events Breton happens to encounter stimulate his involuntary response. The walk then is like an automatic text, unfolding by chance or perhaps in response to subconscious desires, without the intervention of rational will, and is made up of encounters between the settings and his imagination.[48] Toward the end of *Nadja*, Breton notes how the city engages with the *flâneur* in a reciprocal generation of experiences. With its situational structure, its historical layering and archetypal settings, its moods and its aleatory flow of images, it is the catalyst and the expression of the artist's thoughts and imaginings, and is in turn transformed by them into a poetic world which Breton calls the "true city distracted and abstracted" from the actual Paris:

> It is not for me to ponder what is happening to the "shape of the city," even of the true city distracted and abstracted from the one I live in by the force of an element which is to my mind what air is supposed to be to life [i.e., the imagination]. Without regret, at this moment I see it change and even disappear. It slides, it burns, it sinks into the shudder of weeds along the barricades, into the dream of curtains in its bedrooms, where a man and woman indifferently continue making love. I leave this sketch of a *mental landscape* whose limits discourage me.[49]

The understanding of this reciprocity endows the texts with poetic truth. Perception always involves a dialogue between the embodied perceiver and the collection of interconnected phenomena (or world) in which he is situated and whose spatiality he inhabits.[50] Instead of any "objective assessment" available to a fictive subject, perception always involves interpretation. The assimilation of the meaning which resides for us in things is conditioned by what we already know – by our memory and our imagination – and is deeply metaphorical in nature.

Breton's evocations of urban settings reveal the deep continuity he perceives between corporeal space and that of the city. This sometimes manifests itself in animate or anthropomorphic qualities of places, as in his evocation of the centre of Paris as an erotically outstretched female body.[51] There is also a blurring of boundaries between his own autobiographical reflections and a collective consciousness. The city is the stage on which the private and the universal, the inner and outer drama, are enacted (the finite and the individual partaking of the archetypal); it is the form in which both are embodied. In *Nadja*, for example, this phenomenal continuity is evoked by Breton's combination of authentic autobiographical narrative and references to familiar, real places, with philosophical reflection and a fictionalized account of his relationship with the heroine.[52]

The convergence of reality and fantasy is even more dramatic in *Le paysan de Paris*, in which Aragon on his urban strolls frequently drifts off into evocations of oneiric images, the materialization of reverie or recollection set off by an experience of some concrete place in the city. A memorable example is his description of the cane shop he notices on one of his evening visits to the subaqueous world of the Passage de l'Opéra.

> My attention was suddenly attracted by a sort of humming noise which seemed to be coming from the direction of the cane shop, and I was astonished to see that its window was bathed in a greenish, almost submarine light, the source of which remained invisible ... The whole ocean in the Passage de l'Opéra. The canes floated gently like seaweed. I had still not recovered from my enchantment when I noticed that a human form was swimming among the various levels of the window display. Although not quite as tall as an average woman, she did not in the least give the impression of being a dwarf. Her smallness seemed, rather, to derive from distance, and yet the apparition was moving about just behind the windowpane. Her hair floated behind her, her fingers occasionally clutched at one of the canes. At first I thought I must be face to face with a siren in the most conventional sense of the term, for I certainly had the impression that the lower half of this charming spectre, who was naked down to a very low waistline, consisted of a sheath of steel or scales or possibly rose petals.[53]

Characteristically, Aragon's narrative then drifts onward, blending fact and reverie, identifying the mysterious mermaid figure as a singing Rhineland prostitute of his fond memory. Further on, he speaks of the margin between the sober, objective reality of the outside world (characterized by the desire for absolute knowledge) and the shadowy, hallucinatory world of the passage, "the whirlpools of his own being." He likes to linger at their edge, the place where the two worlds merge: "Here the two great movements of the spirit are equivalent and all interpretations of the world have lost their power over me. Two universes begin to fade at their point of contact; like a woman adorned with all the magic spells of love when daybreak has raised her skirt of curtains and penetrated the room gently."[54]

For Aragon, then, these mysterious marginal zones reconcile the artificial dichotomy of fact and fiction, a notion he suggests through the metaphor of erotic experience. Love, involuntary and overwhelming, was for the Surrealists the all-powerful means to their goal, "the very cornerstone of that violent liberation which reaches out for a better life in the heart of the technological age."[55] As the primary source of the beauty of the marvelous, it remains a pre-reflective mode of being, deeply rooted in the primordial unity of mind and body. It thus provided a compelling paradigm for the sought resolution of contradictions inherent in rationalist culture.

The convergence of reality and dream characterizing direct experience, is further approximated in surrealist texts by the incorporation of real found fragments into the fictional narrative. Both Breton and Aragon constantly refer to actual places, dates, and people, and reproduce works of art, photographs and fragments of printed material which document the concreteness of the places and events they describe. Having established the "reality" of their narrative, they obscure the boundaries between it and the imaginative material of thought, reverie and fiction. A great deal of the books' excitement and experiential truth is the result of this tension between the concrete and the imaginary. These real fragments, in their own right or by being selected for publication, are excised from their habitual context, thus displaying a strangeness which appealed to the surrealist imagination. This is the case with many of the fragments of commercial signs and advertisements with which Aragon punctuates *Le paysan de Paris*, or even with individual words (such as the word "pessimism" painted on the bellows of a street musician's accordion: its vowels disappear as the instrument is played)[56] which, by being desituated, disclose a strangeness independent of their usual meaning. Breton tends to prefer daily objects encountered in the city which stimulate his subliminal response or whose mundane appearance conceals an inexplicable dimension of the oracular, such as the "*On signe ici*" placard or his penchant for expectant loitering in the Boulevard Bonne-Nouvelle. He also finds the greatest beauty in things which have lost their function, such as the amputated Porte Saint-Denis. Objectified realities are thus re-situated in a broader field of metaphorical meaning which characterizes human experience in the world. This is memorably the case with architecture, as with the human aquarium of the Passage de l'Opéra or the enigmatic and multivalent beacon of the Tour Saint-Jacques, itself a fragment.[57]

The spatial structure manifest in the surrealist texts is also sequential (although not linear). Unlike a comprehensive perspectival vision, it unfolds gradually, and yields its meaning through the protagonists' spontaneous wandering and embodied participation in the city. Events are always enacted in place and time: both are irreducible parts of each situation and constitute its particular meaning. This is well illustrated by the lovers' allegorical night walk in *L'amour fou*,[58] starting at the visceral Hales market after midnight, linking the Tour Saint-Jacques with the Ile de la Cité, and arriving at the Quai aux Fleurs at the foot of Notre Dame cathedral at dawn.[59] The time evoked also resembles the temporality which characterizes primordial perception. In contrast to the linear progress of objectified time, in which successive events are registered by a fixed observer, phenomenal temporality is experienced as a fluid medium, a continuum of temporal phases in which recollections and daydreams are not necessarily assignable to a particular time, but permeate the present through the faculties of memory and imagination. In a deeper, ontological understanding, the sterility of an isolated event is broken as one is opened up to the world of references. This temporality, particularly characteristic of surrealist dream time, bears close affinity to lived spatiality, with which it is inextricably interrelated.[60] For example, in Aragon's narrative, each shop which attracts his attention during his imaginary stroll through the Passage de l'Opéra acts as a stimulus for a recollection or an atemporal philosophical reflection. The way in which a concrete architectural setting becomes a repository of images and recollections (which can be retrieved by an actual or imagined revisit) is reminiscent of the ancient art of memory, a technique in which rhetoricians used a succession of places in a real building to help them remember images for a speech.[61] Both phenomena are based on the remarkable affinities between the situational topographies of concrete settings and of thought.

The nonperspectival space of surrealist Paris is also characterized by the importance in its structuring movement. As with mythical space, which is constituted through the ritual re-enactment of exemplary situations, the space the surrealists evoke is configured through the body's motility. The way in which the sense of the city is evoked is reminiscent of a primitive kind of corporeal space such as the space of dance.[62] This relates to another favourite surrealist theme, the labyrinth. As the traditional symbol of the order of the city and of human life, it ties into the multi-layered poetic fabric of the texts. The mythical labyrinth has death-dealing but also regenerative powers. It is structured as a series of obstacles and initiations to keep the weak and unworthy away from its sacred centre. Traditionally understood as an equivalent of the alchemical *Opus* and a perennial metaphor for the bypassing of linear logic, its successful negotiation by the hero amounts to the attainment of the philosopher's stone, which in surrealism signifies the ultimate perfection in surreality.[63] In addition the labyrinth is explicitly spatial; its dark, mysterious spaces, inaccessible to instant perspectival visions, must be negotiated through the movement of the body. Traditionally structured through the reciprocity of architectural setting and ritual dances, the nature of its space has been described aptly as "frozen choreography."[64] The theme of the labyrinth is occasionally evoked explicitly in the texts,[65] but is generally implicit in the journey. The "hodological" structure[66] of surrealist space is well suited to the theme of the allegorical journey of self-discovery and trans-formation. This journey begins and ends at particular, significant points,[67] and takes the protagonists and reader along a series of initiatic steps. The journey as a narrative structure and as a means of disclosing meaning is an ancient theme, rooted in archetypal human experience. Surrealist literature consciously returns to it for its primary symbolic and ethical meaning.

As we have seen, lived space is structured not as a neutral, empty container which remains when its contents are removed, but exists only in conjunction with the things it contains. These contents structure it into a series of situations, and endow the space with meaning. Space is constituted as the wanderer participates in it; it comes into being as it is inhabited and perceived. Only in the conceptual realm of perspectivity, which ignores the organic continuity of man and world, and in which the corporeal understanding of space is replaced by a pictorial one, can space be appreciated instantly in its abstract, geometrical entirety. An analogy for this type of instant global vision is an aerial photograph of a city. Its streets, squares, and buildings are showed in a uniform way, at a consistent scale, and from a single hypothetical viewpoint. Relationships between elements are fixed and unequivocal. The size and shape of buildings may vary, but nothing is inherently more significant than anything else. This type of conceptual, cartography approach provides a good analogy for the optical objectivity sought by the scientific attitude.[68] A perspective, visual order (a complete panoramic view) is a manifestation of a kind of omniscient god's-eye view and clearly is detached from lived experience. Similarly, the post-baroque perspectival efforts to bring order to the disorderly, elusive richness of the city by opening up great axial vistas produce only a superficial, visual order. Here objects are conceived as instant visions of a formal whole or as distant stage sets, but have little connection to direct experience and thus with the true meaning of the city. By contrast, direct spatial experience is structured as a flow of situations. Its essential features are the built-in standpoint of the animated body to which everything is related, its movement, and the perceptual processes which are always interpreting the spatial world in terms of meaning. Our spontaneous perception of space thus can be seen as an unending sequence of spatial impressions, each informed not just by physical encounters, but also by our pre-existing experience of the typicality of situations. The meaning of places is informed not only by what we see, but also by what we think, imagine, and remember. Analogy plays a constant and crucial role, it is our chief interpretive tool. Thus the images we happen to encounter on our journey immediately mould the whole experience and contribute to our spatial impressions. The journey narrated in these multi-leveled terms echoes the surging and ebbing movements of the narrator's consciousness.

Surrealist writing shares affinities with space as experienced in mythical consciousness (except, of course, that it is self-consciously interpreted and brought to a personal level). Beginning and end, direction, boundaries, and certain archetypal, symbolically significant places all characterize mytho-poetic space. A paradigm of the symbolic journey in which the city is understood as a microcosm of a larger world is the urban procession. The entry procession of the king into a city, for example, has traditionally been understood as the reconstitution of the order of the city, a re-enactment of the founding ceremony. As the royal procession progressed from the periphery to the centre, from the gate to the cathedral, passing through various places of urban significance such as the city hall and the main square, this re-enactment brought the ideal symbolic order of the city into visibility, thus regenerating its spiritual and social order.[69] For the surrealist, the city has a similar character, except that the order to be reconstituted through the re-articulation of a sacred itinerary is of a more private kind, reflecting the difference between traditional public ceremony and the novel.[70] The protagonists' peregrinations in the city, retracing connections between places of significance, are a means toward the realization of the elusive poetic goal of the revelation of the meaning of existence. Breton suggests the importance of wandering in *Nadja* when he asserts the importance of steps, both literal and figurative, as points of transition in the search for human freedom and deeper meaning. In spite of the tedious necessity of work, according to Breton, man must engage in perpetual unfettering: "But it is also, and perhaps, in human terms, much more, the relatively long but marvelous series of steps which man may make unfettered … For myself, I admit such steps are everything. Where do they lead, that is the real question. Ultimately they all indicate a road, and on this road, who knows if we will not find the means of unfettering or of helping those unable to follow it to unfetter themselves."[71] Clearly, the text unfolds intentionally as the protagonists weave their way through the spatial sequences of the public realm of the city.

We have seen that the non-perspectival spatiality which emerged from the surrealist efforts to represent the full poetic richness of phenomena is situational, rooted in the deep reciprocity of man and the world. The situational topography of the city constitutes a receptacle of constant (archetypal) meaning, which is accessible to our imaginative faculties through metaphor. Through our interaction with architectural places, we are able to participate in our cultural tradition. We have also seen the extent to which primary experience is characterized by the blurring of boundaries between the concrete outer and an inner world. An essential reciprocity between humanities and culture is embodied in the built fabric of cities.[72] We are the makers of that culture, but we are also collectively and in a very real sense "made by it." To retain its traditional ethical dimension and its relevance, architecture must continue to concern itself with the *creative interpretation* of the paradigmatic situations which constitute the thematic field of our existence. This is only possible with a sensitivity to the richness of the non-perspectival space of architectural representation.

NOTES

1 "The street, which I imagined might convey to my life its surprising detours, the street with its disturbances and its glances, was my one true element. There I partook, as nowhere else, of the wind of possibility." André Breton, *Les pas perdus* (Paris: Gallimard 1924, 1969), 11.

2 "Tear open my heart you will find Paris." Louis Aragon, "Le paysan de Paris chante" in *La Diane française suivi de En étrange pays dans mon pays lui-même* (Paris: Seghers 1975).

3 See A. Breton, *Manifestoes of Surrealism*, trans. R. Seaver and H. Lane (Ann Arbor: The University of Michigan Press 1972), 10.

4 This primary surrealist aim is articulated for example by Breton, *Manifestoes*, 14, 123, and *What is Surrealism? Selected Writings*, ed. and trans. F. Rosemont (London: Pluto Press 1978), 126.

5 For a survey of the urban themes permeating surrealist literature, including the writings of Desnos, Soupault, Crevel, and Péret, see Marie-Claire Bancquart, *Paris des surréalistes* (Paris: Seghers 1972).

6 For the possible relationships between surrealism and architecture, it is still useful to see the special issue of *Architectural Design* 2–3 (1978), particularly Dalibor Vesely's article "Surrealism, Myth and Modernity," 87–95 and Roger Cardinal's "Soluble City: The Surrealist Perception of Paris," 143–9.

7 J.F. Geist's *Arcades. The History of a Building Type* (Cambridge, MA: MIT Press 1983), a fairly typical example of this genre, serves as an instructive contrast to Aragon's poetic evocation of the *passage*.

8 In reference to the instrumentalization of space, see Alberto Pérez-Gómez, "Chora: The Space of Architectural Representation," in *Chora 1* (1994), 1–34.

9 Some of Breton's claims of authenticity have been questioned, for example, by R. Cardinal (*Breton: Nadja*, London: Grant and Cutler 1986, 69–77). However, a scrupulous adherence to reality is in my view beside the point, since Breton's professed aim is the obliteration of the largely artificial bound-

aries between objective and poetic "truths." The desire to suggest authenticity is the reason that the central section of *Nadja* is written in the form of a dated journal.

10 A. Breton, *Nadja* (Paris: Gallimard 1928, 1964), trans. Richard Howard (New York: Grove Press 1960), 19. All my quotations from this work are taken from this translation.

11 "I do not take particular note of the empty moments of my life, that it may be unworthy for any man to crystallize those which seem to him to be so. I shall ... *ignore* the description of that room and many more like it." Breton, *Manifestoes*, 8 (original emphasis). He also uses highly atmospheric photographs of particularly strange or significant things in preference to descriptions.

12 On the nature of mythical space, see M. Eliade, *The Sacred and the Profane: The Nature of Religion* (New York: Harcourt Brace Janovich 1959), E. Cassirer, *The Philosophy of Symbolic Forms*, vol. 2 (New Haven: Yale University Press 1953), and G. Gusdorf, *Mythe et métaphysique: Introduction à la philosophie* (Paris: Flammarion 1953).

13 The ancient philosophical discipline of alchemy enjoyed considerable popularity with artists and thinkers of the early decades of the twentieth century. Since the late nineteenth-century occult revival there had been a wealth of literature available on the hermetic sciences (for details, see Los Angeles County Museum of Art, *The Spiritual in Art: Abstract Painting 1890–1985*, New York: Abbeville Press 1986); the surrealists, interested in everything pertaining to the realm of the marvelous, read much of it. (For an interesting discussion of the role of alchemy in surrealist thought and an examination of some alchemical themes in Breton's *L'Amour fou*, see Daphne Becket, "Je cherche l'or du temps," unpublished paper, University of Cambridge, 1989.) The philosophical aims of alchemy as well as its esoteric procedures, based on an alternative mode of understanding to that of logical analysis, provide a potent symbolic paradigm for the surrealist enterprise. Breton writes: "I would appreciate your noting the remarkable analogy, insofar as their goals are concerned, between the Surrealist efforts and those of the alchemists: the philosopher's stone is nothing more or less than that which ... brings us once again ... to the attempt to liberate once and for all the imagination by the 'long, immense, reasoned derangement of the senses,' and all the rest" (*Manifestoes*, 175). The surrealist quest of liberation from the tyranny of logic and the restoration of the primordial unity of the rational and irrational (also physical and psychic, mundane and fantastic, and so on) which would

lead to a renewed poetic existence, was couched in the archetypal imagery of alchemy. Alchemy's series of symbolic operations leading to the transmutation of base matter into higher states of being and to spiritual regeneration offered an appropriate metaphor for the surrealist goal of transforming ordinary language into poetry (Breton acknowledges the surrealist debt to Rimbaud's notion of "Alchemy of the word" in *Manifestoes*, 173) and affecting similar change in wider life. Of the numerous contemporaneous works with alchemical content, the most pertinent in this context is Max Ernst's 1923 painting *Men Shall Know Nothing of This*, which has a quasi-hermetic text on the back and was dedicated to Breton. It hung in his apartment (where he discussed it with Nadja) and was reproduced in the book (*Nadja*, 129, 132). Its themes closely prefigure the alchemical allegories of *Nadja* and *L'amour fou*.

14 See C.G. Jung, *Psychology and Alchemy*, in *The Collected Works of C.G. Jung* (New York: Bollingen Foundation 1953), 12:317.

15 For a discussion of the notion of the original alchemical androgyne and some connections to surrealism see A. Schwarz, "Alchemy, Androgyny and Visual Artists," *Leonardo* (1980):57–61.

16 Breton considered the reconstitution of the "primordial Androgyne" in each human being an important concern (see *Manifestoes*, 301–2), and this metaphorical quest a theme of both *Nadja* and *L'amour fou*.

17 The abyss, labyrinth, hell, and so on.

18 Breton, *Nadja*, 64.

19 See Breton, *Surrealism*, 128.

20 Breton, *Nadja*, 66. This theme of new beginnings is reinforced by the photograph of the Humanité bookshop which Breton places opposite this passage in the book. The door is surmounted by a large sign reading, "On signe ici," with an arrow pointing to the sidewalk below. This signals not only the real invitation to join the Communist party (with its promise, for the idealistic intellectual, of a liberated future) but also an uncanny anticipation of an event which will transform Breton's life.

21 "She carried her head high, unlike everyone else on the sidewalk. And she looked so delicate she scarcely seemed to touch the ground as she walked." Breton, *Nadja*, 64. Her haunting, penetrating eyes foreshadow her visionary powers, while an enigmatic smile of recognition may be playing across her face.

22 Breton, *Nadja*, 66. This is apparently the church of St Vincent de Paul in today's Place Franz Liszt.

23 The preliminary stage of the alchemical *Opus* is the return of matter to an initial state (*massa confusa*).

24 Breton notes the situational character of the city, where places are permanently permeated by the meaning of historical (as well as everyday) events: "Lorsqu'il s'agit d'une ville aussi ancienne et de passé aussi riche que Paris, il me paraît impossible de tenir ces structures pour uniquement physiques. Leur intérêt est qu'elles procèdent pour une grande part de *ce qui a eu lieu* ici ou là." Breton, "Pont Neuf," in *La clé des champs* (Paris: Éditions du Sagittaire 1953), 229–30 (emphasis in original).

25 Cassirer notes that in the space of mythical consciousness "every attribute which adheres to a specific spatial-temporal *place* is immediately transferred to the *content* that is given in it; while conversely the spatial character of the content gives a distinguishing character to the place in which it is situated. Through this mutual determination all reality and all events are gradually spun into a network of the subtlest mythical relations." *Philosophy of Symbolic Forms* 2: 81.

26 Breton's references to the Ile de la Cité conjure up a rich symbolic fabric surrounding the theme of life-giving and regeneration. In "Pont Neuf" he likens it to the beating heart of the whole country (231). In *L'amour fou* he calls it the "cradle" of Paris (*L'amour fou*, Paris: Gallimard 1937, translated as *Mad Love* by M.A. Caws, Lincoln: University of Nebraska Press 1987, 47. My quotations from this work are taken from this translation.) The island is also the archetypal female counterpart to the male Tour Saint-Jacques, the pair being united metaphorically as the couple cross the bridge between them (69–73). This union, reflecting that of the lovers themselves, can be seen as a re-enactment of species of hierogamy. The ritual repetition of the act of creation in mythical consciousness is traditionally linked to the conquest of immortality, a goal also implicit in the alchemical quest for the philosopher's stone.

27 The impression of this square as a kind of spiritual purgatory is further strengthened by Breton's statement that he lived for a time in a nearby hotel which was characterized by "comings and goings at all hours." Breton, *Nadja*, 80. This simultaneously suggests it is a place of erotic activity.

28 The understanding, current in theosophy, of the triangle as a "mystical and magical symbol" which "awakens a sense of uneasiness and even fear in the onlooker" was articulated by Giorgio de Chirico ("Metaphysical Aesthetic," in M. Carrà, *Metaphysical Art*, New York: Praeger 1971, 91). De Chirico's

triangular painting, which Breton calls *An Agonizing Journey* (better known as *The Enigma of Fatality*) hung, as we learn in *Nadja*, in his apartment and is reproduced in the book (see *Nadja*, 122, 128). In alchemy the triangle symbolized the union of sulfur and mercury (man and woman) with salt, the base of the transformative process.

29 Breton writes: "Il me semble, aujourd'hui, difficile d'admettre que d'autres avant moi, s'aventurant sur la place Dauphine par le Pont-Neuf, n'aient pas été saisis à la gorge à l'aspect de sa conformation triangulaire, d'ailleurs légèrement curviligne et de la fente qui la bissecte en deux espaces boisés. C'est ... le sexe de Paris qui se dessine sous ces ombrages" (*La clé des champs*, 232). There are several allusions in his writings to this place as a focus of mysterious erotic intensity (see for example *Manifestoes*, 86–8, *Nadja*, 80, and *La clé des champs*, 233).

30 See M. Eliade, *The Forge and the Crucible* (Chicago: University of Chicago Press 1978) 41–2. The principle is manifest in the name "delta" (the Greek letter Δ), as applied to the fertile, triangular estuaries of rivers. The same understanding of the form is evident in a published photograph of Jacqueline Lamba with her and Breton's baby Aube, which was cropped as a triangle. (Reproduced in the Centre Georges Pompidou, *André Breton* exhibition catalogue, Paris 1990).

31 This is portrayed as explicitly womb-like in the alchemists' diagrams.

32 See Cassirer, *The Philosophy of Symbolic Forms*, 2: 90.

33 Breton, *Nadja*, 83.

34 In "Pont Neuf," Breton gives more explicit expression to the eschatological and soteriological dimension of this place: "La proximité du Lieu du châtiment [i.e., le Palais de justice] – d'ailleurs encadrant la toute précieuse machine d'expiation qu'est la Sainte-Chapelle – fait encore mieux valoir le tabou qui s'attache à la place Dauphine et, pour tout ce qui touche à Paris, la désigne comme le lieu *sacré*" (233).

35 Caves, streams, and mines traditionally symbolize the vagina of the Earth mother.

36 Breton, *Nadja*, 85.

37 "I confess that this place frightens me, as it is beginning to frighten Nadja too. 'How terrible! Can you see what's going on in the trees? The blue and the wind, the blue wind ... And there was a voice saying: "You're going to die, you're going to die." I didn't want to die, but felt so dizzy ... I'd certainly have fallen if he hadn't held me back.' I decide it is high time we leave." Breton, *Nadja*, 84.

38 Nadja foresees one of the black windows in the square lighting up in red colour, the wind is blue. This seems to correspond to the *cauda pavonis* or peacock's tail stage of the alchemical *Opus*.

39 "Here on the right, is a low window that overlooks the moat, and she cannot take her eyes off it. It is in front of this window which looks so forlorn that we must wait ... It is from here that everything can come. It is here that everything begins ... She has not forgotten about the underground tunnel and probably imagines she is at one of its exits." Breton, *Nadja*, 85.

40 The castle was a recurrent surrealist theme. Usually ruined, it was based in the romantic idea of a gothic castle, however there are also suggestions of its links in Breton's thought with the sought philosopher's stone, the product of the alchemical transformation. The dual symbol of crystal/diamond and castle (as in, for example, the "starry castle") also may be interpreted as a veiled reference to the jewel-encrusted, walled Heavenly City of Revelation, which occasionally features in the soteriological iconography of modern art and architecture (as exemplified by Le Corbusier's ambitions for his Villa Stein-de Monzie; see *Une maison – un palais* (Paris: Crès 1928), esp. 70–6). The journeys in both *Nadja* and *L'amour fou* reach crucial stages near such building; for example, in the latter the two wanderers arrive at a point where "On the side of the abyss, made of philosopher's stone, the starry castle opens." *Mad Love*, 97.

41 "She stops again, leans on the stone wall, her eyes and mine gazing into the river that is now sparkling with lights: 'That hand, that hand on the Seine, why is that hand flaming over the water? It's true that fire and water are the same thing ... Of course it's not good luck: fire and water are the same thing, fire and gold are quite different.'" Breton, *Nadja*, 85–6. The imagery of the flickering lights on the dark water is a reference to the ending of the nigredo phase, which, with the dissolution of opposites in the blackness, is characterized by an appearance on the surface of "a starry aspect." S. Klossowski de Rola, *Alchemy: The Secret Art* (London: Thames and Hudson 1973), 11.

42 Breton, *Nadja*, 86.

43 The successful passage is intimated by Breton's identification at this stage with the *Dauphin*, a dolphin but also heir apparent. Breton, *Nadja*, 89. This may be seen to signal his imminent transmutation into the alchemical Red King, and his readiness for the next stage of initiation.

44 The theme of the urban night garden was evoked frequently by the surrealists because darkness endowed such settings with a strong quality of the marvelous. Darkness also obscures perspectival visibility and the rule of reason,

setting the stage for a more primitive involvement of the imagination. For Aragon, it was the central part of the "Modern mythology": "Among the forces of nature, there is one with a power which has always been acknowledged and which remains eternally mysterious and wholly bound up with man: that force is the night ... She is a vast sheet-metal monster pierced by countless knives. The blood of the modern night is a singing light. Night bears tattoos, shifting patterns of tattoos upon her breast ... This palpitating corpse has loosened her hair over the world, and the hesitant phantom of freedoms seeks refuge in this final nest, exhausting its insensate desire for open air and peril, there along the edges of streets illuminated by social sense. Thus, in public gardens the densest part of the darkness is no longer distinguishable from a kind of desperate kiss exchanged between love and rebellion." L. Aragon, *Le paysan de Paris* (Paris: Gallimard, 1923), translated by S.W. Taylor as *Paris Peasant* (London: Picador 1971), 155.

45 Situations are those stable patterns and structures in human existence which have evolved over time and constitute our world and culture. Stemming from a deep cultural understanding of "what is appropriate" in a spectrum of activities, their typicality contains meaning sedimented by events and experiences over time. Through this temporal continuity, they gather and preserve the meaning of events and experiences. They contain the memory of experience (tradition) while anticipating subsequent events. Thus tradition continues to be reinterpreted and lived. Architecture is the most stable and powerful form of embodiment of the typicality of situations. Our language reveals the fundamentally spatial nature of situations (theme or *topos* originally designating "place"). On the notion of situation, see D. Vesely and M. Mostafavi, *Architecture and Continuity* (London: Architectural Association 1982), 9–12.

46 Another rich example in Breton's thought of the way in which things in the world partake for us deep archetypal meaning is the poetic field surrounding the Tour Saint-Jacques. In *L'amour fou* Breton equates the tower with the sunflower (*tournesol*), and through complex wordplay and poetic association, maps out a symbolic field in which the tower/*tournesol* conveys a range of cosmic meanings. It alludes to the sun in its passage through the underworld, and the eventual return to light. The *tournesol*/tower is also veiled in other alchemical significance. It is seen as the alchemical "black sun," the emblem for the *prima materia*, and also as a chemical change detector used in the alchemical process (see *L'amour fou*, 69–70). The name *tournesol* also contains within it both the sun (soleil) and the earth (sol), evoking the

alchemical correspondence of above and below. Finally the tower is the archetypal phallic symbol (see n.26), and is affiliated with Breton himself; when the lovers of the Night of the Sunflower reach their final destination in Jacqueline's room in the Rue du Faubourg Saint-Jacques, the uncanny chance convergence of 'Jacques' and 'Jacqueline' alludes to a mytho-poetic reunion of primordial counterparts and the restoration of wholeness.

47 For example, using the metaphor of fluids' behaviour, Breton writes: "The role of this [capillary] tissue is visibly to assure the constant interchange which must take place in thought between the exterior and interior worlds, an interchange requiring a continual interpenetration of waking and sleeping activity. My only ambition has been to give an idea of its structure." Breton, *Surrealism*, 71.

48 This lack of conscious control is, I think, the reason why Breton, when not wandering on foot, favours travel by taxi; it is involuntary, brought about by an anonymous, unfathomable conductor and thus comparable to the action of fate. The taxi takes the passenger for a ride through unpremeditated, surprising territories, bringing an unsolicited collage of images and experiences his way. See for example *Nadja*, 91.

49 Breton, *Nadja*, 154 (my emphasis). Aragon also alludes to this reciprocity in which the inanimate elements of the setting sometimes assume an active role in human life and become the screens on which reflections and reverie are projected. See *Paris Peasant*, 28.

50 As Maurice Merleau-Ponty writes, "I understand the world because there are for me things near and far, foregrounds and horizons, and because in this way it forms a picture and acquires significance for me, and this finally is because I am situated in it and it understands me." Or, "The world, which I distinguished from myself as the totality of things or of processes linked by causal relationships, I rediscover 'in me' as the permanent horizon of all my *cogitationes* and as a dimension in relation to which I am constantly situating myself (emphasis in original). *Phenomenology of Perception*, 408, xiii. See also 131. These observations are closely related to the phenomenological notion of being-in-the-world, as described for example in M. Heidegger, *History of the Concept of Time: Prolegomena* (Bloomington: Indiana University Press 1986) esp. 135–60, 218–50.

51 Breton, "Pont Neuf," in *La clé des champs*, 228–34. Similarly Aragon's early evocation of the magical subaqueous world of the Passage de l'Opéra compares it to an unexpected erotic encounter, foreshadowing its role as the theatre of desire. It is "a glaucous gleam, seemingly filtered through deep

water, with the special quality of pale brilliance of a leg suddenly revealed under a lifted skirt." Aragon, *Paris Peasant*, 28. The absolute opposition of the realms of the animate and inanimate is an abstraction at odds with direct imaginative experience. The boundaries between them in the world are defined far less clearly.

52 According to Cardinal, Nadja was a real woman with whom Breton had a brief affair in the autumn of 1926 (her letters and drawings are also considered authentic). Her true identity is nevertheless a matter of speculation (see Cardinal, *Breton: Nadja*, 70–2). However, critics' attempts to verify factual details are, in my view, misguided. The person of Nadja is clearly to a large extent an allegorical figure, and an incarnation of an aspect of Breton's own personality; the way in which metaphorical meanings reside for us in real things and people is a significant part of the point of the work. As he writes in *L'amour fou*, "It is only by making evident the intimate relation linking the two terms *real* and *imaginary* that I hope to break down the distinction, which seems to me less and less well founded, between the subjective and the objective" (53).

53 Aragon, *Paris Peasant*, 36–7.

54 Ibid., 60.

55 Members of the surrealist group, "Manifesto on *L'âge d'or*," in Breton, *Surrealism*, 327.

56 Aragon, *Paris Peasant*, 61–2.

57 See n.46. The way in which concrete reality and the imagination intermingle in the perception of meaning is illustrated particularly well by the frottages of Max Ernst. The shapes and textures traced from fragments of ordinary things brought to the artist's attention by fortuitous chance act as catalysts for his ideas and in turn are transformed by them. In the *Histoire naturelle* (Paris 1926) the result is a catalogue of oneiric images, comprising quasi-mythical beasts and other enigmatic phenomena of a marvelous cosmos. This relates to the fact that as human beings we assimilate meaning through metaphor, which gives expression to the latent affinities and contrasts between the things which surround us, thus re-articulating a world of poetic connections. The urban context provides a similar springboard to the imagination.

58 Breton, *Mad Love*, 43–51.

59 The metaphorical journey of completion and regeneration comes to an end in Jacqueline's room opposite a maternity hospital in the Rue du Faubourg-Saint-Jacques (Ibid., 63). There is also deliberate correspondence between

this journey and symbolic royal Entrées into Paris from the Porte Saint-Denis via le Châtelet and culminating at the cathedral. See F.A. Yates, *La joyeuse entrée de Charles lX roy de France en Paris, 1572* (Amsterdam: Theatrum Orbis Terrarum c. 1973).

60 The structure of lived temporality is well characterized by M. Merleau-Ponty in *Phenomenology of Perception*, esp. 410–33. The foundation for an ontological understanding of temporality is still M. Heidegger's *Being and Time*, trans. J. Macquarrie and E. Robinson (London: Basil Blackwell 1962), esp. H 323–30, H 412–28.

61 See F.A. Yates, *The Art of Memory* (London: Ark 1984).

62 In the pre-reflective movement of dance, aided by music, the usual inhibitions inherent in purposive movement dissolve as the body spontaneously opens itself up into a more primitive kind of space. This space is independent of an *a priori* frame, unbounded by the measure of objective space, with its rigid dimensional stability or temporal limits. It is constituted by the moving body's assuming and inhabiting it and is structured as a meaningful topography. Movement plays a primary role, re-enacting the situation as thus articulating it as flesh. The space of dance has qualities of ritual, as a series of stylized, choreographed movements which embody sacred meanings. A similar intent is latent in some of the surrealist promenades. Structured as series of choreographed events, they also aspire to a ritual, sacred dimension. The spatiality of dance is well characterized by E. Strauss, *Phenomenological Psychology* (London 1966).

63 The way in which the traditional continuity of the initiatic themes of alchemy and the labyrinth operated in surrealist thought is evident for example in Breton's 1924 "Introduction to the Paucity of Reality" (in *Surrealism*, 17–28), where he describes himself as a prospector for gold ("I seek the gold of time") and "Theseus, shut up is forever in his crystal labyrinth." For a similar convergence of the two themes, see Breton's poem "Vigilance" in *Le revolver à cheveux blancs* (Paris: Éditions des cahiers libres 1932).

64 Pérez-Gómez, "Chora: The Space of Architectural Representation."

65 In *L'amour fou* the labyrinth is evoked as the hero, setting out on his journey in pursuit of his radiant guide, finds the Montmartre sidewalks coming mysteriously alive in a maze of capricious meanders (*Mad Love*, 43.) In Nadja the strongest allusion to the theme occurs with the imaginary tunnel accompanying the Place Dauphine sequence, which the couple negotiate before emerging into the light (85).

66 Space structured around movement, with the Greek *hodos* meaning "path" or "way," as in traditional procession.

67 In *Nadja* Breton's journey originates around 1918 from the Hotel des Grands Hommes on the Olympian mount of the Pantheon (23). This lofty point of departure suggests the theme of the hero setting out on an initiatic journey. This reading is consistent with Nadja's later comparison of Breton to the god of the sun (i.e., reason but also life), to her free spirit (i.e., the marvelous) (111), and with the alchemical subtext in which the male and female principles are equivalent to the solar and lunar, and ends the night of 12 October 1926 at Saint-Germain, where, near a castle and accompanied by an eruption of phosphorescent crystals, their relationship is apparently consummated (107–8).

68 There is a passage in the kaleidoscopic *Le paysan de Paris* which mimics this kind of detached, objective description. Before moving on to his own highly objective and poetic evocation of the night garden, Aragon describes its topography in terms of its geometrical layout, showing, among other things, how distant such an approach is from direct human experience. In itself, the passage is almost meaningless. However, the opening simile serves to subvert the aridity of its perspectival matter-of-factness, showing the pervasiveness of metaphoricity in human perception and hinting at the marvelous hidden beneath the surface: "Seen from above, the Parc des Buttes-Chaumont is shaped like a nightcap, the axis of which would clearly run from west to east and join where the Rue Priestly debouches into the Rue Manin to the point where the Rue d'Hautpoul debouches into the Rue de Crimée, the rectilinear base being formed by the Rue de Crimée which runs north-south, slanting slightly towards the south-east from the Rue Manin to the Rue Général-Brunot. Of the two curvilinear sides of this figure, the northern one is convex in a north-westerly direction and formed by the Rue Manin, while the southern one is concave in a south-easterly direction and formed by the Rue Botzaris. Furthermore, the point, the angle opposite the base, formed by the meeting of these two sides, bends southwards and slightly eastward, forming a horn which extends the park southwards between the Rue Manin." Aragon, *Paris Peasant*, 151–2.

69 See Yates, *La joyeuse entrée*. Similarly, in north European medieval theatre, the stories of the scriptures were regularly re-enacted using the body of the church and later the complex existing network of places in the city as the real and symbolic setting. For the duration of the sacred festival the whole

city would be transformed into the Heavenly City, its earthly inhabitants becoming the real protagonists in the sacred drama, its architectural places the concrete embodiment of sacred *topoi*. Again, the implicit ideal order during these special festivals would be revealed in the ritual re-enactment, the ideal topography of the Christian myths becoming one with the topography of the actual city.

70 The problem of the adoption of pre-conceptual phenomena such as symbols or ritual by self-conscious modern man is common to much art of the modern era. It is epitomized by the embarrassingly monumental vision of private life manifest in the phenomenon of the "secular sacred" (where banal daily activities and objects were raised to a quasi-sacred status, and where, as for Le Corbusier, the house could become interchangeable with the temple). While primary symbols and paradigmatic situations arise spontaneously due to their archetypal character, some of the "symbols" of modern art have a private, contrived dimension which reveals a confusion between the authentically symbolic and the instrumental. A complex surrealist symbol, such as Tour Saint-Jacques, comes perhaps a little close to this category, but is rescued by the sense for the authentically archetypal in Breton's intensely poetic vision.

71 Breton, *Nadja*, 69. Later he reiterates the theme of self-discovery through urban wandering when he asks: "Is the real Nadja this always inspired and inspiring creature who enjoyed being nowhere but in the streets, the only region of valid experience to her, in the street, accessible to interrogation from any human being launched upon some great chimera, or ... the one who sometimes *fell*" (113; emphasis in original).

72 This realization reveals the emptiness of the kind of de-situated, *tabula rasa* architecture which requires the inhabitant to supply "life" and culture (generally in the form of personal paraphernalia) to an amnesic, instrumentally conceived setting. As for the city, a number of modernist efforts has amply demonstrated how difficult it is for an individual to create an authentic culture in isolation from a symbolic ground such as is embodied in the complex world of the traditional city.

The Metaphoric Architecture of the Diorama

Stephen Parcell

Chora

WITH ITS STUFFED ANIMALS and artificial terrain, the diorama is an earnest representation of nature. During the past century it has become a familiar part of dozens of natural history museums across North America and northern Europe, where it continues to be an enticing spectacle, a benign curiosity.

This spectacle, however, is sustained by practices that verge on the grotesque and the incongruous. A diorama manipulates corpses and surrounds them with model materials and paint. Its execution employs forgery techniques, camouflage, and illusion. By combining relics and fabrications, it hovers somewhere between fact and fiction. Once these production practices are recognized, questions and suspicions begin to arise. As a comprehensive operation – and not just an enticing spectacle – the diorama is a more malignant affair.

While surveying the territory in a diorama and pondering its production, an observer may also be reminded metaphorically of similar human situations that have nothing to do with animals or their habitats – memorable experiences that were equally incongruous and enigmatic. The diorama's particular representational status enables it to sustain such metaphoric interpretations amid the didactic objectivity of its natural history lesson. By examining the diorama's architecture – through its definition, circumstances, techniques, and intentions, then back again along a refracted, metaphoric route – one can trace these two lines of thought and see how they reinforce one another.

DEFINITION ONE

By emulating the familiar domestic experience of standing in a dark room and looking through a window at the great outdoors, the diorama imports exotic situations into urban museums. In a space no bigger than a front porch, it expands into a partially inflated landscape filled with animals, plants, earth and sky.[1] Its spatial paradox – that something so vast could exist within such a small container – has become familiar to us through generations of perspective-based institutions, including photography, stereography, panoramas, cinema, and television. The diorama's basic architecture is equally familiar: a distant reality is transformed into an image in a framed window, and witnessed by an observer.

An engraving by Albrecht Dürer (fig. 9.2) succinctly portrays this perspectival architecture and can serve as a benchmark reference along-

9.1 Diorama window, American Museum of Natural History, New York; photograph by author.

side the diorama. By cleverly doubling the observer-window-image-landscape schema, through a combined frontal and side view, this engraving both illustrates the geometric alignment of elements in perspective and offers a wry commentary on the whole affair.

During most of the nineteenth century, before Carl Akeley installed stuffed muskrats in a *trompe-l'œil* landscape at the Milwaukee Public Museum, natural history museums had exhibited stuffed animals in display cases.[2] From a museum's classified collection of artifacts gathered from around the world, these specimens would have been selected for their potential interest to the public and displayed securely like framed pictures or mounted trophies.[3] However, contemporary criticism pointed out "the sadly neglected art of taxidermy, which continues to fill the cases of our museums with wretched and repulsive caricatures of mam-

9.2 A partially clad woman is reclined on a table surface and examined by a disheveled man seated at the head of the table. They are separated by a transparent, gridded window. Dürer's oblique view emphasizes the perspective device between them and clearly distinguishes the two different realms in which they are situated. Because of the woman's dormant position, it is unclear if she is gazing back seductively at her observer, or if she is asleep, dead, or comatose. At other times, her position may be occupied by a lute, an urn, or a curvaceous landscape like the one in the window behind her – anything that can remain stationary within the pyramid of vision defined by the frame.

With one eye fixed at the end of a pointed stake, the man records the woman's visual contours on a flat surface. He invokes muscles in one arm and one eye, while the rest of his body remains as immobile as the disheveled plant on the window sill behind him. He cannot touch what he sees because the perspective screen stands in the way. Once he has captured the woman's contours on the surface of the screen (or its surrogate, the paper), she is free to leave. With her perspective image held in suspension, however, she remains vicariously present. He may decide to return the image to her as a memento, thereby consummating the encounter, or he may use it later to construe new realities of his own in the virtual space beyond the screen.

Albrecht Dürer, perspective illustration from *Treatise on Measurement* (second edition, 1538); reproduced from *The Complete Woodcuts of Albrecht Dürer,* edited by Dr. Willi Kurth (New York: Bonanza Books 1946), plate 340.

mals and birds, out of all natural proportions, shrunken here and bloated there, and in attitudes absolutely impossible for the creature to have assumed when alive."[4] Although the diorama continued to present stuffed animals, its new vivid poses and background settings suddenly resurrected these creatures into an intermediate state somewhere between life and death.[5] As this new exhibition format effectively pushed back the rear wall of the display case, it also reached forward to envelope the observer.[6] As if hidden inside a hunter's blind, an observer could now witness these animals pausing during their everyday activities, oblivious to being watched by a human voyeur.

CIRCUMSTANCES ONE

The word "diorama" invokes Greek roots: *dia-* (through) + *horama* (that which is seen).[7] Initially it referred to an elaborate stage-set presentation introduced in Paris in 1822 and London in 1823 by Charles Marie Bouton and by L.J.M. Daguerre, who would later become one of the founders of photography. In front of a large audience, their dioramas portrayed distant places and changing atmospheric conditions by means of large diaphanous veils, layered paintings, controlled lighting, and sound effects.[8] This early version of the diorama was unique in its choreographed performance and its phantasmagorical illusions, anticipating cinema. The habitat diorama, on the other hand, more closely resembles a radial segment of a panorama ("cyclorama" in the United States) because of the stillness of its presentation and because of its spatial openness from foreground to background.[9] Historically, it is a rich conjunction of disciplines, including taxidermy, sculpture, perspective, still-life painting, *trompe-l'œil*, stage design, zoology, biology, and museology.

Although the habitat diorama was developed incrementally by several nineteenth-century individuals, one figure – Carl Akeley – looms especially large in its history.[10] Akeley was born in New York State in 1864, learned the craft of taxidermy in his youth, and while still an apprentice, assisted in the effort to stuff Jumbo, the famous P.T. Barnum circus elephant killed by a train in Canada. As a taxidermist whose interests later expanded to include habitat reconstructions, he introduced dioramas into the Milwaukee Public Museum, the Field Museum in Chicago, and the American Museum of Natural History in New York.

The turning point in Akeley's career was an African expedition in 1896, when he was struck by the radical difference between Africa and his North American homeland. Arising one morning, he reflected on the situation in which he had become immersed: "Everything was waking up ... There was not a breath of air. I had gone back a million years; the birds were calling back and forth, the monkeys were calling to one another, a troop of chimpanzees in the open screamed."[11] Akeley's autobiography, *In Brightest Africa*, describes his gradual ingestion of the

9.3 African landscape; photograph by Carl Akeley, from *In Brightest Africa* (London: William Heinemann 1924).

African wilderness and his transformation from North American observer to African inhabitant. Once he had internalized his new situation, the legendary "deep, dark Africa" became illuminated from within. Toward the end of his life, he noted the changes that had occurred since his arrival: "Africa today is a modern Africa, the Africa of the Age of Man. Africa then was still the Africa of the Age of Mammals."[12]

Akeley regarded himself not as a big game hunter who kills for sport, but as a "preservationist" who gathers valuable fragments of a world before they disappear. "Naturalists and scientists two hundred years from now will find [in the African Hall at the American Museum of Natural History] the only existent record of some of the animals which today we are able to photograph and to study in the forest environment."[13] He also insisted that these artifacts be protected in their own climate-controlled environment within the museum: "[The] animal groups ... cannot be exposed. [They must be] hermetically sealed off from the hall proper and also from the outside atmosphere."[14]

TECHNIQUES ONE

Hunting and gathering

Akeley's expeditions used cameras and weapons to capture animals. To track fleet-footed creatures, he invented a portable movie camera resembling a machine gun, with a "telephoto lens [that] brings a distant object into the foreground on the screen."[15] Before guns finally apprehended the bodies of animals, cameras would capture their poses and activities. Photographs of this previous life would later help the taxidermist design a new artificial life for the animal that would overcome its intermediary state of death. "The size of a lion's leg ... measured as it hangs limp after the animal's death is not accurate data for the leg with the muscles ready for action. Nor is an animal's body the same size with its lungs deflated in death as when the breath of life [is] in its body."[16] Despite the usefulness of photography, Akeley found on-site experience to be crucial: "A real taxidermist ... must be a field man who can collect his own specimens, for other people's measurements are never very satisfactory, and actual study of the animals in their own environment is necessary in making natural groups."[17]

Taxidermy

After being shot, preferably in an inconspicuous place where the bullet does not damage the hide, the animal is approached and examined. To confirm the kill, the hunter may use another optical technique: "[The elephant] was dead, but as we approached there was a reflex action which twitched his trunk from time to time ... I went up and slapped the elephant's eye, the customary test, and ... there was no reaction."[18] The taxidermist then receives the animal's corpse, together with any documentation gathered in the field, and prepares to breathe a new trace of life into it. Like all crafts, taxidermy relies on techniques developed over time by many individuals. The particular procedure depends on the animal's size and characteristics:

> The technique of preparing mammals and birds begins at the animal's death, with taking its measurements, noting any colours liable to fade (eyes, mucous membranes) and cutting up the body, while noting all anatomical features relating to the skeleton, the positioning of the muscles and their relief. The skin is treated separately by tanning in alum; in small animals, parts of the skeleton

9.4 Figures in an African diorama, American Museum of Natural History, New York; photograph by author.

such as the skull or leg bones may remain attached. With small or medium-sized animals, up to the size of a German shepherd dog, a wire framework is used to reconstruct the shape of the animal. This is then covered by the skin and stuffed full of tow and wood fibre. This operation is followed by modeling, and here the taxidermist must use all his talent in order to give a dead animal the appearance of life. With larger animals, the technique is to use mannequins made of wire mesh and plaster.[19]

Animals larger than humans present greater difficulty. Akeley reported that he "was able to photograph, measure, and skin an elephant and have his hide salted in eight hours ... A green skin like this weighs a ton and a quarter and in places is as much as two and a half inches thick. There is about four days' work in thinning it."[20] If techniques appropriate to small animals are used on large, hairless animals, their hides and their expressions become stiff before mounting is complete, thereby risking regression to taxidermy's earlier status as "muscular upholstery."[21] In response, Akeley devised a new tanning technique that enables the skin to remain flexible for days while it is modeled on a clay armature of the body, "giv[ing] the entire semblance of life to mounted

9.5 Taxidermy mount under construction; from John Rowley, *Taxidermy and Museum Exhibition* (New York: Appleton 1925), fig. 2.

animals, especially the delicate display of the muscles of the face, of the eyes, and of the nostrils."[22]

To preserve creatures from places even more exotic, such as the ocean, taxidermy relies on artificial substances and extraordinary processes. For example: "Molluscs … are represented in museums only by their shells because the soft part is difficult to preserve. However, there are ways of keeping the whole animal for display. The problem is to keep them fully extended until death; in other words, to keep the soft part outside the shell. This can be done by using barbiturates, but the dose needed varies with the species, the age of the specimen and the muscles to be treated … Once the animal is dead in the fully extended state … the tissues can be dehydrated by freeze-drying."[23]

In dioramas where appearance is more important than authenticity, small animals may be substituted by replicas or casts. Live snakes, for example, may be anaesthetized with chloroform and then covered in plaster. In this state, their muscles are not yet limp and distorted. Once the plaster mold has hardened and is ready for casting, the snake revives and crawls away.[24]

Although a stuffed animal appears to be suspended at one point in time, natural processes inevitably continue. Before taxidermy techniques were adjusted, animal hides often hardened and crumbled after a few years in a dry museum, much to the distress of taxidermists and curators. "Of what avail to make an animal live again if its second lifetime [is] to be no longer than the first, possibly even shorter."[25] Even now, animals that have been mounted and installed in a museum need to be protected from parasites by periodic treatment with a pesticide such as naphthalene.[26]

Situation

Because a diorama is largely a fabrication rather than an obedient reproduction of a particular place and time, its composition must be devised like a fiction. Although diorama artists are obliged to remain within credible limits, they are free to choreograph poses and activities for their characters. To present an individual event – one place and one time – the animals are simply arranged into a tableau, like a group portrait. To present a series of highlights in the life of a species – many places and many times – different events are combined into a virtual storyboard and incorporated into a composite landscape; many individual animals then play the continuing roles of a few characters. Occasionally a single place – such as a beaver lodge – may be sufficient for an entire life story.

Although it may seem that a diorama has scrupulously reproduced a real situation that has been captured, frozen and exported, the history of its physical production may be quite different. "Old displays include veritable armies of animals of the same species – though it should not be forgotten that the slaughter will have been spread over a period."[27] Because animals may be killed and stuffed at different times, the older possum in a diorama may really be the offspring of the younger one.[28] Despite their obligation to credibility, diorama artists may stretch natural limits by portraying "special situations in nature which bring together an unusual diversity of animals that would avoid one another's presence at all other times."[29]

A diorama is usually designed as a generic habitat for typical animals, based on written and photographic evidence compiled by many individuals in the field. It could alternately represent a real situation in which the animals occupy their original positions and recreate the moment when they were shot. Similarly, a diorama could be a reconstruction of

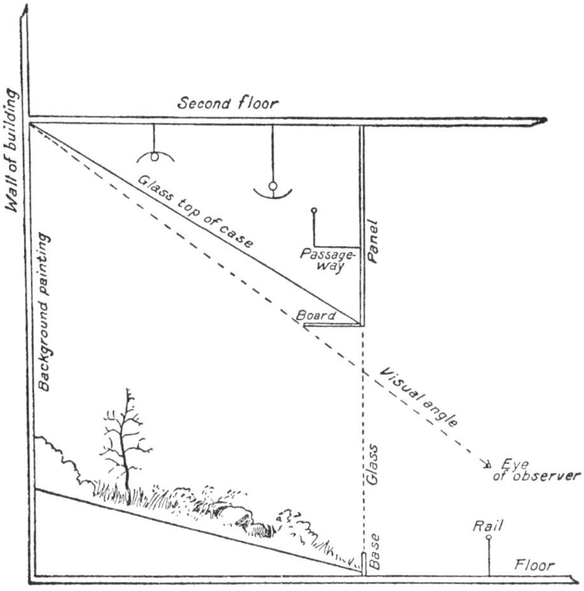

9.6 Section through a typical diorama; from John Rowley, *Taxidermy and Museum Exhibition* (New York: Appleton 1925), fig. 17.

a memory that is loaded with personal significance. After finally capturing his primate nemesis, Carl Akeley declared, "I realized that the search for a background and a setting for the gorilla group was ended. We will reproduce this scene on canvas as a background for the gorillas when they are mounted in the Museum. The foreground will be a reproduction of the old dead tree with its wealth of vegetation in the midst of which the old gorilla died."[30]

Foreground

While some parts of a stuffed animal are bound to be real, the entire foreground of most dioramas is simulated. Nevertheless, its appearance is expected to remain faithful to the natural environment it portrays. "It is unthinkable that an orchid which grows in chalky soil should ever be shown in a diorama where the substrate [is] siliceous!"[31] Because nature seems to construct its own foregrounds so effortlessly, and because a diorama foreground stands out only when parts of it have broken or dust has accumulated, we tend to take for granted the human effort required to construct a model that is so large and complex. For example, a typical diorama at the Denver Museum of Natural History was reported to contain 43,935 leaves, 2,069 flowers, and 157 buds – all made individually by hand.[32]

9.7 Foreground detail of a Canadian diorama, Canadian Museum of Nature, Ottawa, Canada; photograph by author.

Real plants may be included in a foreground if their original forms and colours can be preserved. The chemical baths that were commonplace years ago have been largely superseded by a freeze-drying process that dehydrates the plant slowly without damaging its tissues.[33] The plant is frozen to solidify its liquids, then placed in a vacuum, where its water content is sublimated from solid to gas without passing again through the liquid state. A plant that is successfully freeze-dried should be protected from subsequent humidity and oxygen to retain its colour – ideally in an environment filled with an inert gas such as nitrogen or anhydrous argon.[34]

Constructing artificial plants with a lifelike appearance requires clever substitutions for nature's materials and processes. A book on taxidermy and exhibition techniques, published in 1925 and still used as a standard reference, recommends a palette of materials that includes steel wire, beeswax, paraffin wax, cotton, crêpe paper, silk crepe, oil paint, shellac, rosin, linseed oil, and glue. To substitute for the processes of nature, it suggests an elaborate choreography of human actions: cut, fold, bend, twirl, curl, wrap, clamp, break, notch, tear, tie, trim, hold, pry, pinch, flatten, scratch, scrape, grind, file, scour, stamp, spear, drill, melt, stretch, knead, press, rub, sift, mix, pickle, soak, strain, hang, drain, wash, spray, rinse, wipe, brush, clean, polish, pour, stipple, spatter, and strip.[35]

The same reference describes how to make artificial snow from cotton and spattered paraffin wax. Ice is made from plate glass and molten paraffin. Water is made from liquid celluloid, either cast into a film or applied as a varnish. Rocks are made by casting plaster panels and supporting them on a framework of studs and cross braces, as in drywall construction; the joints are taped and filled, and finally the surfaces are painted.[36] Everything must appear real to the eye but not necessarily to the touch. Consequently, sandy surfaces can be made from real sand, and stones from real stones. When real materials are expedient, there is no reason not to intersperse them among the artificial ones.

As the middle person on this construction site, the foreground modeler must negotiate the difficult geometric transition between the full-scale, full-bodied, three-dimensional state of the animals and the compressed, atmospheric, two-dimensional state of the background painting. A familiar strategy involves the "ha-ha" technique, by which the receding foreground surface falls away into a canyon and then reappears as a vista. Alternately, if the natural setting is especially dense, as in a jungle, the cluttered foreground layers simply prevent the observer from focusing on the background with both eyes. A terrain that is fully visible, however, must rely on accelerated perspective to carry the foreground smoothly into the background. In its nebulous middle ground, somewhere between 3D and 2D, the model parts and their compositional rhythms become smaller and more compressed. Into this space the modeler may introduce smaller animal specimens whose size appears to be a function of distance rather than stature.

Background

Although the background painting is only a few meters away from the observer, it is expected to suggest extreme depth. By adjusting sharpness, contrast, tint, and colour saturation, portions of the background can advance or recede through the apparent atmosphere. Similar painterly effects can make compressed forms in the rear of the foreground seem more distant, especially if their reductions in colour are matched by reductions in scale. Although the background painter and foreground modeler are usually different people, their individual work must blend into one continuous landscape.[37]

A basic geometric armature underlies the diorama's composition. The curved background vista emulates the observer's hemispherical field of vision – the front half of the perceptual globe that surrounds us optically at all times.[38] The eye height of an average observer establishes the horizon of the painting and the "vanishing line" for the perspectival geometry of the whole diorama. The rest is left to the eye of the artist, informed by sketches in the field, and assisted by slide projectors, grid transfer systems, or scale models of the diorama's alcove.[39]

Making a convincing landscape illusion is complicated by the shallowness of the alcove, the changing curvature of the back wall, and any inconsistencies in lighting. To compound these difficulties, the painting is expected to appear credible from the wide range of viewpoints permitted by the picture window in front. Fortunately, the left and right edges of the window frame prohibit sight lines beyond a three-quarter view that would clearly expose how the illusion is staged. Because natural landscapes are irregular and diverse rather than geometric and uniform, discrepancies in perspective can usually be masked. A habitat diorama is not obliged to include buildings, whose parallel lines would demand to be resolved at a particular vanishing point. Above all, because a diorama is not intended to trick the eye completely, its perspectival composition is usually rough enough that the observer must work actively to consolidate the illusion.

INTENTIONS ONE

The diorama's intentions parallel the mandate of the contemporary museum: it is a safe place to preserve treasures and conduct research, and a vehicle for public education and amusement.[40]

Preservation and research

According to Carl Akeley and others, dioramas safeguard portions of the world that are in danger of disappearing forever. Like Lord Elgin seizing chunks of the Parthenon for the British Museum, North Americans brought back animals from the wilderness. By feverishly retrieving artifacts on behalf of future generations, they presumed that the locals (whether man or beast) were unwilling or unable to do so. A curious corollary, as Donna Haraway has pointed out, is that once the colonial treasures have been gathered or recorded, the rest of the estate seems to be expendable.[41] Even within the museum, some artifacts are destined to remain forever in the permanent collection, while others are retained

9.8 Diorama under construction, with scale model, Nova Scotia Museum of National History, Halifax, Canada; photograph by Ron E. Merrick.

only long enough for current research to be carried out. Haraway's recent analysis of historical conduct at the American Museum of Natural History has revealed some significant socio-political circumstances surrounding Carl Akeley and his compatriots, including their capitalist sponsorship by individuals such as Theodore Roosevelt and George Eastman (of Eastman-Kodak fame), latent symbolism in hunting and photography, and implicit narratives in the composition of dioramas that present killing and resurrection as a masculine form of creation.[42]

Although the habitat diorama has been a common feature in natural history museums during the past century, its introduction was troubling for those who regarded it as an artificial fabrication rather than as a real artifact. For these individuals, the diorama's stuffed animals were acceptable as genuine relics extracted from nature, but the rest was dismissed as artistic fakery. To them, museums were supposed to be dedicated to historical authenticity and scientific fact. Their opponents proclaimed that the diorama indeed portrays a real situation (or a generic composite of many situations) that is important for the public to see, but is simply too large and remote to bring into a museum. In its own way, a diorama would then be historically and scientifically authentic, and therefore worth including in the collection. Besides, public education is part of a museum's mission but this is not achieved by presenting boring displays of inert specimens.[43]

This discovery-versus-invention issue is still being played out in an ongoing debate about whether the names of diorama artists should be displayed alongside their diorama. "Currently there is a tendency not to acknowledge the producers [of a diorama], partly due to the desire to restrict the subject of natural history to its objective and scientific counterparts."[44] "The whole purpose ... is to visually eliminate the flat wall surface. The signature destroys this illusion and calls attention to the wall ... A signature would be like graffiti on the walls of the Grand Canyon."[45]

Education

Like a travel brochure, or the perspective being drawn by Albrecht Dürer's observer, a diorama carries one's attention to the distant situation it portrays. "The diorama artist is successful if, even for an instant, the viewer loses his perceptual ability to distinguish between reality and the scene before him. 'I'm always trying to make the wall transparent,' remarked William Traher, a long-time diorama painter at the Denver Museum of Natural History."[46] Even if the diorama does not portray a real situation, the observer assumes that there are others sufficiently like it in the world to warrant its exhibition in a museum.

Once the observer's attention is captured, the diorama is expected to follow through with a lesson about nature. To uphold this responsibility, accuracy is essential: "Not only must the backgrounds be correct, but they must be as typical of the continent as were the beasts they accompanied; in fauna and flora, in geology and geography, we must give as comprehensive a sense of the essence of Africa as possible within our limitations. We must produce complete pictures, faultless history, perfect science."[47] Even with a diorama's wealth of visual evidence, some have

9.9 Diorama background under construction, Nova Scotia Museum of Natural History, Halifax, Canada; photograph by Ron E. Merrick.

declared that it is incomplete without written captions to consolidate the lesson: "Museum exhibits should, of course, be supplemented with good explanatory labels, telling in a straight-forward way and without the use of any more technical or scientific terms than are absolutely necessary, as complete a short story as possible of the group."[48]

Despite these educational efforts, recent studies have revealed that the diorama is the least didactic mode of presentation in natural history museums.[49] It is high in evocation but low in information. In competition with audio-visual presentations, multi-media exhibits, and scientific models, the diorama is understandably outmatched in the race to transmit information about animals and their habitats. In response, some museums have been "upgrading" their dioramas by appending lengthy captions, maps, diagrams, and even audio tracks.[50] Compounding this indictment, dioramas are also among the most expensive exhibits to construct because of the labour involved. Amid these pressures, one might expect that museums would be replacing dioramas with other exhibits or even treating the dioramas themselves as historical artifacts to preserve, but this has not yet happened. New dioramas continue to be built. "It is almost as if dioramas are their own justification, somehow exempt from the research and evaluation that exhibit designers are attempting to apply to other museum exhibits."[51]

Amusement

The diorama's perspectival heritage introduces another set of intentions. "In certain circumstances the diorama 'is more important for the esthetic pleasure it gives than for the amount and significance of the information it adds to the display of the species.' [This] view is not commonly shared by other museum professionals for whom an aesthetic experience has no place in a natural history museum. The public, on the other hand, responds most immediately not to the didactic information but rather to the optical effect of the diorama."[52] The diorama's strange, hybrid mode of representation lies somewhere between the fullness of a body and the flatness of an image – between presence and absence.[53] One might wonder about its original state: is it a painting that has been delaminated or a room that has been compressed? This instability prompts odd statements such as "the diorama is a stereoscopic painting rather than a coloured model."[54]

In its suspended state between presence and absence, the diorama resembles other perspective-based modes such as photography and cinema. Each seems to be "a trace, something directly stenciled off the real, like a footprint or a death mask"[55] – a chunk of the world that has been captured and suspended in its own time.[56] An observer can inflate this world perspectivally, and inhabit it vicariously, but despite the apparent consciousness of the individuals who reside just beyond the picture plane, our actions here-and-now cannot reach them.

The diorama's mode of presence does not quite belong to the full-bodied world, but neither is it grounded in the world of photography. Its suspended time and spatial shallowness are apparent to the eyes of an observer, but a camera is easily fooled. A photograph of a well-built diorama looks exactly like a photograph of a real landscape. Unlike human vision, photography is an instantaneous phenomenon with a fixed monocular viewpoint and a constant depth of field. It cannot detect the slope of a foreground terrain or its transition into a vertical background painting. To a camera, this transition is as smooth as the no-seam photographic backdrops that let models float freely in space.

A diorama is animated partly by the actions of an observer standing in front of it. The movement of the eyes introduces a virtual cinematic animation, even in flat compositions.[57] This is compounded when a momentary sway by the observer induces an unexpected parallax shift between foreground and background. If this prompts the observer to wonder momentarily if taxidermy is reversible, the living status of the diorama becomes even more ambiguous. Of course, any tendency toward animation must remain subtle and inconclusive; if a diorama's animals suddenly began to move like automata or live creatures, the observer's participation would be terminated.[58]

Promotional claims such as "attraction," "pleasure," and "excitement" emphasize amusement, not information.[59] Being close enough to touch a gorilla begins to explain this attraction, but earlier display-case exhibits would have offered the same degree of proximity. What the diorama adds is a raw perspectival effect that induces vertigo as one anticipates falling into a virtual space. Some writers have also noted refined aesthetic qualities that "inspire the viewer's imagination" with "scenes of artistic beauty [that] unconsciously instruct the spectator."[60] Although the diorama's visual attraction pales in comparison with the more sophisticated visual media and compositions to which we are now accustomed, something about it continues to be compelling.

At this point, the diorama's explicit intentions – preservation and research, education, and amusement – are evident, along with the techniques and circumstances that support these intentions and help to define the diorama. Our interpretive expedition could very well end here, unless we suspect that these factors alone do not account entirely for the diorama's origin or for its continuing allure. Now it may be useful to refract the trajectory of the expedition and head back across the diorama's museological territory in search of what previously remained implicit.

INTENTIONS TWO

The habitat diorama is located in a darkened hall – a quiet area away from the rest of the museum. The only substantial light comes from the diorama itself. With little else to focus on, one draws near and engages its perspectival mechanism to inflate the shallow scene into a deeper space. One's station-point in the museum is gradually superseded by a pair of hovering eyes roaming around within the diorama. As the eyes become immersed in this new situation, the rest of the body is carried along.[61] When portions of the diorama are apprehended, the phenomenal body adopts the poses of the stuffed figures inside, or flexes its way throughout the hollows of the interior space. One's muscles are aroused involuntarily, just as the sight of an impending collision prompts the body to respond metonymically, with sympathetic body language.[62] The diorama may also invoke physical memories that rely on senses other than sight – archaic personal memories that are triggered when previous encounters are repeated.[63]

While the phenomenal body can roam freely through any remote space – including older, display-case exhibits – the diorama's perspectival geometry offers an extra allure. Although perspective may seem to privilege the eye exclusively, it presupposes the involvement of the rest of the body. Its pyramid of space and logarithmic foreshortening make sense to the eye only because the observer recognizes them as distortions of orthogonal volumes and regular rhythms previously experienced in the world of flesh and bone. Forms that are completely irregular cannot be recognized in this bodily way, and therefore cannot convey perspective to the eye. Although a natural history diorama rarely includes precise horizontal lines or exact repetitions of elements, such features are evident in an approximate way. Consequently, its natural scenes are able to convey perspective, although less systematically than scenes that include forms based on a more Euclidean geometry.

As the diorama is gradually ingested by the observer, its architectural

9.10 African diorama, American Museum of Natural History, New York; photograph by author.

conditions – silent, illuminated, atmospheric, self-contained, temporally suspended, suspiciously solid, and ambiguously deep – may resonate with other enigmatic situations we have glimpsed in life or in fiction, one step beyond our normal habitat. From time to time, we may even imagine our own immersion in these situations: different vital states (coma, paralysis, ecstasy, death), different social situations (imprisonment, quarantine, stardom, freedom), different atmospheric conditions (liquid, gas, intense cold, vacuum), and different temporal conditions (slow motion, ancestry, déjà vu, timelessness). Each of these forms of habitation remains within the realm of secular possibility, without crossing over into the fantastic or the sacred. By invoking these situations, the diorama enables them to be witnessed vicariously, as worlds-next-door. Of course, such situations could remain merely implicit, as subtle aesthetic overtones colouring an otherwise didactic display, but they could also rise to an explicit level, since there is no way for a suspicious observer to disprove that they exist behind the glass.

For the diorama to embody such a wide range of situations seems unlikely unless one realizes that its basic representational mode (suspended ambiguously between body and image, between room and painting) parallels a similar bodily experience that is shared by all of these

9.11 Yves Tanguy, *Multiplication of the Arcs* (1954), oil on canvas, 40″ × 60″; Museum of Modern Art, New York, Mrs Simon Guggenheim Fund; photograph © 1995, Museum of Modern Art.

situations: in their own ways, all of them suggest a suspension between presence and absence. Even familiar expressions weave together various states of life, social orders, physical places, and temporal conditions. For example, *Roget's Thesaurus* refers metaphorically to death (a vital state) as: falling into the big sleep, joining the choir invisible, going to a better place, and being launched into eternity.

What makes the diorama compelling is its capacity to manifest these enigmatic situations in a physical way. Normally we carry such things around with us as memories, or encounter them indirectly through literature and painting. "Metaphor gives a body, a contour, a face to discourse" and relies on "some visualizable phenomenon ... which serves as a vehicle for expressing something about the inner life of man."[64] The diorama's extraordinary status as a worldly stepping-stone is based on its particular representational architecture, which is neither here nor there.[65] Equally important is the metonymic disposition of its observers. That initial metonymic step from museum to diorama prepares the way for a subsequent metaphoric infusion "by which we understand and structure one domain of experience in terms of another domain of a different kind."[66] Metaphor "describ[es] a less known domain – human reality – in light of relationships with a ... better known domain."[67] To the extent that the diorama vividly invokes this larger realm of "human reality," its explicit museological intentions must be accompanied by implicit metaphoric ones.

TECHNIQUES TWO

The diorama's metaphoric capacity to invoke other situations is sustained by a well-defined set of design characteristics. It is unclear to what degree this is a fortuitous byproduct of museological imperatives (preservation, education, amusement) or a deliberate strategy guided by the insight of diorama artists. While scientific discrepancies would be noticed only by experts, most observers bring a sharp, critical eye to any aesthetic discrepancies that threaten to undermine the diorama's basic operation – criticisms that are guided not by formal principles but by an underlying metaphoric cohesion.

Creatures

During the past century, habitat dioramas have presented a veritable menagerie of creatures – mammals, molluscs, insects, birds, fish, reptiles, and amphibians – but mammals have always been the most compelling subjects.[68] While birds remain rather remote, perhaps because of their ability to fly, we enjoy a much closer rapport with mammals. Their bodies differ from ours but we are joined at the eyes.[69] We personify them, too – by naming them when we adopt them, and by attributing human intentions to them when we include them in our fictions.[70] On the evolutionary ladder from slime to humans, our neighbours are mammals, one step away. We recognize scientific experiments conducted on them because we can picture them as surrogate humans, and anxiously observe their reactions in exotic situations that we ourselves are not yet prepared to endure.

Despite the bond between humans and mammals, a substantial gap separates us.[71] Animals from the wilderness clearly belong to a remote world that we visit only temporarily as campers and hikers. Even then, we rarely encounter them in the wild. At home, even our pets remain

9.12 Canadian diorama: Muskoxen with Inuit sled dog, Canadian Museum of Nature, Ottawa, Canada; photograph reproduced courtesy of the Canadian Museum of Nature.

somewhat remote: they are surrounded by subtle smells and high-pitched sounds we cannot detect, and communicate in ways we cannot fully understand.

Poses

A stuffed animal aggressively frozen in the middle of a leap is incongruous enough to undermine a diorama's illusion. "Violent action is better avoided. In painting or in sculpture, this may be done to a good purpose, as the piece represents only the subject and no illusion is intended. But to represent two mounted animals in violent action, as fighting each other, and no movement actually taking place, betrays at once that the thing is unreal."[72] Only with difficulty can an observer's imagination thaw out a frozen pose vigorously enough to re-animate the scene and become absorbed in it. However, lifelike poses that suggest a rhythmic continuity – such as strolling and digging – are quite acceptable; they are less incongruous than frozen poses that await an impending conclusion.[73]

9.13 Underwater diorama under construction, Nova Scotia Museum of Natural History, Halifax, Canada; photograph by Ron E. Merrick.

Far more compelling are poses that suggest a pregnant pause that the observer is free to develop. From everyday life we know that a crisp moment of silence instills a heightened awareness, since ambient static no longer distracts us. Such moments are casually timeless, as if the moment could be extruded endlessly; there is no temptation to force the narrative by asking, "Then what happened?" When this moment of expectation is sustained, the diorama's still-life transforms fluidly into slow-motion rhythms of a different kind, as if steered by unforeseen currents. With the privilege of fiction, the observer's own story line may depart freely from the standard trajectory of action that the poses presume.

Foreground/background

Although the background painter is expected to suggest infinite depth, and the foreground modeler is expected to make lifelike objects, virtuosity is not essential for a diorama to invoke metaphoric situations. An observer need not be completely fooled nor marvel at the artists'

9.14 A moose enters its diorama, Nova Scotia Museum of National History, Halifax, Canada; photograph by Ron E. Merrick.

technical abilities. Although anyone can see that the painted horizon is only a few meters away, this is not a problem. In fact, the painting only needs to be convincing enough to oscillate between presence and absence – to be a painting or a vista. The same applies to the foreground: it only needs to be convincing enough to oscillate between a model and a terrain.

The critical detail, however, is the edge where the background and foreground meet. Dioramas are most compelling when the general transition zone is visible but the actual joint cannot be detected. To heighten the paradox – that the scene is unified, yet the background is a painting and the foreground is a model – each mode must flow imperceptibly into the other. Dusty surfaces cannot be permitted to give it away, and shadows cannot be allowed to fall onto the sky. A well-camouflaged joint between foreground and background permits the entire diorama

9.15 Benvenuto di Giovanni, *Passion of Our Lord; Christ in Limbo* (ca. 1490), wood, 17″ × 19″; National Gallery of Art, Washington, Samuel H. Kress Collection; photograph © 1995, Board of Trustees, National Gallery of Art.

to oscillate smoothly from two-dimensional to three-dimensional and back again through various intermediate states. This fluid spatial transition may also assist the diorama's temporal fluidity between stasis and animation.

Window

Recent educational impulses have promoted "open dioramas" that entice visitors to believe they are in a Jamaican bat cave or a southern Ontario wetland. Despite their exotic decor and multi-media effects, these stage-sets clearly share the "here-and-now" with the observer.[74] A diorama that retains the customary window format is more amenable to metaphor. Because a window distinguishes sharply between the domain of the observer and the domain of the diorama, yet permits a vicarious crossing of its threshold, it enables the observer to imagine this interior/exterior as a virtual world ("there-and-then") where other conditions prevail – a world that is inhabited phenomenally rather than physically.[75]

By framing a vista for an observer, the window appeals to a desire for worldly knowledge through vision. To some of our ancestors, the window was also a threshold that the soul crosses on its way from the world of the living to the world of the dead – or from the world of the living to a suspended state of limbo.[76] To André Breton, the window's capacity for bisection was illustrated by his anxiety about being cut in two when leaning out.[77] Northrop Frye was haunted by the window's double capacity to reflect our domestic interior as "a mirror of our own concerns" and to look out onto "an indifferent nature that got along for untold aeons of time without us, seems to have produced us only by accident, and, if it were conscious, could only regret having done so."[78] Paul Virilio suggests that because doorways predated windows in ancient dwellings, the window is a vestigial doorway that admits light and view but denies physical access.[79]

An open window initiates this distinction between inside and out, but glass consolidates it. As in Dürer's engraving, glass separates the observer from the scene that lies beyond. Although glass has now become a familiar substance, its paradoxical materiality is still evident from time to time – "a mirage which inhibits the free flow of air."[80] Behind glass we may suspect different temperatures and different atmospheres, or faint sounds and subtle smells. By privileging sight over the other, more local senses, glass ensures that we can look and imagine but not touch and confirm. Desires and fears remain unrequited. Reflections in glass normally remind us of our physical form and location, but when the glass in front of a diorama is tilted forward to minimize reflections, the observer fades away as the diorama becomes clear.

CIRCUMSTANCES TWO

A diorama engages the observer by its very mode, not just by its synthesis of design techniques. Just as a literary work must be read actively to be perceived at all, the diorama demands that the observer meet it half-way. Otherwise it remains a mere spectacle, with no metaphoric overtones.

On the epistemological spectrum where histories and fictions are situated, the diorama occupies a middle position, somewhere between the absence of historical reproduction and the presence of fictional production. It also reminds us that the history-versus-fiction debate is not necessarily polarized; all histories tell a selective story, all fictions draw from history, and both provide peripheral benchmarks alongside our daily life.[81] Because a diorama is not necessarily a historical reconstruction, its retains a potential for fiction. Without an authorized narrator to explain the diorama, it is up to the observer to occupy this position by devising a credible narrative from the evidence provided. This new interpretation may remain within conventional stories about the animals and their habitat, but the particular design of a diorama may also permit other story lines.

For a metaphoric situation to arise, a diorama's design must not deny the observer's involvement. Animals that are stiff like mannequins, or overly expressive like bad actors, suppress alternate narratives by dominating the scene with their own apparent self-consciousness. When characters (and/or authors) appear to be watching themselves perform, they become both actor and spectator. This interpretive short-circuit leaves little room for an observer to participate. The same limitation is evident in picturesque landscapes and picturesque assemblies of animals. These preconceived compositions simply wait for a passive observer to arrive at the designated spot and receive a visual reward. In such cases, further exploration appears to be futile; the observer assumes that there is nothing to see but what has been seen already by the author.

Metaphor brings together situations that would otherwise remain independent, whether they are separated by a pane of glass in a museum, by a disciplinary border between fields such as zoology and architecture, or by a specialized division between activities such as painting and building. In seeking what is shared by these situations, it circumvents the boundaries that guard conventional categories. Metaphor operates with a complex topology that resists being compressed into a flat epistemological map with a hierarchic composition of elements.[82]

DEFINITION TWO

The two contexts of the diorama – museological and metaphoric – reinforce one another in an eccentric manner. The scientific classification program of natural history is destabilized by philosophical declarations that metaphor is the origin of logical thought and the root of all classification.[83] Although metaphor had been consigned to the field of litera-

9.16 Oblique view of a South American diorama, National Museum of National History, Washington; photograph by author.

ture by the nineteenth century, and demeaned as a subjective embellishment applied to (and therefore detachable from) an otherwise objective statement, recent probes into its ancient status and its continuing operation in language assign it a central role in the very concept of worldly order.[84] Metaphor is "not only ... a propositional connection of two highly delineated, already determinate domains of experience, but ... also a projective structure by means of which many experiential connections and relations are established in the first place."[85] This tense state of equilibrium is characteristic of metaphor's "predicative impertinence ... [its] clash between semantic fields."[86]

The case of the diorama suggests that metaphoric situations are not vague and nebulous; they can be examined and discussed clearly when appropriate terms and contexts are introduced. They are open to aesthetic discussions that are based on a synaesthetic awareness of the entire body, rather than just its visual capacity. They are open to historical discussions that acknowledge operational details of design and construction, rather than just terminal forms. They are open to philosophical discussions of transcendence that are based on secular human experience rather than sacred belief. They are open to theoretical discussions that are interdisciplinary rather than autonomous.

Acknowledging this metaphoric line of thought and its likely role in the diorama's origin and longevity prompts the architecture of the diorama to be redefined in a more comprehensive way. The three basic elements in Dürer's perspective – observer, window, landscape – remain intact, along with the geometric order and rules of conduct that keep them all in line. Assisted by this mechanism, we continue to be introduced to Carl Akeley's wilderness and the natural history lesson it delivers. Meanwhile, the metaphoric situations that flow into the silence of the diorama – as an observer keeps it suspended in that precarious state between presence and absence – open up another, oblique order that refracts away from the axis of its museological intentions. Energized by the grotesque procedures of its production and the incongruous characteristics of its design, the diorama invokes remote situations that border on our own domestic habitat: different states of life, social situations, atmospheric conditions, and temporalities.

Because of the diorama's particular representational architecture, its metaphors can thrive. Such situations can be portrayed vividly in literature and painting, but a diorama is as concrete and habitable as a world-next-door. In its own quiet way, the diorama disrupts familiar dichotomies – interior/exterior, subject/object, nature/artifice, science/art, history/fiction, presence/absence, discovery/invention, human/beast, life/death – and opens up a monstrous domain in which other enigmatic orders can reside.

NOTES

1 Miniature dioramas occupy a smaller volume because they are not obliged to incorporate the full scale of real animals. Although wildlife habitats are the most common subject, dioramas also present geological formations, historical scenes, and biblical events.

2 These displays grew out of the cosmologically organized collections of specimens in sixteenth- and seventeenth-century European cabinets of curiosity. See Oliver Impey and Arthur MacGregor, eds., *The Origins of Museums* (Oxford: Clarendon Press 1985).

3 George Gaylord Simpson, *Principles of Animal Taxonomy* (New York:

Columbia University Press 1961) examines the concept of taxonomy and the classification systems that have arisen from it. John Berger, "Why Look At Animals?" in *About Looking* (New York: Pantheon Books 1980), 1–26, describes the zoo as a live taxonomic organization in which each animal species is isolated in its own compartment within a larger classification system – an imposed conceptual framework that departs radically from the complex interaction of animal species in nature.

4 This comment is attributed to Henry Flower, who became director of the Natural History Museum in London in 1884. From Charles J. Cornish, *Sir William Henry Flower: A Personal Memoir* (London: Macmillan 1904), 140; cited in Kenneth Hudson, *Museums of Influence* (Cambridge: Cambridge University Press 1987), 73.

5 The history of art includes many skeletons and corpses adopting living poses in worldly situations: for example, some of the engravings in Andreas Vesalius's anatomical treatise, *De Humani Corporis Fabrica* (1543). Edgar Allan Poe's tale "The Facts in the Case of M. Valdemar" describes an extended interval of mesmeric life between two stages of death.

6 The diorama can be situated in the history of *trompe-l'œil* painting and modeling, initiated when Masaccio's *Trinità* (c. 1425) occupied the shallow apse of Santa Maria Novella in Milan and appeared to extend the interior space of the church.

7 The etymology of "diorama" resembles the Latin roots of "perspective": *per* (through) + *specere* (to look). While perspective presumed a view through a window, the first dioramas added layered paintings on transparent veils beyond the window.

8 Helmut Gernsheim and Alison Gernsheim, *L.J.M. Daguerre: The History of the Diorama and the Daguerreotype* (New York: Dover 1968), ch. 2. London's first diorama building, designed by John Nash and Augustus Charles Pugin, still exists on the east side of Regent's Park. Since its final diorama presentation in 1851, the building has been used for many purposes, most recently as artists' studios. Plans to restore it were announced in "Diorama Appeal," *Building Design* 970 (26 Jan. 1990):12.

9 See Stephen Parcell, "The Momentary Modern Magic of the Panorama," in *Chora 1*, ed. Alberto Pérez-Gómez and Stephen Parcell (Montreal: McGill-Queen's University Press 1994), 167–88.

10 A.E. Parr, "The Habitat Group," *Curator* 2 no. 2 (1959):107–28, and Karen Wonders, "Exhibiting Fauna – From Spectacle to Habitat Group," *Curator*

33 no. 2 (1989):131–56, both present the habitat diorama as a series of small developments by many individuals, rather than as one decisive move in 1890 by Carl Akeley, as suggested by James Kelly, "Gallery of Discovery," *Museum News* 70, no. 2 (1991):49–50, and by Akeley himself, in Carl Akeley, *In Brightest Africa* (London: William Heinemann 1924), 1.

11 Akeley, *In Brightest Africa*, 23.

12 Ibid., 254.

13 Ibid.

14 Ibid., 260. In a cinematic parallel, the prospect of worldly air invading a sealed compartment is vividly illustrated by the scene in Federico Fellini's *Roma* in which bright ancient frescoes fade away suddenly after being exposed to fresh air during excavation for a subway tunnel.

15 This camera-as-weapon analogy is illustrated by Akeley's story (166) about a group of German soldiers surrendering during World War I when confronted by one of his movie cameras.

16 Akeley, *In Brightest Africa*, 17.

17 Ibid., 15.

18 Ibid., 28.

19 Geneviève Meurges, "The Preservation of Natural History Specimens," *Museum* 38, no. 2 (1986):95.

20 Akeley, *In Brightest Africa*, 16.

21 Frederic Lucas, "Akeley as a Taxidermist," *Natural History* 27, no. 2 (1927):146; Robert Cushman Murphy, "Carl Ethan Akeley, 1864–1926," *Curator* 7, no. 4 (1964):308.

22 Henry Fairfield Osborn, "Epilogue," *Natural History* 27, no. 2 (1927):173–4; Lucas, "Akeley as a Taxidermist," 148.

23 Meurges, "The Preservation of Natural History Specimens," 95. Freeze-drying also can be used to preserve larger animals.

24 John Rowley, *Taxidermy and Museum Exhibition* (New York: Appleton 1925), 198–200.

25 Lucas, "Akeley as a Taxidermist," 148.

26 Meurges, "The Preservation of Natural History Specimens," 95. Commercial furriers, on the other hand, protect fur coats from parasites by storing them in freezers rather than treating them with chemicals.

27 Meurges, "The Preservation of Natural History Specimens," 92.

28 The anachronistic potential of representations is illustrated in Roland Barthes's remarks about a photograph of his mother as a child in part 2 of

Camera Lucida: Reflections on Photography (New York: Hill and Wang 1981).

29 A.E. Parr, "Habitat Group and Period Room," *Curator* 4, no. 4 (1963):326.

30 Akeley, *In Brightest Africa*, 231. In a literary parallel, Raymond Roussel, *Locus Solus* (London: John Calder 1983), 118–85, describes a comparable episode in which a professor discovers that a double injection of vitalium and resurrectine causes preserved corpses to re-enact memorable events from their lives. In a large ice hall, he reconstructs authentic settings for eight of these figures, who are induced to perform their memories as observers stroll by.

31 Meurges, "The Preservation of Natural History Specimens," 96.

32 Karen Wonders, "The Illusionary Art of Background Painting in Habitat Dioramas," *Curator* 33, no. 2 (1990):101.

33 Chemical techniques for preserving and preparing plants are described in Rowley, *Taxidermy and Museum Exhibition,* 222–56.

34 Meurges, "The Preservation of Natural History Specimens," 93.

35 Excerpts from Rowley, *Taxidermy and Museum Exhibition*, 256–99.

36 Ibid., 24–37. Some of these materials and techniques have been superseded now that convenient synthetic materials such as styrofoam and polyester resins are available.

37 Wonders, "The Illusionary Art of Background Painting in Habitat Dioramas," 90–118, includes biographical profiles of five noted diorama background painters.

38 Tensions between the hemispherical field of the eyes and the orthogonal field of the rest of the body may be compared to tensions between the ancient hemispherical vault of the sky and the orthogonal matrix inscribed on the ground. See José Ortega y Gasset, "On Point of View in the Arts," in *The Dehumanization of Art* (Garden City, NY: Doubleday Anchor Books 1956), 103–4, and E.H. Gombrich, *The Image and the Eye* (Ithaca, NY: Cornell University Press 1982), 162–71. In *The Magic Mirror of M.C. Escher* (New York: Ballantine Books 1976), 49–57, Bruno Ernst examines the curved perspective grids used by Escher to imitate this concave optical field.

39 Wonders, "The Illusionary Art of Background Painting in Habitat Dioramas," 107, 112.

40 This double mission has been an ongoing source of debate within natural history museums. See Hudson, *Museums of Influence*, 70–6; and Susan Sheets-Pyenson, *Cathedrals of Science* (Montreal: McGill-Queen's University Press 1988), 4–8, 100–1.

41 Donna Haraway, "Teddy Bear Patriarchy: Taxidermy in the Garden of Eden, New York City, 1908–36," in *Primate Visions* (New York & London: Routledge 1989), 45.

42 Ibid., 26–58.

43 This debate is noted in Sheets-Pyenson, *Cathedrals of Science*, 69.

44 Wonders, "The Illusionary Art of Background Painting in Habitat Dioramas," 102.

45 These comments were made by contemporary diorama painters, Ray de Lucia and Terry Shortt, cited in Wonders, "The Illusionary Art of Background Painting in Habitat Dioramas," 112.

46 Ibid., 93.

47 W.R. Leigh, "Painting the Backgrounds for the African Hall Groups," *Natural History* 30 (1930):575, cited in Wonders, "The Illusionary Art of Background Painting in Habitat Dioramas," 105.

48 Rowley, *Taxidermy and Museum Exhibition*, 316.

49 B. Peart and R. Kool, "Analysis of a natural history exhibit: are dioramas the answer?" *Journal of Museum Management and Curatorship* 7 (June 1988):117–28.

50 See Jennifer Dyer, "New Life for an Old Hall," *Curator* 35, no. 4 (1992):268–84.

51 Paul Martinovich, *Dioramas: A New Point-of-View* (unpublished Master of Museum Studies thesis, University of Toronto 1986), 21.

52 A.E. Parr, cited in Wonders, "The Illusionary Art of Background Painting in Habitat Dioramas," 90–1.

53 José Ortega y Gasset, "Consciousness, The Object, and its Three Distances," in *Phenomenology and Art* (New York: Norton 1975), 116–24, discusses these two modes. In a literary parallel, Alain Robbe-Grillet, *In the Labyrinth*, trans. Richard Howard (New York: Grove Press 1960), 38–48, offers an extremely smooth transition from a description of a painted scene to a narration of live action.

54 W.F.P. McLintock, "Geological Dioramas in the Museum of Practical Geology," *Museums Journal* 36 (June 1936):90. H.A. Groenewegen-Frankfort, *Arrest and Movement* (New York: Hacker Art Books 1978), 1–11, describes corporeal and spatial ambiguity in several examples of ancient representational art. Fictional accounts of humans dwelling in odd dimensions include Edwin Abbott, *Flatland* (New York: Dover 1952), and A.K. Dewdney, *The Planiverse* (Toronto: McClelland & Stewart 1984).

55 Susan Sontag, *On Photography* (New York: Dell 1973), 154.

56 Stephen Parcell, "The Represented World of the Stereograph," *The Fifth Column* 7, no. 3 (1989): 30–3, describes phenomenal conditions that an observer might encounter in a stereographic photo.

57 See Anne Hollander, *Moving Pictures* (Cambridge, MA: Harvard University Press 1991), 25–32; and Carla Gottlieb, "Movement in Painting," *Journal of Aesthetics and Art Criticism* 17, no. 1 (1958):22–33.

58 See Gianni Vattimo's criticism of naive animism in "Myth and the Fate of Secularization," *Res* 9 (Spring 1985):29–35.

59 Akeley, *In Brightest Africa*, 267; Parr, "The Habitat Group," 108; A.E. Parr, "Realism and Romanticism in Museum Exhibits," *Curator* 6, no. 2 (1963):184.

60 A.E. Parr, cited in Wonders, "The Illusionary Art of Background Painting in Habitat Dioramas," 100; *Scientific American* (10 February 1917:155), cited in Wonders, "The Illusionary Art of Background Painting in Habitat Dioramas," 90.

61 Drew Leder, *The Absent Body* (Chicago: University of Chicago Press 1990), ch. 1, describes a familiar example of bodily absence: the "disappearance" of portions of the body when one's attention is focused on something else. The implicit tactile capacity of vision is described in José Ortega y Gasset, "On Point of View in the Arts," 102–3, and Leder, *The Absent Body*, 17–20.

62 Maurice Merleau-Ponty, *Phenomenology of Perception* (London: Routledge & Kegan Paul 1962), 139–47, discusses the phenomenal engagement that occurs between the body and what it perceives. The interior volume of Le Corbusier's chapel at Ronchamp is a prime example of architectural metonymy. Upon entering the chapel, the observer's body metonymically expands and "becomes" the interior, contorting along with the contortions of the interior space and the implicit trajectories of the window openings.

63 A vivid account of body memory dating from childhood is attributed to Jean Cocteau in J.H. van den Berg, *The Changing Nature of Man* (New York: Norton 1961), 211–12.

64 Paul Ricoeur, "The Function of Fiction in Shaping Reality," *Man and World* 12 (1979):130; Douglas Berggren, "The Use and Abuse of Metaphor," *Review of Metaphysics* 16, no. 2 (1962):248, cited in Paul Ricoeur, *The Rule of Metaphor* (Toronto: University of Toronto Press 1977), 246.

65 This suspended condition recalls Nietzsche's aphorism, cited in Vattimo, "Myth and the Fate of Secularization," 29–35, that to go on dreaming with the knowledge that one is dreaming is not the same thing as pure and simple dreaming. Metaphoric thought cannot return naïvely to the animistic state

of primitive myth described in Henri Frankfort, *The Intellectual Adventure of Ancient Man* (Chicago: University of Chicago Press 1946), ch. 1. Revealing metaphoric qualities in the here-and-now is a more daunting task, attempted by André Breton in *Nadja* (New York: Grove Press 1960), with its surreal descriptions of everyday Parisian objects and places. To reveal metaphoric capacity in something familiar and local, it must be temporarily framed and recomposed, as if the object of one's attention were installed in its own virtual diorama.

66 Mark Johnson, *The Body in the Mind* (Chicago: University of Chicago Press 1987), 15.

67 Ricoeur, *The Rule of Metaphor*, 244.

68 A popular fascination with gorillas is noted in Sheets-Pyenson, *Cathedrals of Science*, 78. The allegedly small evolutionary step from gorilla to human makes the *Man in Africa* dioramas in New York somewhat disturbing because of a lingering suspicion that we are looking at stuffed humans rather than sculpted models, recalling a historical time when natives indeed were regarded as animals. See Thomas D. Nicholson, "The hall of *Man in Africa* of the American Museum of Natural History, New York," *Museum* 25, no. 2 (1973):74–8.

69 Ironically, because the appearance of real eyes is difficult for a taxidermist to preserve, the eyes of a stuffed animal are usually the only visible part that is not real.

70 See Steve Baker, *Picturing the Beast: Animals, Identity and Representation* (Manchester: Manchester University Press 1993). In a section on "animals as metaphor" (81), Baker suggests that some extraordinary human situations would remain indescribable without the example of animals. See also Harriet Ritvo, "The Animal Connection," in James J. Sheehan and Morton Sosna, eds., *The Boundaries of Humanity: Humans, Animals, Machines* (Berkeley: University of California 1991), 68–84.

71 This gap is maintained even when we eat animals, since their names have been changed from *cow* to *beef*, from *pig* to *pork*, from *deer* to *venison*, etc.

72 Rowley, *Taxidermy and Museum Exhibition*, 313.

73 A.E. Parr, "The Problem of Arrested Movement in Static Exhibits," *Curator* 4, no. 1 (1961):382. See also Groenewegen-Frankfort, *Arrest and Movement*, 1–11. The compatibility of stuffed animals and accelerated perspectives is paralleled by the unlikely prospect of two alternatives: live animals in a diorama alcove (the bull-in-a-china-shop scenario) and stuffed animals in the wilderness.

74 Newly constructed open dioramas that abolish the window format and encompass the observer are intended to promote an ecological concept that regards humans as an integral part of a comprehensive natural system. The two examples mentioned are installed at the Royal Ontario Museum in Toronto.

75 Donald Kunze, "Architecture as Reading: Virtuality, Secrecy, Monstrosity," *Journal of Architectural Education* 41, no. 4 (1988):28–37, discusses the concept of virtual space, and notes that half of the visitors to the Vietnam Veterans' Memorial in Washington are visually embedded in the virtual space of the polished black wall.

76 This state of limbo has been proclaimed intermittently in Catholic theology as a middle place between heaven and hell, where unbaptised children and Old Testament saints could dwell in perfect natural happiness while awaiting Christ's redemption.

77 Carla Gottlieb, *The Window in Art* (New York: Aberis Books 1981), 301, 313, 325, 362.

78 Northrop Frye, *Creation and Recreation* (Toronto: University of Toronto Press 1980), 6.

79 Paul Virilio, *The Lost Dimension* (New York: Semiotext(e) 1991), 79.

80 Gottlieb, *The Window in Art*, 341.

81 For a discussion of relations between history and fiction, see Paul Ricoeur, *Time and Narrative*, vol. 3 (Chicago: University of Chicago Press 1988). Stephen Parcell, "The World in Front of the Work," *Journal of Architectural Education* 46, no. 4 (1993):249–59, includes some related remarks pertaining to architecture.

82 Michel Foucault, *The Order of Things* (New York: Random House 1970), ch. 5, discusses the eighteenth-century classification of animals in natural history and its relation to the encyclopedic impulse in the Classical era.

83 Hans-Georg Gadamer, *Truth and Method* (New York: Crossroad 1975), 389, cited in Ricoeur, *The Rule of Metaphor*, 22. In a poignant parallel, Leder, *The Absent Body*, 11, quotes Maurice Merleau-Ponty: "What [consciousness] does not see is what makes it see ... as the retina is blind at the point where the fibers that will permit the vision spread out into it."

84 Ricoeur, *The Rule of Metaphor*, ch. 1, examines Aristotle's writings on metaphor and notes that two of its three basic capacities had been forgotten by the nineteenth century.

85 Johnson, *The Body in the Mind*, 104.

86 Ricoeur, "The Function of Fiction in Shaping Reality," 130.

The Legend of the Golem

Bram Ratner

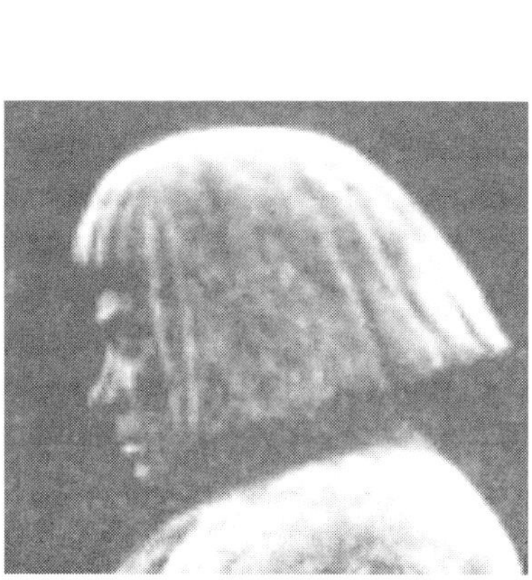

Chora

MODERN MANIFESTATIONS

IN THE HEBREW YEAR 5340 (1580 C.E.) the great Rabbi Judah Loew ben Bezalel, or as he is more commonly known, the Maharal[1] of Prague, undertook the making of a Golem to combat the continued attempt of the fanatical priest Thaddeus to cause mischief toward the Jewish community of Prague. On the second day of the month of Adar, after midnight, Rabbi Loew took his son-in-law, Isaac ben Simson, and his pupil, Jacob ben Chayim Sasson, to the outskirts of town and the banks of the river. There, by torchlight and amid the chanting of Psalms, they worked to form a giant figure out of clay. The three men placed themselves at its feet, and Rabbi Loew bade Isaac to walk seven times around the clay body, from right to left, while reciting specific teachings from the *Sefer Yetzirah* (*Book of Formation/Creation*). When this was done the clay body became red like fire. It was then Jacob's turn to circumnavigate the clay figure seven times, only this time from left to right, and again with the appropriate recitations. As he completed this task, the fire redness was extinguished and water flowed through the clay body. Then the rabbi himself walked once around the figure and placed in its mouth a piece of parchment inscribed with the name of God. The three together bowed to the east, west, south and north, and recited, "And he breathed into his nostrils the breath of life; and man became a living soul" (Genesis 2:7). Fire, water, and air brought to life the fourth element, earth, and the Golem opened his eyes and looked about.

To all appearances the Golem was ordinary except that the faculty of speech was lacking in him. He was told by Rabbi Loew that his task was to protect the Jews from persecution and that he must obey the rabbi's commands at all times. As well, he was to be called Joseph.

Over the next several years Joseph Golem performed his function flawlessly, saving the Jewish community of Prague several times from blood libel accusations and plots.[2] But one Friday afternoon, Rabbi Loew forgot to give instructions to Joseph Golem for the upcoming Sabbath, as was his custom. Generally, Rabbi Loew ordered him to do nothing else on the Sabbath but to serve as a guard. On this particular Sabbath, the Golem began running about the Jewish quarter of Prague like a mad

10.1 "Child offering the Golem an Apple." Scene from *Der Golem: Wie er in die Welt Kam*, Museum of Modern Art / Film Stills Archive, New York.

man, threatening to destroy everything. The panicked public reached Rabbi Loew and told him of the Golem's rampage, and although it was the Sabbath, this was a danger to human life and thus the profanation of the Sabbath was allowed. Rabbi Loew rushed out and commanded Joseph Golem to stop, preventing any further mishaps and evil consequences. The Golem obeyed and peace was restored, but to his confidential friends the rabbi said worriedly "The Golem could have laid waste all Prague, if I had not calmed him down in time."[3]

After a long time had passed since the community had been molested by blood accusations, Rabbi Loew called on his son-in-law, Rabbi Isaac, and his disciple, Jacob Sasson, and told them, "Now the Golem has become superfluous, for blood impeachment can by this time no longer occur in any country. This wrong needs no longer be feared. We will therefore destroy the Golem."[4] It was the year 5353 (1593 C.E.) when the three men went to the garret of the Altneu Synagogue, where the Golem had been told to wait. In destroying the Golem, they reversed the order by which they had created him. Even the words of the *Sefer Yetzirah* were read backwards. After this task was accomplished, the Golem was transformed back into a clod of clay. The body of the Golem remained in the garret of the Altneu Synagogue, and it was strictly forbidden for anyone to enter.

Sixteen years after the destruction of the Golem, Rabbi Judah Loew ben Bezalel died following a dramatic encounter with a terrible giant (the Angel of Death) who threatened the entire community. Although Rabbi Loew was able to save his congregation, he could not save himself, for his name had been earmarked for death.[5]

This account of the Golem is based on Chayim Bloch's 1917 novel *The Golem: Legends of the Ghetto of Prague*, which demonstrates a modern understanding of the legend of the Golem. The Golem of Prague is the most famous in modern times and the prototype of most "Golemim" in the twentieth century. Although the form of this Golem in its various accounts has been altered, the appeal of the Golem to the imagination of twentieth-century artists and their audiences is undeniable.

Chayim Bloch's version of the Golem of Prague, presented as an original letter written by the Maharal himself to a Rabbi Jacob Ginzburg of Friedburg, differed only in detail from a 1909 document entitled *Niflaos Maharal: HaGolem M'Prague (The Wonders of the Maharal:*

The Golem of Prague) published by Rabbi Yudel Rosenberg of Warsaw. These two texts provide the most important literary account of the legend of the Golem of Prague with respect to Jewish mysticism. Rosenberg's account is presented as a copy of a manuscript he found in the archives of the main library of Metz, France around the turn of the century. The manuscript is said to be authored by Rabbi Loew's disciple and son-in-law, Rabbi Isaac ben Simson HaKohen Katz, who had participated with the Maharal in the creation of the Golem. Whether the author is Rosenberg and not the sixteenth-century eyewitness may never be known, although most modern scholarship on the subject doubts Rosenberg's story of the sixteenth-century origins of his 1909 publication. It is known that the author was well acquainted with the printed material about the Golem. His story combines Kabbalistic material with Hasidic terminology and themes to produce an elaborate description of the Golem of Prague. Rosenberg provided what seems to be the first systematic discussion of this topic and also the most influential one. Together with Bloch, this creative literary genius contributed to the spread of the Golem legend of Prague to wider and more secular audiences.

The eagerness of the Ghetto Jew to believe in the authenticity of such stories led the Maharal's Golem to become an unquestioned Jewish patrimony. This is exemplified by a story told in 1945 to a Jewish soldier in Bologna by a holocaust survivor born in Prague:

> The Golem did not disappear and even in the time of the war it went out of its hiding place in order to safeguard its synagogue. When the Germans occupied Prague, they decided to destroy the Altneuschul. They came to do it; suddenly, in the silence of the synagogue, the steps of a giant walking on the roof began to be heard. They saw a shadow of a giant hand falling from the window onto the floor ... The Germans were terrified and they threw away their tools and fled away in panic.
>
> I know that there is a rational explanation for everything; the synagogue is ancient and each and every slight knock generates an echo that reverberates many times, like steps or thunder. Also the glasses of the windows are old, the window-panes are crooked and they distort the shadows, forming strange shades on the floor. A bird's leg generates a shade of a giant hand on the floor ... and nevertheless ... there is something.[6]

In this development of the Golem legend, Jewish folk tradition translated Kabbalistic spiritual speculations into down-to-earth tales. This has become our contemporary understanding of the Golem legend, in which the Golem is a technical servant of human needs, humanly controlled in an uneasy and precarious equilibrium. The Golem, created to help insure our physical safety and comfort, ultimately may become a threat. The creative act creates the potential for self-harm or self-destruction.

This modern understanding of the Golem, as a famulus with the potential to harm its creator, can be traced back to the legends of German Hasidism in the first half of the sixteenth century. It was then that Nehemiah Brull found the story that Samuel the Pious (father of Judah the Pious, the central figure among these Hasidim) "had created a Golem, who could not speak but who accompanied him on his long journeys through Germany and France and waited on him." In another report, published in 1614 by Samuel Friedrich Brenz, it is written that the Jews had a magical device called *Hamor Golim*. It was a figure of mud that was able to walk when certain spells were whispered in its ears.[7]

However, it is the tradition originated by Rabbi Elijah Baal Shem of Chelm that is the blueprint for the modern Golem legend of Rabbi Elijah's famous contemporary, Rabbi Judah Loew of Prague. The story of Rabbi Elijah, as recorded by a probable Polish Kabbalist between 1630 and 1650, is as follows:

> It is known that whoever is an expert in *Sefer Yezirah* is able to perform operations by the holy names, and out of elements, dust of a virgin soil and water, a matter and form [Golem] will emerge, which has vitality; even so it is called dead, since he cannot confer upon it knowledge ... and speech, since knowledge and speech are the Life of the Worlds ... And I have heard, in a certain and explicit way, from several respectable persons that one man [living] close to our time, in the holy community of Chelm, whose name is Rabbi Elijah, the master of the name, who made a creature out of matter and form and it performed hard work for him, for a long period, and the name of *emeth* was hanging upon its neck, until he finally removed for a certain reason, the name from his neck and it turned to dust.[8]

Since the author states that the legend was known to several people, it was probably in circulation before being committed to writing. It may have originated in the generation immediately following the death of Rabbi Elijah in 1583.

Although this creation of a Golem recalls the modern concept of the Golem as a famulus, it displays a strong linkage to past traditions. First, the term "Golem" is not used in its later designation as a creature but instead follows the standard medieval terminology as a representation of matter. There is also an emphasis on the creature being dead, which reflects the earlier nonhuman, ahistorical nature of the Golem. As a transitional piece, this account also lacks many seminal features of the modern legend. The dangerous nature of the Golem and its "tellurian" powers are not mentioned, nor is the creator worried about his creation. Also, the name *emeth* (truth) is written neither on the forehead nor on parchment attached to the forehead. It seems to be hanging from his neck on an amulet. It should be noted that, although Rabbi Elijah takes away the name *emeth,* he does not indicate the precise reason for this act.

The concept of the Golem as a physical threat to its creator first appears in the writings of German students of Jewish lore in the seventeenth century. A letter written in 1674 by Christoph Arnold describes the activities of Rabbi Elijah:

> After saying certain prayers and holding certain fast days, they make the figure of a man from clay, and when they have said the *shem ha-meforash* (the most sacred name of God) over it, the image comes to life. And although the image itself cannot speak, it understands what is said to it and commanded; among the Polish Jews it does all kinds of housework, but is not allowed to leave the house. On the forehead of the image, they write: *emeth*, that is, truth. But an image of this kind grows each day; though very small at first, it ends by becoming larger than all those in the house. In order to take away his strength, which ultimately becomes a threat to all those in the house, they quickly erase the first letter *aleph* from the word *emeth* on his forehead, so that there remains only the word *meth*, that is, dead. When this is done, the golem collapses and dissolves into the clay or mud that he was ... They say that a *baal shem* in Poland, by the name of Rabbi Elias, made a golem who became so large that the Rabbi could no longer reach his forehead to erase the letter *aleph*. He thought up a trick, namely that the golem, being his servant, should remove his boots, supposing that when the golem bent over, he would erase the letter. And so it happened, but when the

golem became mud again, his whole weight fell on the Rabbi, who was sitting on the bench, and crushed him.[9]

Jacob Emden, a descendant of Rabbi Elijah, tells a similar story almost one hundred years later. In it he recounts how Rabbi Elijah saw that the creature he had made kept growing larger and stronger by virtue of the name which was written on parchment and fastened to his forehead. Rabbi Elijah grew afraid that the Golem might wreak havoc and destruction. (In a similar account, the same author writes that the Golem might destroy the world.) Rabbi Elijah eventually summoned up the courage to tear the parchment with the name of God from the Golem's forehead. The Golem then collapsed like a clod of earth, injuring his master and scratching his face.[10]

In both cases the creator is faced with a quandary because his creation is growing in such a way that he can no longer control the process, and is therefore compelled to stop it. The two accounts differ only in the degree of damage inflicted upon the Golem creator in his attempt to stop the Golem's fury. Other contemporary variations also emphasize this new feature of the dangerous character of the Golem. This Golem has prodigious strength and grows beyond measure. He has the ability to destroy the world, or at the very least, cause a considerable degree of damage. It appears that this is due to the power of the tellurian element, aroused and set in motion by the name of God. Unless this tellurian force is held in check by the divine name, it rises up in a blind and destructive fury. This earth magic awakens chaotic and very powerful forces that must be kept within a proper ethical framework for them to be affirmative and not destructive.

This variation of the Golem legend of Rabbi Elijah Baal Shem of Chelm is updated further by Jakob Grimm, who wrote extensively on the Golem phenomenon in the beginning of the nineteenth century.[11] It must have been shortly before Grimm's day that the Polish legend about the Rabbi Elijah of Chelm reached Prague and attached itself to the great Rabbi Loew of Prague, who was much more famous. The legend then became associated with certain special features of the Sabbath Eve liturgy. Accounting to the story, Rabbi Loew fashioned a Golem who did all manner of work for his master during the week, but because all creatures rest on the Sabbath, Rabbi Loew turned his Golem back to clay every Friday evening by taking away the name of God. Once, however, the Rabbi forgot to remove the name. The congregation was assembled for services in the synagogue and already had recited the ninety-second Psalm when the mighty Golem ran amuck, shaking houses and threatening to destroy everything. When Rabbi Loew was summoned, it was still dusk and the Sabbath had not really begun. He rushed toward the raging Golem and tore away the name, whereupon the Golem crumbled into dust. The Rabbi then ordered that the Sabbath Psalm be repeated, a custom which has remained to this day in that synagogue, the Altneu Schul. The Rabbi never brought the Golem back to life, but buried his remains in the attic of the synagogue. Once, after much fasting, Rabbi Ezekiel Landau, one of Rabbi Loew's most prominent successors, is said to have gone up to look at the remains of the Golem. On his return he gave an order, binding on all future generations, that no mortal must ever go up to that attic.[12]

ORIGIN AND DEVELOPMENT

Before delving into the origins of the Golem tradition and its modern metamorphosis, several utterances by Chayim Bloch should be kept in mind. First, the actions of the Golem are like those of an automatic machine that fulfils the will of its creator. In itself, it has no good or evil instincts. When it ran amuck it did not realize it was committing an evil act. The Golem also was an incomplete creation, unworthy of *Neshamah* (the light of God) but inhabited by *Nefesh* (sensory being) and *Ruach* (spirit). Since there was no *Neshamah*, the Golem could possess only a small portion of intelligence, *Daat* (knowledge). The two other intelligences, *Chochmah* (wisdom) and *Bina* (judgment), could not be supplied at all. Finally, the creator of the Golem must be not only a learned man but also a *Zadik* (righteous man) if he is to collect the hidden rays concealed in the letters of the *Sefer Yetzirah* through which it is possible to give life to a lifeless body.[13]

The importance of the *Sefer Yetzirah* as a generating text for the creation of a Golem is evident not only in the above passage by Bloch (as well as his modern colleagues) but also throughout the history of the Golem legend. Almost all medieval and modern authors who have written about the Golem have mentioned this text, yet the creation of an anthropoid is not mentioned explicitly in this short, ancient cosmogonic and cosmological treatise. The *Sefer Yetzirah*, probably written by a

Jewish neo-Pythagorean in the third century, deals in part with some aspects of the Genesis story. It describes, with astronomico-astrological and anatomical detail, how the cosmos was built, essentially from appropriate combinations of the twenty-two letters of the Hebrew alphabet, along with the four letters of the Tetragrammaton. These letters (or elementary letters) were the structural elements upon which Creation was built. Humanity is presented as a microcosm of the greater world.

Although the treatise is presented as a theoretical guide to the structure of the universe, it may have been intended as a manual of magical practices. Certainly medieval commentaries on the book, especially in the traditions of French and German Jews, interpreted it in a magico-mystical way. The final chapter of the treatise, in which "Abraham our father" is mentioned for the first time, seems to point in this direction. In the final *Mishnah* (a unit of study) it is written that:

> When Abraham our father, may he rest in peace, came: he looked and saw, and understood, and explored, and engraved, and hewed out, and succeeded at Creation as it is said, "And the bodies they had made at Haran" (Genesis 12:5). The Lord of all – may His Name be praised forever – was revealed to him, and He set him in His bosom, and He kissed him on his head, and He called him "Abraham, my beloved" (Isaiah 41:8), and He cut a covenant with him and with his seed forever, as it is said, "And he believed in YHVH, and He considered it to him for righteousness" (Genesis 15:6), and He cut a covenant with him between the ten fingers of his hands, and that is the covenant of the tongue, and between the ten toes of his feet, and that is the covenant of the circumcision, and He tied the twenty-two letters of the Torah in his tongue and He revealed to him His secret: He drew them through Water, He burned them in Fire, He shook them through the Air, He kindled them in the Seven Stars, He led them through the twelve constellations.[14]

This passage promotes the notion that Abraham, on the strength of his insight into the system of things and the potencies of letters, was able to imitate and, in a certain sense, repeat God's act of creation. It also provides a plausible interpretation of Genesis 12:5, that Abraham actually made bodies or souls with his knowledge of the principles set out in the *Sefer Yetzirah*.

This interpretation of Abraham is qualified later in many commentaries that attempt to establish the uniqueness and unity of the Creator. The assumption that *Sefer Yetzirah* serves this purpose is noted clearly in the following discussion of the relationship between Abraham and the cosmological gnosis found in the treatise. According to this source, Abraham:

> sat alone and meditated on it, but could understand nothing until a heavenly voice went forth and said to him: "Are you trying to set yourself up as my equal? I am one and have created the *Sefer Yetzirah* and studied it; but you by yourself cannot understand it. Therefore take a companion and meditate on it together, and you will understand it." Thereupon, Abraham went to his teacher Shem, the son of Noah, and sat with him for three years and they meditated on it until they knew how to create a world. And to this day, there is no one who can understand it alone, two scholars [are needed], and even they understand it only after three years, whereupon they can make everything their hearts desire. Rava, too, wished to understand the book alone. Then Rabbi Zeira said to him: It is written, "A sword is upon the single, and they shall dote," that is to say: a sword is upon the scholars who sit individually, each by himself, and concern themselves with the Torah. Let us then meet and busy ourselves with *Sefer Yetzirah*. And so they sat and meditated on it for three years and came to understand it.[15]

Here the ability to understand the *Sefer Yetzirah* and its correlative implications by oneself is solely the prerogative of God. Humans can acquire the utmost knowledge of creative powers – even the creation of a world – but this knowledge must be acquired with a companion. The hierarchy thus is made explicit, and the context in which man's creative powers can flourish is clearly delineated.

The reference to Rava, who also wanted to create alone, and to Rabbi Zeira derives from the most influential and explicit passage about the possibility of creating an artificial human being, which gave credence to the exegesis above on Genesis 12:5. The passage is found in the following Talmudic verse: "Rava said: If the righteous desired it, they could be creators, for it is written, 'Your iniquities have distinguished between you and your God' (Isaiah 59:2). For Rava created a man and sent him to Rabbi Zeira. The Rabbi spoke to him but received no answer. Thereupon he said unto him: 'Thou art a creature of the magicians. Return to your dust.'"[16] Thus the creative power of the righteous, the pietists, is limited. Rava is able to create a man who can go to Rabbi Zeira but he cannot endow this man with speech, and by his silence Rabbi Zeira recognizes his nature. This artificial or magical man is always lacking in some essential function. We are not told how the artificial man was created but it may be inferred that he was made out of dust. There is a clear similarity between this act and the creation of Adam by God. The various Genesis exegeses on Adam's creation provide the basis of the Golem legend. A man makes a Golem and God makes Adam: human creative power and the creative power of God necessarily enter into a relationship, whether of emulation or antagonism.

This creation of an artificial man, and its evolution into the Golem legend, is a metaphor of Man's (Adam's) own creation at the hand and breath of God, and also recalls Adam's subsequent act of transgression in seeking to be like God and to know of good and evil and the power of creation. For this discussion, the rabbinical and talmudic commentaries on Genesis are important for the evolution of the Golem legend, for at certain stages in Adam's creation he is actually referred to as a Golem. These commentaries add another layer (which is later developed and accentuated in the Middle Ages) beyond the more obvious connection between the making of Adam and the making of a Golem, namely that they were both formed "of the dust of the ground" (Genesis 2:7). In these passages the term "Golem" is adopted from the Hebrew word that occurs only once in the Bible (Psalm 139:16), where it meant shapeless or unformed matter and is mentioned by the speaker who praises the Creator, acknowledging how he secretly formed the human body "in the lowest parts of the earth," from which came his golem (amorphous matter).

In one such talmudic passage, where the term "Golem" refers to the creation of Adam, the first twelve hours of Adam's first day are described: "In the first hour, the dust was gathered; in the second, it was kneaded into a golem, a still unformed mass; in the third, his limbs were shaped; in the fourth, the soul was infused into him; in the fifth, he stood on his feet; in the sixth, he gave names (to all living things); in the seventh, Eve was given him for a mate; in the eighth, the two lay down in bed and when they left they were four; in the ninth, the prohibition was communicated to him; in the tenth, he transgressed it; in the eleventh, he was judged; in the twelfth, he was expelled and went out of Paradise."[17]

Adam here is perceived as a Golem, a mass that has not yet obtained a form, a soul or the ability to speak. A further development is found in a *midrash* from the second and third centuries on Genesis 5:1. Here Adam is described not only as a Golem, but a Golem of cosmic size and strength to whom God showed all future generations: "In the hour when God created Adam, He created him as a Golem, and he spread from one end of the world to the other, as it is written 'Thine eyes did see my Golem' (Psalm 139:16). Rabbi Judah bar Simeon said: While Adam still lay as a Golem before Him who spoke and brought the world into being, He showed him each generation and its wise men, each generation and its judges, its scribes, its expositors and its leaders."[18]

According to Gershom Scholem, while Adam was in this Golemic state, a tellurian power flowed into him out of the earth from which he was made and allowed him to receive such a vision.[19] Adam's size also suggests that the power of the whole cosmos was concentrated in him, and is reflected in this later *midrash*:

> When God wished to create the world, He began His creation with nothing other than man and made him as a Golem. When He prepared to cast a soul into him, He said: If I set him down now, it will be said that he was my companion in the work of Creation; so I will leave him as a Golem, until I have finished everything else. When He had created everything, the angels said to Him: Aren't you going to make the man you spoke of? He replied: I made him long ago, only the soul is missing. Then He cast the soul into him and set him down and concentrated the whole world in him. With him He began, with him He concluded, as it is written: "Thou hast formed me before and behind" (Psalm 139:5).[20]

There is evidence here of the trepidation surrounding man's potential threat to God's unique position that becomes a prominent feature in many later versions of Golem-making. These sources also show that the biblical verse mentioning the word "Golem" was interpreted by rabbinical sources as a reference to the creation of Adam. In these commentaries, elements of actions foreshadow later discussions of the creation of an artificial man or Golem. The magical/mystical power of the combination of the Hebrew letters (as displayed above with the *Sefer Yetzirah*) was superimposed onto these Adam/Golem elements of creation at a later stage.

The development of the Golem legend – through its origins and roots in the Bible (Psalm 139:16), *Sefer Yetzirah,* talmudic passages, and exegeses on the creation of an artificial man and the connection of Adam and Golem – led to the medieval concept of the Golem that sprang up among the strong esoteric movements of French and German Jews in the age of the crusades. They were eager to perpetuate, if only in rites of initiation that gave the adept a mystical experience of the creative power inherent in the pious, the achievement attributed to Abraham and Rava and other righteous men of old apocryphal legends. In the twelfth century, the Golem was conceived as a man-like creature produced by the magical powers of man,[21] following a set procedure that varies slightly in different accounts. It had become the object of a mystical ritual designed to confirm the adept in his mastery over secret knowledge. The creation of a Golem here is an end in itself; it serves no practical purpose. The act of making a Golem is regarded as a ritual of initiation into the secret of creation.[22] This notion perhaps is exemplified best in the ecstatic Kabbalah of Abraham Abulafia (1240–ca 1292), in which the mystical experience of the act of creation by the adept culminates in ecstasy. Describing the creation of a creature, Abulafia writes:

At the beginning of the creation, the person must be acquainted with the quality of the weight, the combination and the variation. And he has to be acquainted with the construction and all the alphabets, the 231 gates of the alphabets, which are engraved in the ninth sphere (or wheel), divided into sixty parts. And he has to be acquainted with the combination of all the letters, and all the alphabets, each one per se, until all the gates will be completed. And he shall take pure dust and flour, turn the wheel in the middle, and begin to combine until the 231 gates are computed, and then he will receive the influx of wisdom. Afterwards let him take a bowl full of pure water and a small spoon and fill it with earth. He should know the weight of the earth before he begins to stir it and the size of the spoon. When he has filled it, he should scatter it and slowly blow it over the water. While beginning to blow the first spoonful of earth, he should recite loudly a letter of the divine name and pronounce it in a single breath until he will be exhausted and his face should be turned to the earth. And so, beginning with the combinations that constitute the parts of the head, he should form all the members in a definite order, until a figure emerges ... It is forbidden to do like the deed of the Creator, and you shall not learn it in order to perform it, but you shall learn it in order to understand and to teach and to cleave to the great name of God, praised be He.[23]

The above text is based on the recitation of combinations of letters of the alphabet, to receive the influx of wisdom, and the letters of the divine name, to create the figure. The process of creation is not corporeal but conceptual. It emphasizes the contemplation of the act and not its instrumentality. Golem-making is a mystical, spiritual experience for Abulafia and is not concerned with actually creating a Golem. Abulafia and his medieval contemporaries use biblical and talmudic passages only as a starting point for their present experience. As soon as the Golem is created, it is dissolved back into the earth from which it was born; with the initiation of its creator, it has served its purely psychic role. Abulafia takes this one step further by completely ignoring the need to annihilate the creature. He did not conceive it as a lasting entity and therefore did not worry about its ontological status after the end of the mystical experience. The creature apparently dissipates when the Kabbalist returns from the paranormal state of consciousness induced by Golem-making. Abulafia also departs from more traditional forms of Jewish mysticism which call for more than one participant to make a Golem. This demonstrates the individualistic nature of ecstatic Kabbalah.

The concept of the Golem illustrated above is an ecstatic experience in which the figure of clay is infused with radiations of the human mind deriving from combinations of the Hebrew alphabet and the name of God. The clay figure becomes alive for only a fleeting moment of ecstasy. It should be noted that other notions concerning early Golem practices did exist. The particular nuances in Golem-making changed forms in accordance with the particular metaphysical system serving as its background.

The emergence of the Golem legend in Prague follows the particular leanings of thirteenth-century Franco-Ashkenazi mystics who embraced the ritual of creating a Golem. In contemporary Sefardi texts, on the other hand, material creation is an inferior activity to be transcended by intellectual creation; they preferred the spiritual over the material and thought over action. As a result of this fundamental difference, deep concern for the Golem in the thirteenth century among Franco-Ashkenazi Jews (which continues to the present) is strongly contrasted with the indifference of the Sefardi mystics who, apart from Abraham Abulafia, did not pay much attention to this tradition. It is significant that the most luxuriant production of Kabbalist literature, the *Zohar*, a work of thirteenth-century Sefardic mystics, is indifferent to the practice of creating a Golem. This is also the case with Safedian Kabbalah. The only important Safedian Kabbalist, Rabbi Moses Cordovero, is rather reticent in attributing any spiritual value to the Golem; he regards this act of creation as totally meaningless from a spiritual point of view. The Safed Kabbalists of the sixteenth century speak of the Golem as a phenomenon situated in the remote past, and their discussion of the matter is of a purely theoretical nature.[24]

It is important to distinguish between two historical concepts of the Golem: pre-modern and modern. In modern times the Golem emerges as a practical, autonomous (and potentially dangerous) being. The Golem becomes a saviour and a labourer. This concept is unknown in the medieval tradition. When the populace took up the old stories of the Golem ritual, the nature of the Golem underwent a metamorphosis. Prominent religious contemporaries then became Golem makers, whereas twelfth- and thirteenth-century legends related primarily to persons of Jewish antiquity (e.g., Abraham, Rava, Jeremiah and Ben Sira). Later developments, such as Rosenberg and Bloch's account, for the first time refer to the Golem by a proper name, Yosele (Joseph) Golem. This lends a quality of affectionate familiarity to the creature, almost as one would treat a contemporary friend. This familiarity could lull the creator into a false sense of security over his creation. When the Golem turns against his maker and society it would be all the more distressing.

Classical versions of the Golem story did not describe the creature in detail, nor did they address his inner thoughts. The Golem remained an abstract idea as opposed to a personalized, subjective one that we see in the modern account. The Golem was traditionally neither a part of nature nor a mishap of biology but an unnatural exception, a *transitory* being whose emergence and annihilation were premeditated. The Golem was not a person, nor were its idiosyncracies described in a personal way. It had no particular name and its disappearance was of no consequence to its human creator. It served as a silent witness of the creative endeavours of both God and humanity, and helped certain men to appreciate the divine way of creating.[25]

The muteness of the Golem also reflects the transformations of the Golem legend (ancient to medieval to modern). This flaw in the nature of the Golem demonstrates the limited power of the human creator, compared to the Supreme Creator. As humanity remains inferior to God, although created in his image, the Golem lags behind its human creator, although created in his image. The value attributed to the lack of speech depended on the particular era in which the legend was told. In ancient Judaism, orality was very important in communication and study. The highest worship had to be performed in an oral manner; silent prayer was not adequate. This was also true in the last phase of Jewish mysticism, Hasidism, which emphasized the importance of loud prayer and study of torah in almost an ecstatic manner. However, in the medieval period, the absence of speech was related to reason, which was then conceived as the highest human faculty. The silence of the Golem thus did not indicate an inability to create a speaking being, but rather an inability to create a rational being. The faculty of speech stands between the animal faculty and the rational one.[26] The modern version picked up on this tradition and used the Golem's lack of speech to reinforce its subservient role as a famulus to his master. To those who were unaware of its creation, the Golem is passed off as a dumb stranger and rabbinical bodyservant. In Yiddish the term *golem* came to mean an ignorant person or dummy, and is often uttered as an affectionate insult.[27]

In the medieval ritual, knowledge of the esoteric Hebrew language – the effective formative elements of all that is created – bestowed upon the operator a state which transcended the magical operation. The operator shared cosmological secrets with the Creator, and became a demiurge. This act fulfilled the need felt by Judaism, in contact and conflict with other dominant religions during its formative development, to ensure its value and uniqueness, not only through its canonical texts but also by competing with the "technology" and magic of other religions. The Golem ritual in this light was an act of self-affirmation. It was intended initially for the masters themselves, but in the later translation of the legend the populace drew confidence from the fact that their hostile environment of Christians, pogroms, and blood-libels could be met effectively by the magical achievement of their religious leadership.[28]

WARNING OF GOLEM-MAKING

The inherent danger of the modern Golem reflects a profound transformation of the original concept, but this is at least partially inherited from the warning of Golem-making in many medieval texts on the subject. This warning, in all its various nuances, sheds some light on the modern condition that is born out of it. In its modern and pre-modern variations, creativity is a double-edged sword. Aside from its real, necessary and possible benefits, the creative endeavour is replete with dangers. In the pre-modern version the danger is in Golem-making itself; only later is this danger transferred directly to the Golem as it becomes a historical figure.

In the medieval texts, the awareness of the sanctity of reciting the powerful letters of the Hebrew alphabet combined with the name of God was matched by an awareness of the dangers of faults occurring during this recitation. In the Pseudo-Sa'adyan commentary on the *Sefer Yetzirah*, the creator may even sink into the earth. In this thirteenth-century text it is written that:

> They make a circle around the creature and walk around the circle and recite the 231 alphabets, as they are noted, and some say that the creator put power in the letters, so that a man makes a creature from virgin earth and kneads it and buries it in the ground, draws a circle and a sphere around the creature, and each time he goes around it recites one of the alphabets. This he should do 462 times. If he walks forward, the creature rises to life, by virtue of the power inherent in the recitations of the letters. But if he wishes to destroy what he has made, he goes around backwards, reciting the same alphabets from end to beginning. Then the creature sinks into the ground of itself and dies. And so it happened once to R.I.B.E. [not known to whom this refers] and his students who studied the *Sefer Yetzirah* and by mistake went around backward, until they themselves by the power of the letters sank up to their navels in the earth. They were unable to escape and screamed out. Their teacher heard them and said: Recite the letters of the alphabets and walk forward, instead of going backward as you have been doing. They did so and were released.[29]

Aside from the warning, it is also interesting to note that the Golem is buried in the earth, from which it eventually rises. In this respect, the earth serves as the womb for the embryo (the initial Golem mentioned in Psalms in the Bible). The ritual which follows causes the Golem to emerge from the earth (or alternately extracts it from the womb) and then animates the body.

In the case of Abraham Abulafia, a mistaken recitation actually may cause bodily harm to the recitator. Abulafia stresses that there is an organic affinity between the Hebrew letters and the limbs of the body, so that the correct pronunciation of the orders of letters is necessary for the well-being of the mystic. He writes that: "If the person who recites the letter errs, God save us, in his pronunciation of the letter that is appointed upon the limb that is on the head of the person who reads, that limb is separated from its place and changes its place, its nature being immediately transformed, another form being conferred to it and the person becoming injured."[30] In another passage, Abulafia directly relates the pronunciation of the letter to the corresponding limb of the mystic himself. The pronunciation therefore includes an act of self-contemplation. This combination of vocalization and introspection is a powerful technique that may be pernicious if inaccurate.

This preoccupation with danger characterizes anomian techniques in general. In Judaism, nomian practices do not involve any danger in themselves. These are necessary prescriptions to conduct one's life in accordance with God's will. This is, of course, not the case in anomian practices. They were rarely an imperative for the masses and commonly were regarded as the enterprise of a few exceptional individuals who deliberately chose to confront an inherently dangerous situation in order to attain a higher religious experience (as in ecstatic Kabbalah). The greater the spiritual achievement and the stronger the means to attain it, the greater are the dangers the mystic has to confront.[31] Therefore, the attempt to appropriate the ultimate human act of religious experience, Divine Creation of humanity itself, bears with it the ultimate consequence of this act: death.

Two thirteenth-century versions of the Golem legend vividly displayed another variant of the destructive power of Golem-making, involving idolatry and its possible implications. These stories are attributed to the biblical prophet Jeremiah and his son Ben Sira.[32] One version is found in the *Sefer ha-Gematri'ot*, a collection of traditions gathered by the disciples of Rabbi Yehudah he-Hasid and composed probably in the mid-thirteenth century:

Ben Sira wished to study the *Sefer Yetzirah*. Then a heavenly voice went forth: You cannot do it alone. He went to his father Jeremiah. They busied themselves with it, and at the end of three years a man was created to them, upon whose forehead stood *emeth*, as on Adam's forehead. Then the man they had made said to them: God alone created Adam, and when he wished to let Adam die, he erased the letter *aleph* from *emeth* and he remained *meth*, dead. That is what you should do with me and not create another man lest the world succumb to idolatry as in the days of Enosh. The created man said to them: Reverse the combinations of letters and erase the *aleph* of the word *emeth* from my forehead – and immediately he fell to dust.[33]

The above passage is amplified in a text from the early Kabbalists of Languedoc, attributed to the Tannaite Judah ben Bathyra. It is written that:

The prophet Jeremiah busied himself alone with the *Sefer Yetzirah*. Then a heavenly voice went forth and said: Take a companion. He went to his son Sira, and they studied the book for three years. Afterward they set about combining the alphabets in accordance with the Kabbalistic principles of combination, grouping and word formation, and a man was created to them, on whose forehead stood the letters YHWH *Elohim Emeth* (God the Lord is Truth). But this newly created man had a knife in his hand with which he erased the *aleph* from *emeth*; there remained: *meth*. Then Jeremiah rent his garments (because of this blasphemy: God the Lord is Dead, now implied by the inscription) and said: Why have you erased the *aleph* from *emeth*? He replied: I will tell you a parable. An architect built many houses, cities, and squares, but no one could copy his art and compete with him in knowledge and skill until two men persuaded him. Then he taught them the secret of his art, and they knew how to do everything in the right way. When they had learned his secret and his abilities, they began to anger him with words. Finally, they broke with him and became architects like him, except that what he charged a thaler for, they did for six groats. When people noticed this, they ceased to honour the artists and came to them and honoured them and gave them commissions when they required to have something built. So God has made you in His image and His shape and form. But now that you have created a man like Him, people will say: There is no God in the world beside these two [referring to the architect's renegade pupils of the parable, and by extension Jeremiah]! Then Jeremiah said: What solution is there? He said: Write the alphabets backward on the earth you have strewn with intense concentration. Only do not mediate in the sense of building up, but the other way around. So they did, and the man became dust and ashes before their eyes. Then Jeremiah said: Truly, one should study these things only in order to know the power and omnipotence of the Creator of this world, but not in order really to practice them.[34]

In these Kabbalistic interpretations of the legend, two fundamentally contradictory motifs of Golem-making meet. On one side, the creation of a Golem is a confirmation of humanity's likeness to God; on the other side, the creation of a Golem is a death sentence to that very God and the replacement of God by humans.

The warning expressed so dramatically in the passage above is not made because of the dangerous powers concealed in the Golem (as in modern versions of the legend) but because this creation might lead to polytheistic confusion and undermine the central principle of monotheism in Judaism. In this respect, the Golem story is connected to the discussion of idolatry current in these circles (and noted explicitly in the first account of Jeremiah and Ben Sira above). It was said that Enosh was the first idolater. Enosh questioned his father, Seth, about his grandfather, Adam, and became aware that Adam had neither a father nor a mother but was created by God's breathing into the earth. When Enosh learned this he proceeded to make a figure of mud and to breathe upon it. Satan then slipped into the figure and gave it an appearance of life. Thus, the name of God was desacrated, and idolatry began when the generation of Enosh worshipped this figure. This account, along with its archetype – Adam's initial transgression (seeking to be like God) and subsequent demise into an historical time, subject to unending conflict – vividly apprise us of the dangers attached to man's attempt to imitate God's power of creation. Creativity can lead to spiritual rapture, but it can also be an invitation to idolatry. One may begin to worship and adore what one creates, thereby replacing the uniqueness and unity of God (integral to the existence of Judaism) with polytheism.

What we witness here is a deeply rooted suspicion of the mimetic powers of the creative imagination. If humanity, created in God's image, uses his imagination to create a new creature (Golem) in his own image, is this not tantamount to the killing or dissolution of God by humans and the idolatrous birth of humanity as God? Although the story of Enosh shows the Golem as the focus of worship, it is implicit in the parables above that those who created the Golem, and not the Golem itself, are a challenge to God's supremacy. What these parables do not yet presume is the corollary of the death of Man at the hand of its creation. As noted in the documents above, Golem-making endangers the life of the creator. The source of the danger is not the Golem or the forces emanating from him, but the tension which the creative process arouses in the creator. Mistakes in carrying out the directions do not impair the Golem; they destroy its creator. This inner conflict on the part of the creator is developed further in twentieth-century accounts, adding a rich new dimension to the legend. Bloch writes, "God knows what could have happened if a Golem had been given the faculty of speech also!"[35]

CONTEMPORARY IMPLICATIONS

The Golem legend returns in a variety of forms to confront our modern sensibilities. Many of the moral, psychological, and spiritual problems that we struggle with today seem to have been anticipated by the Golem legend in both its medieval and modern variations.

Two important themes arise in recent versions of the legend. First, there is a warning from the Golem itself not to be made, and second, there is a feeling of doubt or remorse by the Golem creator. Both reveal a contemporary paranoia and fear of possible implications of the creation.

Abraham Rothberg's *The Sword of the Golem* offers a post-Holocaust viewpoint on the legend and exemplifies the first of these two themes. Rothberg's Golem objects to being born. "The very earth resisted his creation and lay limp and diffuse, refusing to be formed out of the chaos into that which was human ... An anguish in the clay pulsed to [Rabbi Loew's] fingers, speaking without speech, 'Do not rip me from this womb of clay ... If you bring me to life, my rage shall devour the living, my strength shall lay waste the earth.'" Rabbi Loew explains that neither of them can resist his destiny while the grey corpse laments his fate as "a clenched fist, a hulk, a golem!"[36]

The second theme, in which the creator doubts his creation, is eloquently displayed in the poetry of Jorge Luis Borges. In a poem entitled "The Golem" (1958) the final three of eighteen quatrains express the ambiguity of the Golem legend, as well as Borges's own questioning skepticism:

> The Rabbi gazed fondly on his creature
> And with some terror. *How* (he asked himself)
> *Could I have engendered this grievous son,*
> *And let off inaction, which is wisdom?*
>
> *Why did I decide to add to the infinite*
> *Series one more symbol? Why, to the vain*
> *Skein which unwinds in eternity*
> *Did I add another cause, effect, and woe?*
>
> At the hour of anguish and vague light
> He would rest his eyes on his Golem.
> Who can tell us what God felt,
> As he gazed on his Rabbi in Prague?[37]

The contemporary notion of Golem-making in all its ramifications is expressed no more vividly than in genetic engineering. A United States government report entitled "Splicing Life" (November 1982) investigated the social and ethical implications of genetic engineering. In reviewing its possible dangers, the report refers to the Golem legend and the "difficulty of restoring order if a creation intended to be helpful proves harmful instead." The report reflects on the painful irony of this situation when people "in seeking to extend their control over the world ... may lessen it. The artifices they create to do their bidding may rebound destructively against them – the slave may become the master." The suspicions reflected in this report are mirrored by the public who, in a National Science Foundation study, opposed most restrictions on scientific research in all areas but one: the creation of new life-forms and genetic engineering with human beings.[38]

The apprehension that the golem-slave will become the master of its creator and lead to the death of humanity is a recurrent theme in contemporary literature. Joseph and Karel Capek's play *R.U.R.* (act 3) warns that "Mankind will never cope with the Robots, and will never have control over them. Mankind will be overwhelmed in the deluge of these dreadful living machines, will be their slave, will live at their mercy."[39] It is reasonable to assume that the Capek brothers, who were from Prague, were influenced by contemporary Golem legends. It is in this work that the term "Robot" is first coined. It derives from a Czech root, meaning a "worker" in the sense of a slave labourer.

The play takes place at an R.U.R. (Rossum's Universal Robots) factory, which manufactures robots. In the course of the play, the robots take over both the factory and the world. After the robots have all but destroyed the human race, a clerk at the R.U.R. factory asks the robots, "Why did you murder us?" One of the robots offers the sobering reply, "Slaughter and domination are necessary if you want to be like men. Read history, read human books. You must domineer and murder if you want to be like men."[40] As artificially created beings reflect back on their creator, our creations may tell us much more about human nature than about themselves. The creation of a Golem is not only an expression of human achievement, but an exercise in human self-understanding ("we are what we make"). The fear of unchecked technological achievement running amuck can be interpreted as a fear of our own unchecked creative making. In light of the ever-present nuclear threat (a Golem created to serve and defend that may ultimately destroy us) and environmental destruction, this is a fear with which we must reckon.

The technological Golem may not only reflect human proclivities, but may cause us to alter the manner in which we think of human nature. In his *Economic and Philosophical Manuscripts* (1844), Marx writes that "as machines become more human, men will become more like machines."[41] The proclivity of modern Western thought to define the human being as a machine, and conversely to grant human status to machines, is based on a mechanistic and reductive view of reality. In the eighteenth century, humanity began to be defined as a machine of reason seeking self-perfection. Once internalized, this philosophical position becomes a determining factor in human behaviour.

Jerzy Kosinski amply illustrates this concept of the self as a machine-like instrument in his *Passion Play*:

> They appeared to him, most of them, to have consented to the manufacture of their lives at some common mint, each day struck from the master mold, without change, a duplicate of what had gone before and was yet to come. Only some

> accident could bring to pass upheaval in the unchallenged round of their lives.
>
> It was not contempt he felt for them, merely regret that they had allowed the die of life to be cast so early and so finally. He preferred individuals whose singularity gave him insight into himself ... people (are) so programmed to be efficient, civil, ready with a practised smile, that the very juices of life had been leeched from their bodies. Like the cash machines that were posted in the bank lobbies... the men and women who worked in banks were ... as functional as the currency itself.[42]

What Kosinski attacks is the dehumanization of individual human sanctity, the self-negation that accompanies a human being's acquiescence, explicitly or implicitly, to becoming a variety of machine.

This theme of humanity's becoming indistinguishable from the Golem it has made is brought out in a story of a wealthy American Jew who visited Prague after World War II to see the remains of the Golem in the attic of the Altneu synagogue. When his request was rejected by the shammes, he slipped the clergyman a considerable amount of money. The American entered but returned fifteen minutes later, complaining angrily that he had wasted his time and money because he found nothing in the attic but old, worn tallisim, torn prayer books and mounds of dust. When the shammes asked if there was anything else in the attic, he remembered one other thing: an old mirror on the wall. The shammes quickly replied, "Then you did see the Golem!"[43]

When Gershom Scholem heard of a newly built Israeli computer in 1965, he told Dr Chaim Pekeris, who "fathered" the computer, that the most appropriate name for it would be Golem No.1 (Golem Aleph). Dr Pekeris agreed, on the condition that Scholem would dedicate the computer and explain why it should be so named. Scholem, in his dedication speech, makes a direct link between the legendary activities of the sixteenth-century Rabbi Judah Loew of Prague and the computer created at the Weizmann Institute at Rehevot. Scholem then compares the Golem of Prague with that of Rehevot. He cites the modern electronic engineer or applied mathematician as a latter day disciple of the rabbis of Poland and Prague, concocting his own computerized Golem, but without the theological and ethical context of his rabbinical ancestors. He concludes his address by resigning himself to say, "To the Golem and its creator: develop peacefully and don't destroy the world."[44]

The ultimate conclusion of our Golems of course remains uncertain. Meanwhile we have various contemplative theories about the legend of the Golem, from the Bible to present day novels, poetry, plays and films. In a 1920s film directed by Paul Wegener, *Der Golem: Wie er in die Welt Kam* (The Golem: How he Came into the World), we see for the first time the introduction of children at a critical juncture in the story's denouement. This version proceeds in the usual manner until it is time to destroy the dangerous Golem who went on a rampage in the Prague ghetto. Traditionally, it is the creator himself who is able to halt the Golem. But in a striking twist of plot, a child assumes this role. The Golem, who reappears at the city gates after his fury has somewhat subsided, watches a group of children playing in the bright sunlight. The children flee in terror from the giant, except for one girl who remains frozen. As the Golem approaches, the girl offers him an apple. The Golem picks her up and holds her in his arms. Fascinated by the amulet on the Golem's chest (which gives him his power), she removes it and reduces the Golem to a lifeless statue. The returning children play with the amulet until it is lost. The rabbi eventually arrives to find the children sitting on the inert body, now covered with flowers.

NOTES

1 Maharal was an acronym for *Moreynu HaRav Loevy* or Our Teacher, Rabbi Loew. See Gershon Winkler, *The Golem of Prague* (New York: Judaica 1980), 29.

2 The Blood Libel was the accusation that Jews murder non-Jews in a religious ritual and drink their blood. It originated in twelfth-century England, partly due to the belief that Jews were responsible for the crucifixion of Christ. By the fourteenth century, the ritual murder charge had become associated with Passover; Jews were accused of mixing Christian blood into their matzah and wine. These accusations lasted right into the twentieth century and led to the murder of tens of thousands of Jews.

3 Chayim Bloch, *The Golem*, trans. H. Schneiderman (Vienna: Vernay 1925), 191.

4 Ibid., 192.

5 Rabbi Loew's death at the hands of this terrible giant may be Bloch's device for alluding to the Golem and its ability to destroy its maker.

6 Document No. 11383 of the Archives of Jewish folklore in Haifa, Israel; quoted in Moshe Idel, *Golem* (Albany: State University of New York Press 1990), 256.

7 Gershom Scholem, *On the Kabbalah and Its Symbolism*, trans. R. Manheim (New York: Schocken 1971), 198–9.

8 Ms. Oxford 1309, fols. 90b-91a; quoted in Idel, *Golem*, 207–8.

9 Letter to J. Christoph Wagenseil, quoted in Scholem, *On the Kabbalah*, 200–1.

10 Ibid., 201.

11 In 1808 Grimm wrote on the Golem legend in his *Journal for Hermits*. Only eight years later Mary Wollstonecraft Shelley (1785–1851) published *Frankenstein*. It is not unreasonable to assume that she was influenced by the Golem legend. Although she lived in England, she had access to German literature, and in fact in one of her letters, she attributes her inspiration for "Frankenstein" to German "ghost tales" she had read. The Golem is clearly the closest in theme to the Frankenstein story and it is difficult to imagine that a literary figure such as Shelley at some point should not have come across the numerous Golem tales in German literature that existed before and during her time. See Winkler, *Golem of Prague*, 19, 20.

12 Scholem, *On the Kabbalah*, 202–3.

13 Bloch, *Golem*, 199–203.

14 *Sefer Yetzirah*, trans. D. R. Blumenthal, in *Understanding Jewish Mysticism* (New York: Ktav Publishing House 1978), 43–4.

15 Quoted in Scholem, *On the Kabbalah*, 176.

16 Isadore Epstein, ed. "Sanhedrin" in *The Babylonian Talmud* (London: Soncino Press 1935), 446.

17 Ibid., 242.

18 Jacob Neusner, ed., *Genesis Rabbah* (Atlanta: Scholars Press 1985), 264.

19 Scholem, *On the Kabbalah*, 162.

20 Quoted in ibid.

21 This magical knowledge is not seen as a perversion, but a pure and sacred knowledge which belongs to man as God's image.

22 This notion is central to the idea that Gershom Scholem stresses is the one underlying point of the Golem legend in his essay, "The Idea of the Golem."

23 *Tehilat ha-Yezirah*, quoted in Idel, *Golem*, 97.

24 Ibid., 275.

25 Ibid., 261.

26 Ibid., 265–6.
27 Arnold Goldsmith, *The Golem Remembered, 1909–1980* (Detroit: Wayne State University Press 1981), 16.
28 Idel, *Golem*, 266.
29 Commentary on *Sefer Yetzirah*, quoted in Scholem, *On the Kabbalah*, 186–7.
30 Ms. Oxford 1582, fol. 14b. quoted in Idel, *Golem*, 100.
31 Ibid., 264.
32 The association of the prophet Jeremiah to these stories can be related to his Biblical role to warn against the evil and idolatrous behaviour of the people of Israel at this time (ca 600 B.C.E.). The prophet's pleas are disregarded and a causal link then is made between their behaviour and their subsequent defeat, their destroyed Temple, and Exile at the hands of the Babylonians.
33 Quoted in Scholem, *On the Kabbalah*, 179.
34 Ibid., 180.
35 Bloch, *Golem*, 69.
36 Abraham Rothberg, *The Sword of the Golem* (New York: McCall 1970), 5–7.
37 Jorge Luis Borges, "The Golem," in *A Personal Anthology*, ed. Anthony Kerrigan (New York: Grove Press 1967), 79.
38 Byron Sherwin, *The Golem Legend* (Lanham, MD: University Press of America 1985), 25–8.
39 Joseph Capek, Karl Capek, *R.U.R.*, trans. R. Selver (London: Oxford University Press 1961), 71.
40 Ibid., 94.
41 Karl Marx, *Economic and Philosophical Manuscripts*. Quoted in Sherwin, *Golem Legend*, 44.
42 Jerzy Kosinski, *Passion Play* (New York: St Martin's Press 1979), 126, 244.
43 Goldsmith, *Golem Remembered*, 142.
44 Gershom Scholem, "The Golem of Prague and the Golem of Rehovot," in *The Messianic Idea in Judaism* (New York: Schocken 1971), 340.

Paradoxical Spaces in Literature, Film and Architecture: A Dialogue with Alain Robbe-Grillet

Alain Robbe-Grillet/
Alberto Pérez-Gómez

Chora

THIS TEXT ORIGINATED from a conversation between the novelist and filmmaker Alain Robbe-Grillet and Alberto Pérez-Gómez. The public interview was organized by l'Institut de recherche en histoire de l'architecture, and held in Montreal at the Canadian Centre for Architecture on October 16, 1992. The transcript was edited in French by Louise Pelletier, translated by Franca Trubiano, and edited in English by Stephen Parcell and Alberto Pérez-Gómez.

Alberto Pérez-Gómez: During the past several decades, architects such as John Hejduk, Peter Eisenman, and Daniel Libeskind, have found inspiration in the *new novel* for both their theoretical and building projects. In my opinion this fascination stems partly from the tendency of the *new novel* to frame its narratives within an architecture that is objectified, but in no way stripped bare of its sensuality. In order to generate their buildings, architects work with plans and elevations, representations of lived space that necessarily objectify its geometric quality. This requirement, however, has been set by these talented architects against the expectation of technology and engineering to use the same sorts of geometrical projections exclusively for the purpose of efficient control and the prosaic manipulation of building operations. Although devoid of romantic or classical sentimentality, their austere architecture, while embracing abstraction, has been able to communicate polysemic human values, construing a world propitious for mystery and reverie. Amidst the encroaching technological demands of the late twentieth century, these and other architects have turned their attention to theoretical spaces in other disciplines such as cinema and literature, in search of a new manner of inhabiting spaces and a particular dimension appropriate to the "post-modern" work of architecture.

Both your novels and films, such as *L'année dernière à Marienbad,* present labyrinthine theoretical spaces that appear to resemble the temporal experience of architectural space. As we can travel through the spaces of a building with our own itinerary, the narratives in your work invite us to wander through their own literary and cinematic spaces. Both the *new novel* and your cinematic work invites a much greater participation on the part of the observer. One can also see an attempt to oppose the linear narratives of the nineteenth-century novel, to establish a new alternative for the contemporary reader.

My first question concerns this transformation of literary form from the nineteenth-century novel to the *new novel*. Whereas the nineteenth-century novel describes the subjective experience of the author or the characters, the *new novel* objectively describes the totality of the character's spatial situations, in a manner analogous to the spaces proposed by the architect for human action. Emotions are never named in the *new novel*, just like the architect must expect emotions to be elicited through the interaction of the inhabitant and the proposed formal and geometrical spatial order of the building. Nineteenth-century Beaux Arts design also established linear narratives – processional routes with sequences of rooms unfolding in a predetermined order and at a constant scale. In opposition, contemporary architecture has been exploring fragmented sequences and juxtapositions that resemble spatial perceptions in your novels and films. Do you believe it is possible for built architecture to communicate that which is otherwise left unsaid?

Alain Robbe-Grillet: To begin, there are some clarifications I wish to make. It is quite difficult for me to speak in general terms about the *new novel* and its relation to architecture. The *new novel* is a group collection of writers – Marguerite Duras, Nathalie Saraute, Claude Simon, Michel Butor, Robert Pinget, and myself – and this group is not very homogeneous. Our treatment of architecture is also highly diversified. The novels of Nathalie Saraute, for example, make hardly any reference to what you have called the "objectification of the setting." Therefore, I will speak only for myself, and I will also differentiate between the novelist and the filmmaker. Due to the very nature in which these two modes of narration are practised, the issues present themselves differently when one is writing a novel and when one is making a film. Having said this, it is true that space does play a predominant role in my novels, whereas with Balzac it is time that is predominant. During the fifties and sixties, the *new novel* was discussed as being appropriate to the times – unsettled times, but times nonetheless. Rather, I think of it as a time in which temporality is substituted by space. This would explain the frequent occurrence of dreams or oneiric impressions in my literary works. A dream is not a temporal unfolding. Technicians of the dream psyche know that a dream is instantaneous. It has no duration; at most, it is an extremely brief instant in which space is developed. In dreams, our normalized daily spaces disappear in favour of a "paradoxical" space where, for example, the notions of exterior and interior are constantly inverted, reversed, subverted, etc. Within the space of the dream, no one needs to use a doorway to cross from the interior to the exterior. Interiority itself appears to transform from exterior to interior through an invagination, whereby all of space is sucked to either one side or the other. On the contrary, the traditional novel attempts to constitute a rational space that resembles the daily world to which we are accustomed. What interests me in the narrative is precisely to explore the operations of the human spirit which hardly, if ever, conform to this rationalized space.

For this reason, I highly object to the diagram of the house in *Jealousy* that was published in an English version of the novel. That diagram is not my doing. Moreover, it conflicts with the very text of the book on several points. The right wing of the terrace should extend to the facade above instead of stopping at the sitting room. However, the very idea of producing a plan is the more serious issue. For example, at certain moments in the text there is a room which exists between the office and the storage space, while at other moments there is nothing there. In other words, in this house, there is an uncertain room and we do not know exactly what it contains – something like the hidden room of a possible crime. This is extremely important and yet the person who made the sketch seems to have had no notion of this. He acted as if my description was clear, tranquil – in effect, Balzac-like. We could make a sketch of Père Goriot's room by placing the furnishings where Balzac had actually placed them, but in a text such as *Jealousy*, things are mobile. At every instant there is a spatial shift, a mobility of space, or the apparition or disappearance of certain elements. The entire room may or may not exist, and this is enormously important to the narrative.

This is why I've protested against the word "objectivity" for over forty years, because for me the issue is exactly the opposite. Every instant in my novels describes a setting which "appears" to be objective, but if we attempt to draw it, we realize that this is impossible. To redefine this appearance of objectivity Professor Van den Heuvel has proposed the word "objectivism." It is a subjectivity supported by objects – an objectivist subjectivity. This confusion between "objectivity" and "objectivism" resulted in serious errors, liberties, and misunderstandings by the literary critics of the time. In large measure this continues today, for when I published some autobiographical pseudo-memoirs that are as fictional as the rest of my narratives, they said: "Well, Monsieur Robbe-Grillet, are we no longer objective today?" My response was: "Well, no, I never was; it was a word invented by the critics" – by the critics who had not read the books but had found the word to be useful. Therefore, when I started to make films they said, "We will finally be able to understand what he is talking about. In the novel he describes a house for well over two hundred pages and at the end we still do not know how it is built, because in effect it is constantly moving around. Therefore we will give him a camera and finally understand what it is all about!"

Pérez-Gómez: Is this how you came to make films?

Robbe-Grillet: Thanks to this, I have been able to make films – but filmmaking finds itself just as confused and misled about rationalized spatiality, whereas for me the making of films continues to be about the building of paradoxical spaces. Naturally, it is simpler in film, in that the standards for film narratives are so deeply rooted in a rationalism that any small transgression is enough to produce an energetic work. To cite a simple example, there is a form of dialogue between two characters that is referred to in cinema as ping-pong: the camera points at the other character, the camera points at me, the camera points at the other character; one view is set off against the other. For the average spectator of commercial cinema it is essential that the camera never cross the famous 180-degree line so that the spectator has the impression that the two actors are looking at each other. In reality, however, nothing prohibits us from doing so. If we walk around them, we would see them from different angles. Therefore, while the actors in the film initially appear to be facing each other, changing the point of view suddenly gives the impression that they have now turned their backs to each other, since we see their opposing profiles. It is quite an elementary example, but at every moment in cinema we can easily create spaces that have more than three dimensions. Although the screen is flat, we can create spaces within it with a considerable number of dimensions.

Pérez-Gómez: Perhaps you could discuss this notion of multi-dimensional spaces by describing your experiences with spatiality in *L'année dernière à Marienbad* and *L'immortelle.*

Robbe-Grillet: In *Marienbad* and *L'immortelle* the sets are indeed an important aspect, although research on spatiality had been more extensive in other films. *Marienbad* was not filmed in Marienbad, but rather in four palaces in Munich, all built by the same architect during the eighteenth century. There is consistency among the sets, even though part of the film was shot in a Paris studio. For example, scenes in which the young woman's room is overloaded with baroque ornamentation were shot at the Billancourt studios in Paris, where we could reproduce and transform elements found in the real palaces where we had shot the beginning of the film. From shot to shot, and from scene to scene, this room is increasingly invaded by stucco mouldings that look like plants, beasts, or octopi, and are in the process of overcrowding the entire room, somewhat like the famous water-lilies of Boris Vian in *L'écume des jours.* Otherwise, the only other fundamental transformation in my project was cut out by Alain Resnais. I will say a few words about this.

I wrote not only the scenario but also the screenplay for *L'année dernière à Marienbad.* That is to say, I described the film shot by shot, including the still frame settings, the camera movements, an imaginary film, the collating, the editing, etc. However, I was not at the shooting; it was shot by Resnais. At the time I was preparing *L'immortelle* in Turkey. Resnais respected almost everything I wrote, but he believed the spectator would not grasp one particular element, and he probably was right; Resnais has a much deeper maternal instinct toward the spectator. You probably know that the film's sounds and images were not recorded simultaneously, except for a few instances when required for certain words. All of the sounds were made by special effects. When you hear a character walking, and even if you see him on the screen, the sounds of the footsteps are not made by the character. It is a studio effect made by a technician, who follows the action with a shoe in each hand, and skilfully presses together the heels and the soles at the moment he sees a footstep occur on the screen. But nothing stops us from derailing this system. As I had imagined that the man would speak of exteriority, while the woman would speak of interiority, and that he would be trying to lead her from the inside toward the outside, I had also imagined that the sounds of their footsteps would continue with their original characteristics. In other words, the sound of the man's footsteps would always be on gravel even when he was walking on carpets in the hallway, whereas the woman would make little carpet sounds even when she was walking on gravel. This would explain why she twists her foot and breaks the heel of her shoe, since there would no longer be any correspondence between the sound and the image. Resnais said, and I think rightly so, "It would simply give the impression that the sound track was dirty," and that it might have been necessary to add subtitles to specify that they were "sounds of footsteps on gravel" at that particular spot in the film. Without the subtitles it probably would have been incomprehensible. However, this shows the continuing attempt to create paradoxical spaces, in this case by contaminating the interior with sounds from the exterior. Interesting idea, but probably difficult to achieve, given that film viewers see little of what is actually on the screen and hear almost nothing of what is on the sound track. They hear only what is identical to the image seen on the screen. In other words, they would think these noises are audio interference and cannot belong to the film itself.

Pérez-Gómez: You have also produced several of your own films. How did you make the transfer from literary space to cinematic space?

Robbe-Grillet: In the films I have made, I have had the opportunity to construct paradoxical spaces on two occasions. The first of these was *L'Éden et après*, half of which was filmed in Bratislava and the other half in Tunisia. The part which takes place in Bratislava was shot in a café called the Eden, but this was not an actual café; it was a studio in Bratislava in which we built a checkered space using rail-mounted moveable panels set at right angles. These panels are all Mondrian reproductions – rectangles separated by black bars. In the reproductions a few liberties were taken, and there are a few subversions, too; some of the rectangles are replaced by posters, mirrors, and things of that sort. But in general, we clearly recognize their Mondrian origins. The panels are moveable not only to change the spatiality between shots, but also during the actual filming of an individual shot. We can imagine a long sequence of shots in this space, during which the camera crosses the space and a panel gets displaced, and when the camera returns to its original position, something else is there instead – somewhat similar to what happens in the oneiric world, in the world of dreams.

The second example is *La belle captive* with the Quebec actress Gabrielle Lazure. It is a story with many diverse settings but everything is filmed in the same house. It is a very curious house – a mock Palladian villa in St-Cloud, named Villa Gounod. The villa itself was one hundred years old and quickly becoming a ruin, so the filmmakers were permitted to break it, demolish it, and do other things with it. In the film, there is a clinic with white walls and a nightclub with black walls. It was the same room which had been repainted black during the night. For myself, this was very important, precisely because the film resembles a dream – everything takes place within the mind of the principal character and therefore within the interior of the same house.

There is one scene in the film that I do not like at all: the scene which takes place in the café. I had been wrongly persuaded, "There is a café just next door which exactly corresponds to what you want. We will film there." I let myself be had, just like that, out of fatigue; it is very tiring shooting a film. And that specific scene angers me today; one gets the impression that it does not take place in the same house.

What is most spectacular in *La belle captive* are the convertible and the motorcycle that are being driven in the middle of the night. In effect, they are not being driven at all, and it is not nighttime; they are also in the house. To bring them inside, we tore down an exterior wall, closed everything up, and set up a play of lights and landscape effects on either side – something that never could have been achieved with a "travelling" car on a nocturnal road where the lighting is always poor. In this case, the head cameraman, Henri Alekan, the most famous of French cameramen, organized it all. What moves is the camera, the sets, the lights, the exhaust, the wind, etc. All is at hand. And Alekan directs it all like an orchestra conductor. But these are rudimentary examples. At every moment, things occur that are more subtle and less perceptible by the spectator.

Pérez-Gómez: As we have seen in your novels and your films, architecture often constitutes both the plot and the means of expression. Do you believe that built architecture possesses this power of expression intrin-

sically and is simply revealed by the narrative, or is this expression "imposed" on the architecture by the fiction?

Robbe-Grillet: If you are asking me whether built architecture can create paradoxical spaces similar to those created in my films and my novels, my answer would be "maybe." Naturally it would be worth trying, but insurance companies would probably find it objectionable, since there are gaps in the narratives in my novels. Often the complete story falls through this gap, as if it were disappearing, sucked by a void within the narrative continuity. We could very easily construct buildings where people would fall through a staircase because the stair would suddenly be displaced. It is technically possible, but is it commercially possible? I do not believe so. This would also represent an enormous risk for the tenants of such a building. Certain paradoxical things are possible in architecture, but I do not believe they can ever be comparable because the oneiric possibilities of film and novels are not handled in the same way.

Pérez-Gómez: What has been your personal connection to architecture?

Robbe-Grillet: This is a question that I am often asked. When I began to be known as a writer in the United States, it was not the writers who welcomed me with open arms. American writers were not at all interested in my work, except for Nabokov, who was half-American. Instead I was welcomed as a brother, or almost as a father, by a whole generation of painters, sculptors, and architects. The plastic artists saw themselves reflected in my work, often in ways which appeared to me rather arbitrary and naïve. Do you know of a painter – perhaps one calls him a painter – Bernard Venet? He has worked with angles for much of his life, but now he has moved on to the arcs of circles. As a matter of fact, some have been built, and there is a magnificent one in Berlin, near the former wall. Once he showed me a large painting which had only two straight lines, and he said to me: "You see, it's exactly like your work. I've drawn an angle of 123 degrees; I assure you that it really measures 123 degrees." I was completely flabbergasted that he could see a relationship between two works that are so dissimilar.

I have sometimes said that I would have been an architect if I could.

But if I had become an architect, what would I have done? It would not have interested me to build housing, for housing by definition must be habitable. Instead I would have designed a monument that would be built according to Klein's topology. When we enter it, we find ourselves in the process of exiting, in a similar way as the water one pours into a Klein bottle is really running along the outside. Klein's bottles have been built and we could also build a building that is similar, but in the end I don't believe this would be of interest.

I would have liked to build an entire city, uninhabitable but spectacular. A city – grandiose, monumental, and eternal. There is one city in this world, in the ruins of antiquity, which absolutely fascinates me. It is well known but rarely visited, since it is situated in Libya, a country which itself is rarely visited. It is Leptis Magna, one of the three cities which formed the Tripolitaine. Leptis Magna is located on the coast, and was built all at once by an African emperor. It was very quickly buried in sand and therefore has been protected from pillage and destruction. Whereas the majority of ancient cities served as stone quarries for constructing churches and other things, this city was not touched because it was completely covered by tens of metres of sand. During the 30s, Mussolini decided that the project of the century would be to clear Leptis Magna. He chose this city because its late architecture, from about the fourth century A.D., was already somewhat Mussolini-like. There was something grandiose and a little mad in Leptis Magna. I have visited this city. It is extraordinary because it is still standing – not like ruins where we find some remaining walls nearly levelled to the ground, or a couple of columns broken here and there. All is standing, but what is particularly stirring is that the sand is returning again little by little, and it is once again in the process of becoming entombed. What fascinates me about this city is its totality, that it was built all at once, entirely in the monumental style, and also that it is nevertheless in a state of ruin. It is a ruin that appears to be almost a recent ruin, as if it had been built this way.

Why is it that ruins fascinate our era? There are many traces of them in both my novels and my films. But one finds traces of ruins everywhere; it is one of the themes most often talked about by post-modern theoreticians. For myself, I think that we have no choice but to build upon ruins. Philosophically, for example, Hegel is built upon the ruins of Kant.

He does not destroy Kant, but he makes ruins of him, and upon those ruins he builds something else: another system in which there will always be a watermark of Kant's philosophy. One could say that my novels were built upon the ruins of Balzac. It is upon the ruins of Père Goriot that *Jealousy* is built. My first published book, *Les gommes*, originally had a provisional title, *Les ruines de Thèbes*. The idea for this book was something like Sophocles' *King Oedipus*, but in a state of ruins. And it was from those ruins that I would construct a new work to be erected partly upon the materials abandoned by history, at the edge of the Mediterranean, as at Leptis Magna.

Pérez-Gómez: It is interesting that you should speak of ruins, since architects are fascinated by possibilities of mystery found in light, and not in the darkness of shadow.

Robbe-Grillet: Yes, of course. Ruins are almost always found in dry, sunny, arid areas. Very few ruins are found in misty landscapes.

Pérez-Gómez: The importance of light and clarity in your work leads me to a second theme. I don't know whether we could redefine the objectivism vs objectivity opposition, of which you have spoken, in terms of the dissolution of the objective/subjective polarity, spoken of by philosophers today. What I think fascinates architects is the rediscovery of oneiric spaces which may appear to be in some way more real than objectified space.

The hallucinatory effects of the work of Franz Kafka, similarly to your own work of which we have been speaking, results not from a vague description of some mysterious atmosphere but rather from the extreme accuracy of the details. Once more we can establish an analogy with the work of some modern and contemporary architects such as Le Corbusier and Alvar Aalto and in contrast to nineteenth-century architectural romanticism. As an applied art, architecture is more highly subject to technological determinism than literature. This situation highlights constraints that are often elaborated upon by philosophers and by yourself as well. For example, I was greatly touched in this regard by your novel *Djinn*. If mystery originates in light, this could then constitute a means of destructuring the reductive effects of technology within architecture,

to allow the creative and poetic potential of architecture to prevail over the simplistic efficiency of the technological tool. Could you elaborate upon the role of the poetic in our technological world?

Robbe-Grillet: While I can imagine that it would be desirable, I see myself ill suited to engage in a discourse that elaborates upon the role of poetics in technology. It is something which one must attempt to make, to fabricate. I do not believe that it would be desirable to conceptualize it, *a priori,* beforehand.

Pérez-Gómez: But it is a concern of yours. You are very conscious of this, nonetheless?

Robbe-Grillet: I am not the only one, of course. I have a famous predecessor, Heidegger, who so greatly struggled against the technological world, precisely for the world of poetics. But, as we say, one actively has to make it. It could just as easily spring forth from the spontaneous invention of a few builders rather than from a preconditioned formulation made by a thinker like you or me. I have a feeling that it requires handiwork.

On the other hand, the technological world is still quite vague in nature. This vague quality is seen very often in Heidegger's texts where he appears to be bringing together science and technology. For myself, it is exactly the opposite. Poetics have already entered particle physics in large measure, to the point where physicists have actually borrowed words from literature. Do you know where the word "quark" comes from? Quarks are particles – probably imaginary ones, since no one has ever seen a quark – that make up, in groups of three, the protons and neutrons within a nucleus. These quarks are constantly moving and are particles with a fractional charge. They do not have a whole unit of charge like electrons; their charges are measured in fractions. Generally, the fractions are 1/3 and 2/3 for *u* and *d* quarks. The inventor of these particles borrowed the word "quark" from James Joyce. It is in *Finnegans Wake* that Joyce cites an English-Irish nursery-rhyme in which there are "Three more quarks for Mister Mark." Even today, in the *Larousse Encyclopedia*, the origin of the word quark is cross-referenced to James Joyce.

This shows the extent to which poetics have been introduced into the basic sciences, especially from the moment when Einstein developed the idea that the presence of a void – a gap – was fundamental to science, and that this was necessary for it to be alive. Of course, this is completely contrary to technological ideas. Contrary to Heidegger, I do see an opposition between science and technology. Science has been aligned with poetics since about 1920 – the time of Einstein's famous declaration on the criteria regarding scientism – whereas technology continues to be bound by constraints that are certainly not shared by researchers in the basic sciences. For them, the questions are not asked in the same way.

Pérez-Gómez: On a different subject, I would like to engage the issues of ritual and sacrifice. Various authors have written about the origins of architecture within the practice of sacrifice, particularly George Hersey, an architectural historian who has published a fine work, *The Lost Meaning of Classical Architecture*, on the origins of Greek architecture as they arise out of ritual practices and more specifically out of sacrificial practices. In your novels it appears obvious that without such a place for ritual, our very humanity risks being thrown into question. Is there a place for ritual and sacrifice in architecture? Do you think it is possible to engage the ritual dimension of built spaces, or is this possible only in the work of fiction? We know that your work is insistent upon these themes. Also, what do you think of the position of Georges Bataille?

Robbe-Grillet: You are alluding to a work by Bataille on architecture which unfortunately I have not read. I was good friends with Bataille during the last part of his life and actually he's the one who protected me at the beginning during my first novels. But there was an issue upon which we disagreed a great deal. He was a deeply religious person. His attack against religion was fundamentally marked by a Catholic education. I did not have a Catholic nor Jewish education, nor any sort, and as a result I have arrived calmly into the world. Therefore the notion of guilt, which is fundamental in Bataille, is largely absent in my case. Nevertheless, if Bataille became interested in my books, and in particular *Le voyeur* – after all, it is thanks to Georges Bataille that I received the critics' award for *Le voyeur*, which in some way launched my public career – what had fascinated Bataille and Blanchot in *Le voyeur* is precisely this ritual crime that takes place in the middle of the book, a crime which may be absent, somewhat like a loss, but which is nonetheless terribly present as it overtakes the whole of the book. "It is from there that the light comes," says Blanchot, referring to *Le voyeur.* I can see very well that there is something in common with the ritual crime, but without guilt, for the voyeur leaves the island completely absolved. On the contrary, with Bataille, there hovers an underlying religiosity.

In my secret boyhood dreams, the monumental city I dreamt of building would naturally be the sacrificial site, of a preferably human sacrifice – the sacrifice of a young boy, for at the time I had not yet discovered my fundamental heterosexuality, which had been transformed further on in my work that followed. Morally the issue of human sacrifice is resolved very easily on paper, or in a film, because we don't actually sacrifice young actresses because of the insurance issue. If you want to introduce this within some sort of daily reality – not only within the real, for I, like you, make a distinction between the real and reality by recovering the definition given by Jacques Lacan, "The real begins where consciousness ends" – you will be obliged to water down completely the notion of sacrifice. You will be confined to making works of parody.

QUESTIONS FROM THE AUDIENCE

Question: You have repeatedly evoked the oneiric world and the world of dreams in your discussion. I was astonished at certain moments for I had the impression that you were presenting your work like some sort of oneiric mimesis.

Robbe-Grillet: I would be careful with the word mimesis. My work is an approximation of what takes place in one's mind during the dream, the dream in the general sense, and of what the imaginary can be. This is a highly creative place, where the reader must himself invent a passage within the interior of the work set before him as a place where multiple routes are possible. But there again I cannot speak of mimesis, for we only know of dreams through Freud and it is obvious that this is actually the opposite of what I want to do, for what Freud teaches us are dream narratives. All is normalized in Freud's dreams. But apart from my disputing the use of the word mimesis, I can agree that my work is an attempt at approximating how things occur internally and how things

occur between this internal state and myself. That is to say, what am I and what am I doing here?

In fact, this is the ultimate question of philosophy. After all, it is the ultimate question of metaphysics to try to understand the workings of Being. Literary or cinematographic works, and to a certain extent architecture, are attempts to represent these workings of the consciousness. They are non-conceptual attempts to represent things that we cannot conceptualize. The problematical exercise of literature, as Borges calls it, or the plastic constructions of cinema, painting and architecture are attempts to investigate these workings that are of interest to us, but which we do not understand.

Question: In the film *L'immortelle* I sensed a strong connection between the main female character and the city. The principal male character seeks both to discover the city and a woman. The city is never completely exposed; the woman remains mysterious. That particular mystery would never be resolved. Can we say that in the final part of the film, the man who heads out in search of the truth about this woman is in fact seeking to discover that which is shared by both the architecture of the city and the woman?

Robbe-Grillet: Well, one can say it that way, but one must nonetheless begin by specifying that the city in question is Istanbul, a city which is already highly identified with a whole array of stereotypes – the Orient as mystery, the woman as mystery, and the immortal city. We never know whether *L'immortelle* is the young woman or the city of Istanbul, and this defines the site of the narrative progression, as well as the site of investigation. I would rather say that during the final part, the man increasingly loses his footing for he finds once again all the material signs which had circumscribed the rest of the film, but these signs have in some way been stripped of their uniqueness. He finds once again the statuette, the exact same one – the same antiquarian has a second one exactly the same; he probably makes them, like all the antiquarians of Istanbul – and he finds once again the white car which has not been damaged. He revisits all the same places which appear to be intact, as if the whole story were glued together by the narrative progression.

I must say that for myself, Istanbul has been extremely important and is at the very origins of the film. The history of the film is quite bizarre; it is the first film which I shot and one should be stunned that producers actually invested money to have a film made by an author who at that time had hardly any readers at all. I asked the producer, "Have you seen the sales figures for my novels? Therefore, you will invest money and you will leave me to do as I please?" And he answers, "Yes. The only thing which is important is to shoot the film in Turkey." And he very calmly explains to me that he has at his disposal a considerable sum of Turkish pounds, at a time when the pound could not be exchanged. He says to me, "It would not bother you to film in Istanbul?" and he did not know that I was greatly attached to this city; that it was there where I had met, several years before, the little girl who would become my wife, and that as a result I was sentimentally attached to this city. And therefore, I settled in Istanbul and I wrote the film for the city of Istanbul. The city itself was the site where it all took place, as Blanchot would say.

Like for Pierre Loti and for the professor who arrived down there in the film, Istanbul for me was also an imaginary city, the city where I had in fact met the little girl who would become my wife. The city itself was terribly well suited for my story. Today the film is valuable as a document of a place that no longer exists, for this whole city built in wood has disappeared, it has burnt away. One can still see the Sinan mosques, but all of the wooden city, which was the real city, is something that no longer exists but in *L'immortelle.*

Question: In your preface to *L'immortelle* you make an important distinction between your notion of the work and that of the cine-novels. If you will allow me, I will quote you: "The work is the film which we can see and hear in a cinema; whereas the cine-novel is an element of precision brought to the performance itself. It is but a description anterior to the film which can be read as a musical score. Therefore, the communication must pass by the intellect of the reader whereas the work addresses itself primarily to his immediate sensibility, which nothing can truly replace." Do you still hold to this distinction? Might this be the reason why you are attracted to architecture as an art form that addresses the immediate sensibility of people?

Robbe-Grillet: In response to the first question, yes, I subscribe in full to what I say there and I would even go further. The description of the image in the cine-novel is nothing without its production. *Marienbad*, for example, was written by one author and filmed by a second author. It is obvious that another director would have made a different film. Regardless, it is the moment when it is produced with the images and the sound that the film crosses into the realm of sensibility. This is very clear to me when I write a screenplay. To write a novel I need two or three years, while *Marienbad* was written in thirty days. The writing does not pose any formal problems. It is simply the expression of the contents which must then be carried out. It is the actual production which tends to be perilous and difficult.

Will architecture be a means? Yes, and moreover you've noted how I immediately said that it is not "to conceptualize" which is needed, but rather the issue is "to do it." That is to say, what will be important is the moment when the sensible creation of something will be perceived with sensuality, with the body, with sensibility, and not in any way through the use of conceptual intelligence.

Question: You have said that Hegel is built on the ruins of Kant, and that your novels are built on the ruins of the ancients. Does a paradox exist for architecture because ruins are precisely those sites upon which nothing is built? When we build on them they are no longer ruins; they are monuments that have been integrated and reappropriated.

Robbe-Grillet: You are quite right. In general, we respect ruins, but this is quite recent. The citadel of Ankara is built almost completely with materials borrowed from Greek monuments, and there are walls in which statues are partly encased, having been used as simple building stones. During that time, the lack of respect for the ruin had already created an early type of post-modernism, as we would call it today – an integration of elements without reference to the original monuments. Another example is the temple of Diana at Ephesus, which for the most part is found in St Mark's Cathedral in Venice. I think there is something vaguely defined in all of these cases. When I speak about this notion of using materials to make other things, it is a little different. When I say, for example, that Hegel is made with the ruins of Kant, one must specify clearly that the core of Kant's work remains whole and intact; those ruins are always present. They are simply surpassed by a system which makes

them outdated but which completely respects them. Similarly, all of Richard Wagner's work can be considered as the ruins of the tonality system invented by Johann Sebastian Bach, since all of Wagner's chords can belong to many tonalities at once. When we listen to *Tristan*, in the first measure we are already within a dissonance that will last four hours and for which there will never be a resolution. The work of Bach is not destroyed; it is present. Bach's whole system, the twelve notes and the well-tempered clavier are still present in the tetralogy and in *Tristan*. Practically speaking, this would be difficult to produce in architecture. Once again, we come up against a problem of technology. Moreover, we have such respect for architecture that this would not be allowed. Suppose that someone takes a monument that I do not like very much – Notre-Dame de Paris, for example – and wishes to do something, by some incredible stroke of genius, that would succeed in respecting the space while at the same time surpassing it. But Jacques Chirac, otherwise an open-minded individual, would never allow it. At the present time, you are right; architectural ruins are respected precisely for being ruins, and as a result we are not allowed to make use of them.

All images are stills from the films *L'année dernière à Marienbad* and *L'immortelle*.

When the Old Mirror is not yet Polished, What Would You Say of it?

(Fragments Toward a Reconstruction of a Weak Myth Through the Passages of the Museum)

Tracey Eve Winton

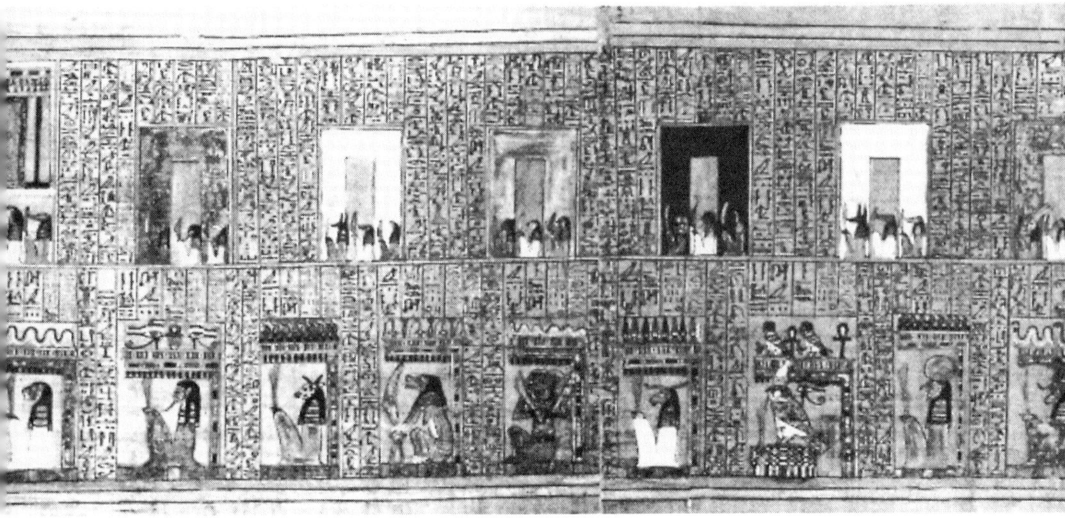

12.1

I THE HISTORY OF THE MUSEUM

1667: Perrault colonizes the Louvre.

1704: Kepler invents infinity.

1772: Diderot and d'Alembert complete the *Encyclopaedia.*

1787: Volume I of *Glossarium comparativum totius orbis* is published.

1789: 2 July The Bastille logbook notes that "the Count de Sade shouted several times from the window of the Bastille that the prisoners were being renumbered and that the people should come to liberate them."[1]

1789: 14 July The Bastille is stormed and Sade's cell sacked, his furniture, his suits and linens, his library and most important, his manuscripts, are "burned, pillaged, torn up and carried off."[2]

1 The Marquis de Sade, *The Complete Justine, Philosophy in the Bedroom and other Writings* (New York: Grove Press 1966), 100.
2 Ibid, 101.

1792: Decision to create the Museum française in the galleries of the Palais du Louvre.

1793: The decapitation of the monarch, after a long tradition of ritual regicide, otherwise practised only by savage tribes under the supervision of Lévi-Strauss.

1794: The Convention reviews the project for the Conservatoire des arts et métiers in St Martin-des-Champs, in place by 1799.

1796: Museum's name is changed to Musée central des arts.

1798: The Convention occupies the interior of the Louvre with statues.

1798: First National Industrial Exhibition takes place at the Champ-de-Mars.

1799: Charles Fourier discovers the germ of the calculus of Attraction.

1822: The next decade and a half sees most of the Parisian arcades constructed.

1839: Daguerre's panorama burns down. In the same year he announces the invention of the daguerreotype.

1853: Baron Haussmann begins his reforms to Paris.

1857: Baudelaire begins to write his *Poèmes nocturnes*.

1889: Eiffel Tower completed.

1914: Raymond Roussel writes *Locus Solus*

1917: Richard Mutt installs a fountain at the Museum without Walls.

1989: I.M. Pei builds a monument to the museum: three glass pyramids in the courtyard of the Louvre.

The meaning of language, like that of gestures … does not lie in the elements composing it.[3]

History is no more external to us than language.[4]

2 HOUSE OF THE MUSES

"The Greek *mousa* is held to derive from the verb μαειν, to seek after, crave, covet, and … to be [an] inventress, invention being inferred from seeking and desiring.

"*Mousa* also may have referred originally to the emotion of "fine frenzy" implied in μαειν and its derivatives (μεμαωζ: excited; μαινεσθαι: to rage, *mania*: frenzy, *mantis*: seer). All these meanings are comprised in the English verb "muse," as the cognate forms in other languages show.

"Desire implies brooding, meditation; meditation implies leisure, and both together give the state of 'bemusement,' and when bemused you are very apt to mumble and mutter. Hence μυζειν, to mutter; in Norwegian *mussa*, *mysja*, whisper; cf. Italian *mussare*.

"The Italian *musare,* to gape at, only implies an intense condition of pondering and wondering. Compare the Italian *muso*, mouth; whence muzzle. The leisure element in musing is given directly in the

3 Maurice Merleau-Ponty, "An Unpublished Text," in *The Primacy of Perception*. (Evanston: Northwestern University Press 1989), 8.

4 Ibid., 9.

German *Musse*, idleness, and indirectly in amusement."[5]

The mother of the nine Muses is Mnemosyne. Two consorts of the goddess of memory were Apollo, the god of the Oracle, and his brother Hermes, the fleet messenger to the Underworld. Through memory, the Muses are related to interpretation and translation. And the museum is the house of the Muses.

"In Greek thought everything 'musical' was closely related to ritual."[6]

"For Plato, indispensable to the production of the best poetry is a type of divine madness defined as possession (κατοκωχη) by the Muses. It was a Muse who took from Demodocus his bodily vision and gave him something better, the gift of song, because she loved him. Epic tradition represented the poet as deriving supernormal knowledge from the Muses ... The gift ... of the Muses ... is the power of true speech."[7]

3 VENUSTAS

"I am not overfond of museums. Many of them are admirable; none are delightful. Delight has little to do with the principles of classification, conservation, and public utility ... It is an absurdity to put together these independent but mutually exclusive marvels, which are most inimical to each other when they are most alike."[8]

4 RELATED INSTITUTIONS

Arcade, Asylum, Bordello, Clinic, Concentration Camp, Department Store, Prison, Zoo. Perhaps others. The difference in program is intentional.

5 English translator's note, Johan Huizinga, *Homo Ludens: A Study of the Play Element in Culture* (Boston: Beacon 1955), 159.

6 Ibid.

7 E.R. Dodds, *The Greeks and the Irrational* (Berkeley: University of California Press 1951), 80–1.

8 Paul Valéry, "The Problems of Museums," in *Degas Manet Morisot* (New York: Pantheon Books 1960), 202.

5 TYPOLOGY HATH MURDERED ARCHETYPE

"In this world beyond death that is staged, everything is like life, its exact image. But it is imperceptibly separated by a thin black layer, the lining [*la doublure*]."[9]

6 FROM MEMORY TO SOUVENIR

"The product of thousands of hours' work consumed in painting and drawing by so many masters, each hour charged with years of research, experiment, concentration, genius, acts upon our senses and minds in a few minutes ... We cannot stand up to it. So what do we do? We grow superficial.

"Or else we grow erudite. And erudition, in art, is a kind of dead end: throwing light on what is least refined, investigating the non-essentials. For direct feeling, it substitutes theories; for the marvellous actuality, an encyclopaedic memory; and the immense museum is further saddled with a limitless library. Aphrodite is transformed into a dossier."[10]

7 ALLES IN WUNDERKAMMERLAND

All things are removed from their natural context and hence from their natural scale. Redoubled, they are brought into proximity with other things that invade and deny their presence. Naturally, they must seek an internal space.

8 PLATO'S TOMB

"Eagle! why soarest thou above that tomb?
To what sublime and starry-paven home
Floatest thou? –
I am the image of swift Plato's spirit,

9 Michel Foucault, *Death and the Labyrinth: The World of Raymond Roussel* (Garden City, New York: Doubleday 1986), 85.

10 Valéry, "The Problems of Museums," 205.

Ascending heaven; Athens doth inherit
His corpse below."[11]

"Philosophical idealism ... was in Plato's case ... the fear of overpowerful senses, the prudence of a prudent Socratic. – Perhaps we moderns are merely not healthy enough to be in need of Plato's idealism. And we are not afraid of the senses because – "[12]

"[Benjamin's] aim was not merely for philosophy to catch up to surrealism, but for it to become surrealistic."[13]

The possibility of Redemptive Geometry: deliverance as removal of weight. The museum is suffering from structural failure: failure to ground itself in its mythology; its foundations are weakened; it has failed to resolve its details at grade. We constantly hear stories of fragments, ruins, falling, complaints of free masonry ... *sic transit gloria mundi.*

9 ABSENCE

"Full fathom five thy father lies;
Of his bones are coral made:
Those are pearls that were his eyes:
Nothing of him that doth fade,
But doth suffer a sea-change
Into something rich and strange."[14]

10 TRUTH AS CORRESPONDENCE

"Before the entrance to the arcade, a mailbox: a last opportunity to give a sign to the world that one is abandoning."[15]

The picture postcard, widespread through the postal system since the Chicago Columbian Exhibition of

11 Percy Bysshe Shelley, "Spirit of Plato," in *The Selected Poetry and Prose of Percy Bysshe Shelley*, ed. H. Bloom (Toronto: Signet 1966), 407.

12 Friedrich Nietzsche, *The Gay Science* (New York: Vintage 1974), 333.

13 Theodor W. Adorno, "A Portrait of Walter Benjamin." in *Prisms.* (Cambridge: MIT Press 1990), 239.

14 William Shakespeare, *The Tempest*, in *The Complete Works of William Shakespeare.* (London: Oxford University Press 1964), 6.

15 Walter Benjamin, *Das Passagen-Werk.* vols. 1, 2 (Frankfurt: Suhrkamp 1983), 42.

1893, is the forerunner of the mail-order museum.

André Malraux's *Museum without Walls* describes those epiphenomena of the reproductive media which enabled all available artifacts to be represented to man across the globe. Decentralizing and collapsing space and time in their sense as qualitative relations, the museum manipulates, changes and modifies the traces of the past. But does this not mean that the museum is itself a great artifact of its time, manifesting the struggle of the present with the past?

When the museum without walls completed the project of representation – the externalization of memory – and the Platonic project of reference to the ideal form through the notion of style, a reversal occurred in representation itself: the system of images re-internalized memory in the individual. And the photograph, entering the space of the museum, then became a work whose reproduction did not, and could not, reduce it to style or homogeneity through manipulation.

It is believed that fragments of The Wall may still be available as souvenirs for collectors, and photographs of the fragments when those are gone.

II INTOXICATION IN DESTRUCTION

The Museum is often destroyed by Acts of God:
lightning, irradiation, spontaneous combustion,
tornadoes, gales, hurricanes,
tidal waves, avalanches, floods,
earthquakes, mudslides, volcanoes,
and linguistic problems.

On occasion, the architect commits arson.

12 THE FOUR CAUSES

"For centuries philosophy has taught that there are four causes: (1) the *causa materialis*, (2) the *causa formalis*, (3) the *causa finalis*, (4) the *causa efficiens*.

"*Causa, casus*, belongs to the verb *cadere*, to fall, and means that which brings it about that something turns out as a result in such and such a way. The doctrine of the four causes goes back to Aristotle."[16]

Effects are often the cause of confusion between causality and synchronicity.

13 THE SPACE-TIME CONTINUUM

Matter is neither created nor destroyed, only transformed. The metamorphic nature of things persists and repeats. Myths are living things. If mythology is grounded in anything, it is in metamorphosis: the transcendence of poetic narrative over natural order.

14 GHOST IN THE MACHINE

"Proust's arguments in favour of museums also have as their point of reference not the thing itself but the observing subject. It is not coincidental that it is something subjective, the abrupt act of production in which the work becomes something different from reality, that Proust considers to be preserved in the work's afterlife in the museum."[17]

15 CIRCULATION

"On Sundays at five o' clock, at the exit to the Louvre, it is interesting to admire the stream of visitors visibly animated by the desire to be similar in every way to the heavenly visions still delighting

16 Martin Heidegger, "The Question Concerning Technology," in *Basic Writings* (San Francisco: Harper Collins 1977), 289–90.

17 Adorno, "Valéry Proust Museum," 183.

their eyes. A museum is like the lungs of a great city: the crowd floods into the museum every Sunday like blood and it leaves purified and fresh."[18]

16 THE ETHICAL DIMENSION OF ARCHITECTURE

"A hideous fellow came in and considered himself in the glass. 'Why look at yourself in the mirror, when you can only see your image with disgust?' The hideous fellow replied, 'Sir, according to the immortal principles of 1789 all men have equal rights; and whether it is with pleasure or displeasure is a matter for my own conscience.' According to common sense I was no doubt right; but from the point of view of the law he was not wrong."[19]

17 ERROR

Without error there could be no chance; without chance, there would be no responsibility, and without responsibility, no need to remake the world by action.

18 THE PSYCHOPATHOLOGY OF MODERN ART

Significantly, the reason Marcel Duchamp was the most infamous architect of the twentieth century is that his first famous intervention in the museum, a fountain, was accidentally installed upside-down by Duchamp, who was bilaterally symmetrical, rendering it functionally useless.

19 THE MUSEUM AND THE CITY

"The modern metropolis had ceased to be a place and had become a condition. Art no longer has any real goal, since the work of art reproduces the

18 Georges Bataille, "Musée," in *Œuvres complètes de Georges Bataille* (Paris: Gallimard 1970), vol. 1, 239–40.

19 Charles Baudelaire, "The Looking Glass," in *The Poems in Prose* (London: Anvil Press Poetry 1989), 101.

metropolis as it is, i.e., without transforming it into anything else."[20]

In what sense has the museum become a model for the city? *Cardo* and *decumanus* cross-slice four-folded Roma Quadrata, between earth and sky, from the central square to the outer limit of circling furrow. The sensible order of the city is the persistent coincidence of time and space: the mythical rhythm in the programme. The representational function is an attempt to map history onto mythology, or to regenerate myth by generating history.

20 THE SORCERER'S APPRENTICE

"The painted animal has the function of a 'double'; by its symbolic slaughter, the hunters attempt to anticipate and ensure the death of the real animal."[21]

Philosophers speculated that the reason that playing cards derived from the Tarot deck were banned in France from the time of the revolution was not simply that its symbolic universe continued to represent the monarchy, but the fear that that universe of the cards would magically recreate the world it now modelled.

21 SEVEN YEARS OF BAD LUCK

"The mirror itself is the instrument of a universal magic that changes things into a spectacle, spectacles into things, myself into another, and another into myself."[22]

"During the oral stage of organization of the libido, the act of obtaining erotic mastery over an object coincides with that object's destruction."[23]

20 Andrea Branzi, *The Hot House: Italian New Wave Design* (Cambridge: MIT Press 1984), 129.

21 Aniela Jaffe, "Symbolism in the Visual Arts," in *Man and his Symbols*, ed. C.G. Jung. (New York: Dell 1968), 266.

22 Merleau-Ponty, "Eye and Mind," in *The Primacy of Perception*, 168.

23 Sigmund Freud, *On Metapsychology: The Theory of Psychoanalysis* (New York: Penguin 1984), 327.

22 COLONIZATION

Cultural enframing is linked to the substitution of walls by columns: the modern museum is characterized by the prevalence, and often predominance, of columns in the architecture. The word *colonization* is related to the word column.

"I placed a jar in Tennessee,
And round it was, upon a hill
It made the slovenly wilderness
Surround that hill.

The wilderness rose up to it,
And sprawled around, no longer wild.
The jar was round upon the ground
And tall and of a port in air.

It took dominion everywhere.
The jar was gray and bare.
It did not give of bird or bush,
Like nothing else in Tennessee."[24]

"Whereas usually a piece of sculpture is an object with space around it (exactly the opposite of a cannon, which is a hole encircled by bronze), Giacometti is now engaged in creating space that contains one or several objects."[25]

Columns have an anthropomorphic nature; they inhabit an area greater than that of their actual matter. They give meaning to space by providing both local centres or foci and radial presence. A column is an *axis mundi*[26] linking heaven and earth. The column is an architectural element which demonstrates *weak truth*'s relationship to technology.

24 Wallace Stevens, "Anecdote of the Jar," in *The Collected Poems of Wallace Stevens* (London: Faber and Faber 1954), 76.

25 Michel Leiris, "Stones for a possible Alberto Giacometti" in *Brisées: Broken Branches* (San Francisco: North Point Press 1989), 132.

26 A cosmic game of Snakes and Ladders.

In the traditional games of chess and go, the former commands space by inhabiting the centre, while the latter commands space by framing it: this suggests why the Great Wall of China differs significantly from the Tower of Babel.

It is said that we dream all the time, but in the daytime our dreams are overrun by our sensory impressions. The glimpse of enlightenment through our engagement with the world is like the momentary clarity preceding "The Falling Sickness" described by Paracelsus and others.

23 THEATRE OF MEMORY

A misleading notion deriving memory from abstract order originates with Simonides, history's first detective. Called out of a dinner party by twin youths, Castor and Pollux, whose praises he had sung at dinner, Simonides escaped death when the dining room's ceiling fell in. The remaining bodies were so deformed that they could be identified for burial only through his memory of their locations at the table.

The theory attributes memory to the visual realm, divesting the sensual body of its haptic orders. The hidden significance of the tale lies in the nature of the twins: one mortal and one immortal.

24 ARS COMBINATORIA

The combinatoric tables of the hermetic arts merged the notions of notation and arrangement of matter in the containment of geometric form – permitting the division of form and content, which, subsequently, could be understood as discretely significant.

25 ON THE INSIDE

In the pre-creative chaos of its interior space, the museum continues to embody the tension between matter which is chaotic and uncontrollable, natural, metamorphic, and monstrous, and ordered, spectacular, disciplined, framed, and controlled form. The primary archetype of this struggle is language.

26 WHERE DO WE DRAW THE LINE?

"Language becomes an infinite museum whose centre is everywhere and whose limits are nowhere."[27]

[Draughts and Notes: Nocturnal Poems: D] "Symptoms of Ruin. Colossal Buildings. Many of them on top of the other – flats and bedrooms, temples, galleries, stairways, cesspools, gazebos, lanterns, fountains, statues – cracks and splits, damp oozing from a cistern up in the sky. – How to warn everybody, warn the nations – alert the most intelligent people, whisper in their ears."[28]

27 THE POSSIBILITY OF CRITICAL HISTORY

"Dreams of this kind, according to Freud, 'endeavour to master the stimulus retroactively, by developing the anxiety whose omission was the cause of the traumatic neurosis.' 'The impressions and sense perceptions of man,' Valery writes, 'actually belong in the category of surprises; they are evidence of an insufficiency in man. Recollection is ... an elemental phenomenon which aims at giving us time for organizing the reception of stimuli which we initially lacked.'"[29]

He who lives by the word shall die by the word.

27 Robert Smithson. "A Museum of Language in the Vicinity of Art." in *The Writings of Robert Smithson*, N. Holt, ed. (New York: New York University Press 1979), 67.

28 Baudelaire, *The Poems in Prose*, 144.

29 Walter Benjamin "On Some Motifs in Baudelaire," *Illuminations: Essays and Reflections* (New York: Schocken 1969), 161–2.

28 MAUSOLEUM

"Only a small part of architecture belongs to art: the monument and the tomb."[30]

Death: the ultimate Other. The irreconcilable, the unfamiliar, the unassimilable – although, in all life the seed of death lies dormant, as the seed of life lies in death.

29 ARCHITECTURE AND MYTHOLOGY

Reading the architecture of the museum means being able to understand the archetypal and mythological attributes of its architectural elements, forms, and programs with respect to ritual. In short, it is being able to orient oneself in the world of architecture, in order to create architecture that allows one to orient oneself in the world. See the hermeneutic circle and other circles.

30 MUSEUM AT THE CENTRE OF WHICH IS A TEMPLE OF FAME

Muséum au centre duquel est un temple de la Renommée destiné à contenir les statues des grands hommes.[31]

Musée Française Projetté contenant les chefs-d'œuvres des Arts en tout genre, tant Antiques que Modernes; également les statues en Marbre des Hommes Célèbres de la Nation et celle de Roi Louis XVI régnant fixée au centre du Monument.[32]

The essential aspect of the program was not aimed at function nor was the form generated by pure representation; the elements acted as universal symbols.

30 Adolf Loos, "Architecture," *Architecture: The Complete Treatises and Manifestos*, ed. Gabriel Monk (Rome: Mercurius 1966), vol. 20, 202.

31 Boullée, 1783. Ibid., vol. 9, 871.

32 Undated, attributed to Boullée.

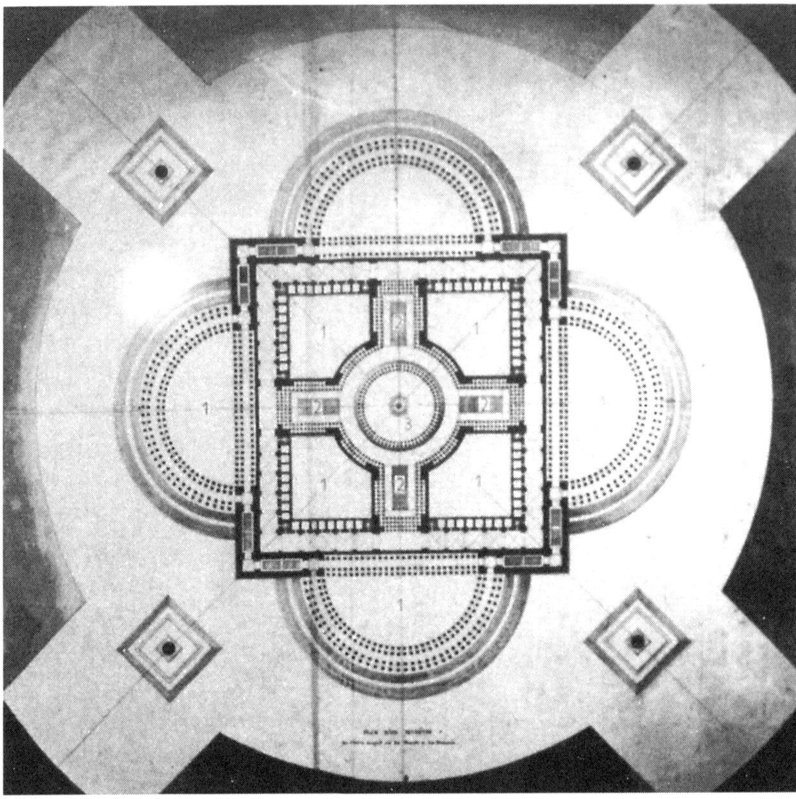

12.2

The colonnades were no longer load-bearing members; they became symbolic divisions.

The Greek Cross was overlaid with the circle, squared, with the four portals: the recognizable form of a mandala.

In the plan is demonstrated the transfer of representational power conferred by the people, the public domain, and the attempt to place new heroes – the actors and makers of the brave new world.

31 THE THEORY CONSPIRACY

Durand's type for the museum is formally derived from Boullée's museum. From Durand it is possible

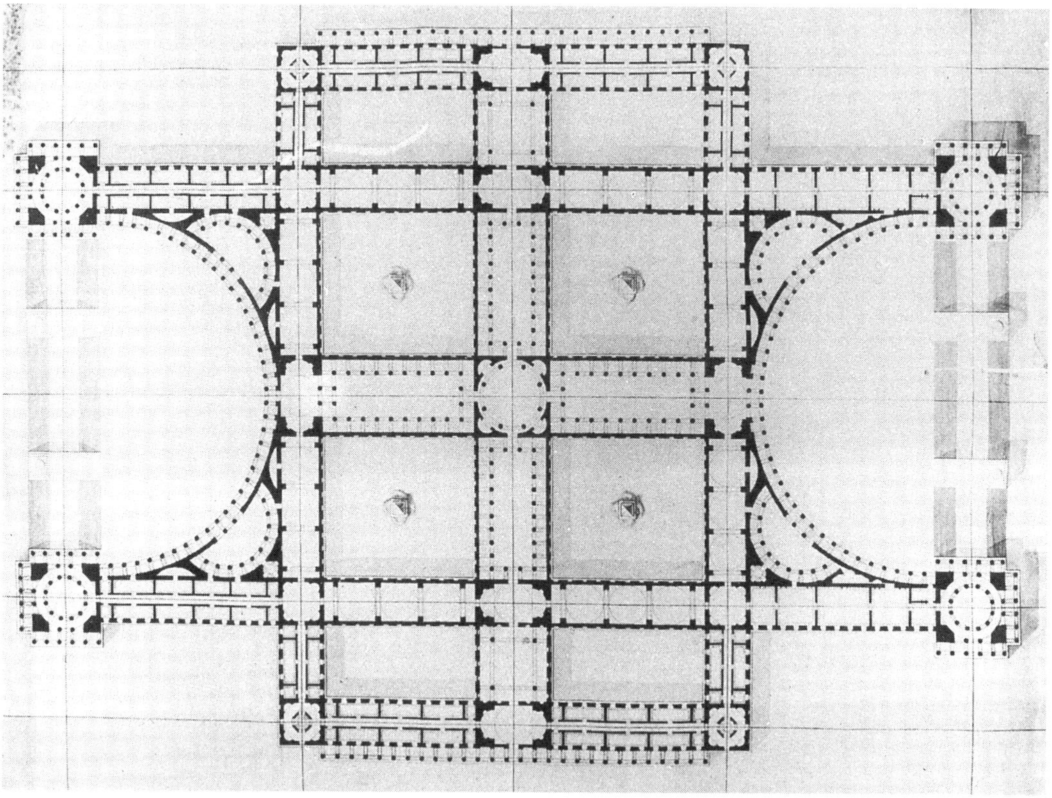

to trace a planimetric lineage of symbolic representation through prominent examples such as Schinkel's Altes Museum and Mies van der Rohe's gallery in Berlin.

"Painting and sculpture, says my Demon of Analysis, are both foundlings. Their mother, Architecture, is dead. So long as she lived, she gave them their place, their function and discipline. They had their exact allotted place and given light, their subjects and their relationships ... While Architecture was alive, they knew their function."[33]

The daily life of a building does not refer "typologically" to another building any more than the rituals of living of one man "refer to" another man.

33 Valéry, "The Problems of Museums," 206.

12.3

32 SQUARING THE CIRCLE

A section through the labyrinth: "[The World Museum is a] tripartite museum: *three naves extending parallel side by side*, with no partition wall separating them. In one nave: human works, those which tradition, the piety of remembrance or archaeology have brought to us here; in the adjacent nave: *all the documents which will fix time and history at a particular moment*, made visual by graphic art, scientific reconstructions, etc. And finally the third nave with all that which shows us what a particular place has to offer, its various conditions, its natural and artificial products, etc.

"This chain of knowledge upon which human works unfold across the thousands of years starts in prehistory and enlarges its links in the recent past *where history has already classified certainties.*"[34]

A Museum without Façades: "Let me tell you about my contribution to the idea of the creation of a museum of modern art for Paris [The Museum of Unlimited Extension].

"It is a means for bringing about, in Paris, the construction of a museum under conditions which are not arbitrary, but on the contrary, follow natural laws of growth in the order in which organic life is manifested: an element capable of being added to harmoniously, *the idea of the ensemble having preceded the idea of the individual part.*

"The museum can be started without money; truly, the first hall can be built for 100,000 francs. It can be continued by one, two or four new halls, during the following months or two or four years afterwards, as desired.

"*The museum has no facade; the visitor will never*

34 Le Corbusier, *The Mundanaeum and the World Museum, 1929*, in Le Corbusier et Pierre Jeanneret, *Œuvres complètes*, W. Boesiger, ed. (London: Thames & Hudson 1964–70), vol. 1, 10.

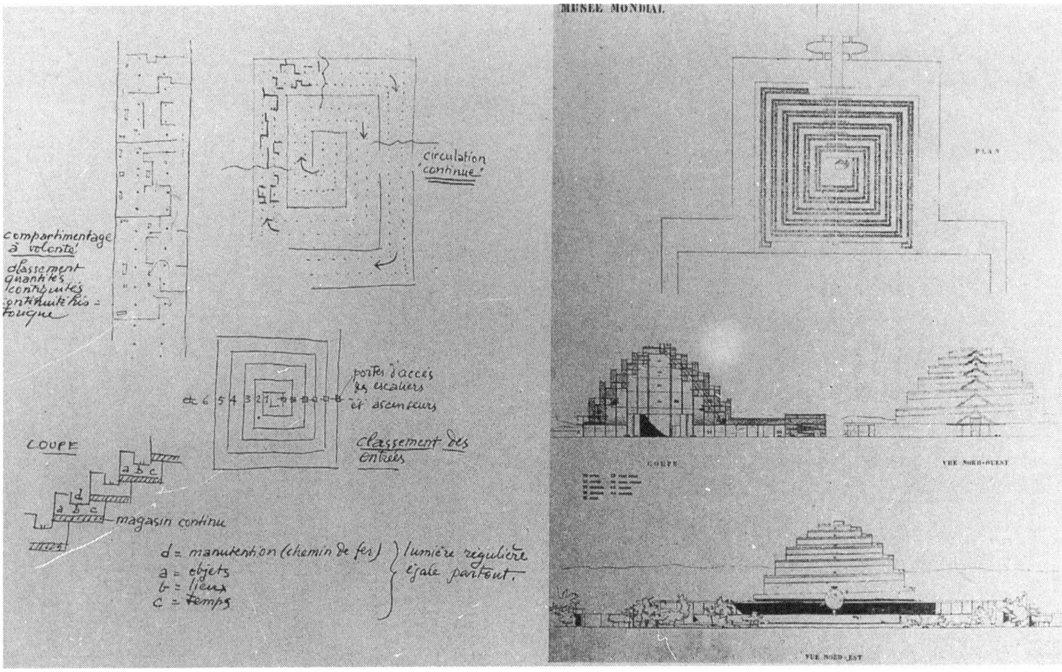

12.4

see a facade; he will only see the interior of the museum."

A Visit to the Underworld: "*One enters the heart of the museum by means of a subterranean passage* of which the entrance door opens in a wall which would, once the museum has reached its full magnificent size, comprise the 9000th metre."[35]

A New Temple of Fame: "Standard columns, fixed or movable partitions, standard ceilings. Maximum economy.

"The museum is extensible at will: *its plan is that of a spiral; a true form of harmonious and regular growth*. The donor of a picture could also donate the wall (or partition) destined to receive his picture; two columns, plus two girders, plus five or six beams, plus several square metres of partition. And this small gift could permit him to attach his name to the room in which his pictures are displayed."[36]

35 Le Corbusier, letter on Museum of Contemporary Art in Paris, 1931, in Le Corbusier et Jeanneret, *Œuvres complètes*, vol. 2, 184.

36 Le Corbusier, *Museum of Contemporary Art in Paris, 1931*, in Le Corbusier et Jeanneret, *Œuvres complètes*, vol. 2, 185.

The Second Cosmogony: "The problem of extension of buildings is a task of our time, for which, until now, no solution has been found. A series of studies over a period of ten years has led to a notable result: complete standardization of structural elements:

- one column
- one beam
- one ceiling element
- one illumination element for the day
- one illumination element for the night.

"The totality is laid out according to the Golden Section and permits an unlimited number of simple harmonious combinations."

The Struggle between Constancy and Flux: "*The fundamental principle of this Museum is that it is built on columns*, the entrance at ground level is in the centre of the building complex where the main hall is located, a true hall of honour, destined to house several masterpieces.

"The squared spiral which starts from there makes for a *discontinuity in the flow of circulation, extremely favourable for attracting the required attention from visitors.*"

Between Nature and God: "The means of *orienting oneself in the museum* is provided by the rooms at half-height which form a 'swastika'; every time a visitor, in the course of his wanderings, finds himself under a lowered ceiling he will see, on one side, *an exit to the garden,* and on the other side, *the way to the central hall.*

"The Museum can be developed to a considerable length without the squared spiral becoming a *labyrinth*. A modular element of about 7 metres in size, and 4.5 metres in height will ensure perfectly uniform lighting on the inside walls encompassing the squared spiral. Occasional interruptions along these side walls can allow communication between the different rooms, open out onto new perspectives, allow for a greater number of different room arrangements. Standardization introduces not only economy here, but also a wealth of combinations necessary for the proper organization of a Museum."[37]

"The museum is *on pilotis*: one enters *underneath the building* into an open court from which a ramp, similarly opened to the sky, leads to the exhibition levels. One enters the main nave in a series of spiral squares 14 metres wide, consisting of double bays of 7 × 7 m."

Locus Solus: "It is assumed that visits to the museum will be made particularly *in the evening and night-time*; they will wind up on the roof which will offer a wonderfully flowered surface formed by 49 basins of 49 m² each, all filled with water to a depth of 49 cm.

"This water is protected from the torrid sun by the shade of thick vegetation; each basin is strewn with leaves or blossoms floating on the surface of the water, the ensemble forming a checkerboard of blue, red, green, white, yellow, etc. ... The water of these basins is nourished by a *special powder* which induces enormous growth, *far beyond normal plant size*."[38]

"Palace-roof of cloudless nights!
Paradise of golden lights!
Deep, immeasurable, vast,

37 Le Corbusier, *The Museum of Unlimited Extension, 1939*, in Le Corbusier et Jeanneret, *Œuvres complètes*, vol. 3, 211.
38 Le Corbusier, *Museum at Ahmedabad*, in Le Corbusier et Pierre Jeanneret, *Œuvres complètes*, vol. 5, 72.

Which art now, and which wert then
Of the Present and the Past,
Of the eternal Where and When,
Presence-chamber, temple, home,
Ever-canopying dome,
Of acts and ages yet to come!"[39]

"The space for electrical installation extends under the entire surface of the ceiling which is placed in shadow, as described above, against the effects of the sun. Henceforth it will be possible to employ the illumination in solo, in duo, in trio, in symphony – uniformly subdued or sharply accented – analogous to the system of a musical score.

"The illumination has become an integral part of the museum's impression on the visitor. It is raised to the level of *emotive power.* It has become a determining element of the architecture."[40]

33 IT IS THE PRIVILEGE OF AN ARCHITECT TO BE LOST IN A BUILDING

Nietzsche saw the meaning of knowledge for the common person as the reduction of the strange to something familiar, reduction of fear of the unknown to the habitual, at which we no longer marvel. For him, the error in thus understanding the world is metaphorical:

"What is familiar is what we are used to; and what we are used to is most difficult to 'know' – that is to see as a problem; that is, to see as strange, as distant, as 'outside us.'"

Symbolically, the reason Marcel Duchamp was the most infamous phenomenologist of the twentieth century is that his first gift from a famous admirer,[41]

39 Shelley, "Ode to Heaven," in *Selected Poetry and Prose*, 118.

40 Le Corbusier, *Museum at Ahmedabad*, in Le Corbusier et Jeanneret, *Œuvres complètes*, vol. 5, 73.

41 R. Mutt: cf. Dogs, cross-breed; also mutation, monsters; also mutter, oracles.

a porcelain plumbing fixture, was erroneously taken for a work of art by the public, critically demonstrating the relationship between intentionality and form.

34 HISTORICAL FICTIONS

"People are always shouting they want to create a better future. It's not true. The future is an apathetic void of no interest to anyone. The past is full of life, eager to irritate us, provoke and insult us, tempt us to destroy or repaint it. The only reason people want to be masters of the future is to change the past."[42]

"All these forms are strange to you, you do not recognize them for what they are. They terrify you beyond words, and yet it is you who have created them. It is from your own mind therefore that all this has sprung. What you see here is but the reflection of the contents of your own mind in the mirror of the Void."[43]

35 TIME IS THE ERROR OF IMMORTALITY

"I am convinced that the future is lost somewhere in the dumps of the non-historical past; it is in yesterday's newspapers, in the *jejune* advertisements of science-fiction movies, in the false mirror of our rejected dreams. Time turns metaphors into *things*, and stacks them up in cold rooms."[44]

"*Historia abscondita* – Every great human being exerts a retroactive force: for his sake all of history is placed in the balance again, and a thousand secrets of the past crawl out of their hiding places – into *his* sunshine. There is no way of telling what may yet become part of history. Perhaps the past is

42 Milan Kundera, *The Book of Laughter and Forgetting* (London: Faber and Faber 1982), 22.
43 *Buddhist Scriptures*, from *The Tibetan Book of the Dead*, trans. Edward Conze (London: Penguin 1960), 229.
44 Smithson, "A Tour of the Monuments of Passaic, New Jersey," in *The Writings of Robert Smithson*, 56.

still essentially undiscovered! So many retroactive forces are still needed!"[45]

36 THE AUTOMATIC WRITING OF HISTORY

Many believed that the camera was viewed as the greatest invention of the modern era. For one, using a camera necessitates closing one eye in order to look through the viewfinder. Second, it is brought so close to the remaining eye that the camera becomes invisible through lack of focal distance. Further, the camera itself is capable of focusing on all depths with an equivalent degree of clarity. Last, the camera magnificently demonstrates the faith that one does not really have to see [vision understood as a passage], but merely to look, in order to gain knowledge. The click of that look in the shutter lets one believe that one has an externalized memory, recording one's body as having been some place at some time. The camera did not displace painting as far as it displaced the mirror.

Others were convinced that the prevalence of photography and the subsequent predominance of photographic prints were an epiphenomenon of the red safelight[46] which warms and enfolds the murky depths of the photographic darkroom, whose soothing timelessness and sound of running water recall the womb, more than any desire for further evidence of the split in black and white.

Consequently, the museum was represented as the greatest invention of the modern era because it gave people an opportunity to use their cameras.

37 THE MYTH OF PROGRESS

"Briefly, Proust compares the train station to a

45 Nietzsche, *The Gay Science*, 104.

46 Red lamps are used architecturally in printing, incubation, and prostitution, in which the red light indicates the bordello.

museum. Both stand outside the framework of conventional pragmatic activity, and, one might add, both are bearers of a death symbolism. In the case of the station it is the ancient symbolism of the voyage; in that of the museum, the symbolism associated with the work of art – 'l'univers nouveau et périssable,' the new and fragile cosmos the artist has created."[47]

Historians speculated that the real reason that playing cards derived from the Tarot deck were banned from the time of the French revolution was not the symbolic universe that continued to represent the monarchy, but the fear that, by reading the future, the people would discover Marxist critiques.

38 THE LEGEND AND THE KEY

Mapping the museum means making progress, not toward the future but toward history.

As the killing of a double or twin is a form of ritual suicide preceding rebirth, so the greatest invention of modernity was history, allegorically prefigured by the invention of allegory itself.

39 THE POWER OF SILENCE

Silence is often imposed on things by an act of rational organization. But then, the effect is often mistaken for the cause.

40 FRAMING THE WORK

Like the movement of a figure in a labyrinth, the definition of an idea by the empirical method circles around a notion, in an idealizing praxis which must necessarily fail or fall short.

47 Adorno, "Valéry Proust Museum," 178.

By constant approximation, the thing begins to spring into clearer focus, the impression always returning, closer to the idea, but never attaining it. Is the idea inherent in the field of objects or external to it?

This idea will never be attained because it is a use of the concrete to speak of the abstract, the finite to speak of the infinite, the personal to speak of the universal. In the movement between the two, the oscillation which never entirely touches either of its two poles, resides the realm of representation and its offspring.

Order is encroached upon to bracket the tangible. Tension develops in a struggle between similarity and difference. Taxonomy and classification divide and label, plunging into individual units, with a loss of any internal commonality: Being in the asymptote.

This return regenerates a heterogeneous situation; thus, full circle, reinvokes the senses. Beyond idea or manifest intention, works are redeemed which do not have the reciprocity of a human subject directly, but bear the latent or manifest imprint of the artifex' hand. Although isolated, a thing has a temporal and spatial context of origin, an aura (*avoir*) because of its natality in the world at a particular moment in time and place.

41 NECESSITY IS THE MOTHER OF INVENTION

Private museums originally situated a patron at the centre of the recreated world. Museums developed from private to public as attributes of the collection became a definition of the self, with the need to have what the collection reflects about the Self echoed in the Other.

42 JOURNEY TO THE CENTRE OF THE EARTH

For the Oracle of Apollo at Delphi, the travellers who arrived with questions were as much the purveyors of information as the seekers of knowledge. The temple was not only the centre of the world but, as at Cumae, also an entrance to the Underworld. As a centre of exchange, verbal instability, madness riddled with wisdom, the universe expanded in distance even as it contracted in depth. On the ambiguous hinge of dream-language, the *Platonic* has fused with the *Plutonic*. The legacy of Platonism can be read as a series of footnotes to the history of Death.

43 MUSAEUM ATHANASIUS

The institution of the museum developed privately in the seventeenth century mainly as a result of the increasing spread of global travel by explorers and missionaries of the Jesuit order. In the works and collections of Athanasius Kircher, a prototype of the modern museum is expressed.

The Museum embodies the long struggle between opposing and complementary forces that has constituted and driven Western culture since the Renaissance. The ostensible conflict between matter (things) and idea (geometric order) is a projection on the external world of the disorderly internal struggle of sense and reflection. Without paradox, there is no struggle, and without struggle, no activity.

"I cannot remember it exactly, but it was something like: 'There is a man cut in two by the window.'"[48]

Kircher's preoccupation with origins and genealogy

48 André Breton, *Manifestoes of Surrealism* (Ann Arbor: The University of Michigan Press 1977), 21.

broach the question of recognition or recollection of the relationship among terms in a series.

"An institution caught in the contradictions of its culture ... the history of the museum is the history of all the various attempts to reduce it to a homogeneous system or series."[49]

44 THE GENIUS OF THE MUSEUM

Kircher's Museum became conventional, and consequently, 'transparent,' for Nature was his model and the only 'intentionality' in Nature was the representation of the Divine Plan of Creation. The fragment, the detail and the ruin hence rose in significance, in the place of the object of knowledge.

The universe became infinite because the empirical world was seen as necessarily incomplete; the key error being that of mistaking infinite possibility for infinity itself. The macrocosm had to be read through the microcosm.

In human works, the Divine Plan was also present or revealed, but by an irony of their mimetic intentionality, they also were classified by formal similarity.

45 THE WHOLE IS GREATER THAN THE SUM OF THE PARTS

The hole is greater than some of the parts. An individual is able to project his fantasy onto a partial construct, in particular, one of which the centre is absent. Thus the museum may be a utopian paradigm.

"Among children, collecting is only one process of

49 Douglas Crimp, "On the Museum's Ruins," in *The Anti-Aesthetic: Essays on Postmodern Culture*, ed. H. Foster (Port Townsend: Bay Press 1983), 49.

renewal; other processes are the painting of objects, the cutting out of figures, the application of decorations – the whole range of childish modes of acquisition, from touching things to giving them names. To renew the old world – that is the collector's deepest desire when he is driven to acquire new things."[50]

46 WEAK ART

In the ruins of myth, the narrative has fractured into probabilities and possibilities; the work, into incomplete systems, partial objects, and whole objects complete with missing parts.

47 RECONSTRUCTIONS

Piranesi's creations of full artifacts from minute fragments were then posited as reconstructions – fictions in the museum – to inspire the poetic potential of architecture's role in history.

48 CALCULATED RISKS

One can take risks in a museum – surreptitiously inserting objects into the collection; it is good if these objects bear a strong resemblance to the objects with which they are going to be placed; it is better if they bear no conceivable similarity or associative relationship to the objects with which you are placing them; it is best if they appear to be, or in fact actually are, fragments of the architecture itself, somehow come loose and fallen into the world of the display.

49 INVOLUNTARY MEMORY

The problem of restoration in museums – as with artifacts, buildings, and people, is always the same:

50 Benjamin, "Unpacking my Library," in *Illuminations: Essays and Reflections*, 61.

restoration to what, at what time? What happens to Sir John Soane's museum on Judgment Day is what happens to the relics of the saints.

50 THE LITERAL MUSEUM

"Six months later they had become archaeologists, and their house looked like a museum. On shelves all round stood torches, locks, bolts, screws. On a table in the middle were exhibited the rarest curiosities: the frame of a bonnet from Caux, two clay urns, some medals, a phial of opaline glass. From his bed Pécuchet could see all this in enfilade and sometimes he even went into Bouvard's room to extend the perspective."[51]

51 ARCHITECTURE OF SHADOWS

"Each substance of a grief hath twenty shadows,
Which show like grief itself, but are not so.
For sorrow's eye, glazed with blinding tears.
Divides one thing entire to many objects;
Like Perspectives, which rightly gaz'd upon
Show nothing but confusion; ey'd awry
Distinguish form."[52]

52 GOD IS IN THE DETAILS

The thing in itself need not be complete. Garden treatises of the Baroque period specified, for the construction of ruins, that the complete form implied by the fragment must be reconstructable by the eye.

"To see the World in a Grain of Sand,
And Heaven in a wild flower;
Hold infinity in the palm of your hand,
And Eternity in an Hour."[53]

51 Gustave Flaubert, *Bouvard and Pécuchet [with the Dictionary of Received Ideas]* (New York: Penguin 1987), 103.

52 William Shakespeare, *The Tragedy of King Richard II*, in *The Complete Works of William Shakespeare* (London: Oxford University Press 1957), 390.

53 William Blake, fragment from "Auguries of Innocence" in *English Literature: The Romantic Age* (New York: Dryden Press 1953), 94.

53 SACRIFICIAL ORDER

"Slaughterhouses, along with the museum, make up a system in which the ambivalence defining the sacred nucleus is at work ... Within the heart of one the other is hidden. At the heart of beauty lies murder, a sacrifice, a killing (no beauty without blood).

"Bataille reminds us that the Louvre is turned into a museum by the Convention when the function of royalty has been put to an end.

"The museum is what the Terror invented to replace the king,[54] to replace the irreplaceable. 'The origin of the modern museum,' he comments, 'would thus be linked to the development of the guillotine.'"[55]

54 THE LONG DARK NIGHT OF THE SOUL

The French Revolution was a mythological deposition of the sun, resulting in the long dark night of the soul prophesied by St John of the Cross:

"O night that guided me,
O night more lovely than the dawn,
O night that joined beloved with lover,
Transfiguring them each into the other."[56]

"History ... is a nightmare from which I am trying to awake."[57]

Madness is created by protracted night-wandering in the Museum.[58]

55 THE SURRATIONAL

"When Hippocrates visited the 'mad Democritus' in Abders, he found him sitting in front of his house

54 Note the significance of the king as a symbol of the sun, hence the reincarnation of Phoebus Apollo, as well as the use of the guillotine to denote the symbolic creation of order by dividing the head from the body. In many cultures, the most important thing about the guillotine is its fall and rise.

55 Denis Hollier, *Against Architecture: The Writings of Georges Bataille* (Cambridge: MIT Press 1989), xiii.

56 St John of the Cross, in *The Poems of St John of the Cross*, trans. R. Campbell (New York: Pantheon 1947), 21.

12.5

surrounded by dead, disemboweled birds. He was writing a treatise on insanity and was dissecting the birds in order to localize the centre of bile, which he believed to be the source of madness."[59]

56 THE FOUR MUSEUMS ARE THE FOUR MIRRORS

"*Metaphor* (from the Greek μεταφορα, transfer) is a figure by which the mind applies the name of one object to another object, because of a shared characteristic that allows them to be put side by side and compared. And yet it is hard to know where metaphor begins and where it ends. An abstract word is formed by the sublimation of a concrete word. A concrete word, which never designates an object by more than one of its qualities, is itself hardly more than a metaphor, or at the very least a figurative expression.

"Not only language but the whole of intellectual life

57 James Joyce, *Ulysses* (London: Penguin 1969), 40.

58 The four types are: (1) Prophetic madness, whose patron god is Apollo; (2) Telestic or ritual madness, whose patron is Dionysius; (3) Poetic madness inspired by the Muses; (4) Erotic madness, inspired by Aphrodite and Eros.

59 Mikhail Bakhtin, *Rabelais and his World* (Bloomington: Indiana University Press 1984), 361.

is based on a play of transpositions, a play of symbols, which can be described as metaphorical. *Then again, knowledge always proceeds by comparison, so that all known objects are connected to one another by relations of interdependency.* [60]

"With any two of them, it is impossible to determine which is designated by the name proper to it and is not a metaphor of the other and vice versa. A man is a moving tree, just as a tree is a rooted man. In the same way, the sky is a rarefied earth, the earth a denser sky. And if I see a dog running, *it is just as much the run that is dogging.*

"Even this article is metaphorical."[61]

57 DEATH COMES AND GOES THROUGH MIRRORS

"The mirror stage involves the child's self-identification through his double: his reflected image. The child recognizes himself as a separate object ... by means of his mirrored image. The self is felt, at this stage, only as an image of the self; and insofar as the child initially recognizes himself as an other, there is inscribed in that experience a primary alienation."[62]

"The mirror's ghost lies outside my body, and by the same token my own body's 'invisibility' can invest the other bodies I see."[63]

58 METAMORPHOSIS AND MONSTROSITY

"The museum is the colossal mirror in which man contemplates himself finally, in all of his faces, finds himself literally admirable and abandons himself to the ecstasy expressed in all the reviewing of art."[64]

60 Emphasis mine.

61 Leiris, "Metaphor," in *Brisées: Broken Branches*, 18.

62 Rosalind Krauss, "Notes on the Index: Seventies Art in America," in Michelson et al, ed. *October: The First Decade, 1976–1986* (Cambridge: MIT Press 1987), 3.

63 Merleau-Ponty. "Eye and Mind," 168.

64 Bataille, "Musée," in *Œuvres complètes*, I: 239–40.

"I am the eye with which the Universe
Beholds itself and knows itself divine."[65]

59 HELIOTROPES

According to the writings of a certain Gabriel Monk, modern man is not "master in his own house." The idea of the *ego* assumes a threshold between two hidden aspects operating the mind and body: the collective unconscious memory, and the instinctive drives. Man, even now as a modern monster, lives on this threshold between being a god and being an ape.

Essentially, the reason Marcel Duchamp was the most infamous alchemist of the twentieth century is that his first famous attempt at the conjunction of opposites in the museum, a fountain which was also a urinal, caused Duchamp, who was a hermaphrodite, to be unjustly accused of ill humour.

60 CRIMES OF DUPLICATION

A building "represents" architectural history only insofar as a man "represents" a monkey.

"The nineteenth-century dislike of Realism is the rage of Caliban seeing his own face in a glass. The nineteenth-century dislike of Romanticism is the rage of Caliban not seeing his own face in a glass."[66]

61 NOTHING OUTSIDE OF THE FLESH

A situation that, for no real reason, is destined to end in tragedy: the artist has fallen in love with his model.

65 Shelley, "Hymn of Apollo," *Selected Poetry and Prose*, 263.

66 Oscar Wilde, *The Picture of Dorian Gray* (London: Octopus 1986), 66.

For the flesh of the world is also a mirror. Looking towards the East, from whence the sun rises, our own reality may be glimpsed, if only momentarily. For the Taoists the world is undifferentiated reality, a world of flesh that is at once transcendent and immanent.

"The secret waits for the insight
Of eyes unclouded by longing;
Those who are bound by desire
See only the outward container."[67]

62 REFLECTIONS

"He who looks from the outside through an open window will never see as many things as he who looks at a closed window."[68]

63 A QUESTION OF JUDGMENT

"Similitude is no longer the form of knowledge, but rather the occasion of error. Resemblance enters an age which is, from the point of view of resemblance, one of madness and imagination."[69]

64 THE REPETITION OF FORMS

"There is in the Cabala a music of numbers, and this music, which reduces the chaos of the material world to its principles, explains by a kind of awesome mathematics how Nature is ordered and how she directs the birth of the forms that she pulls out of chaos.

"And everything I saw seemed to correspond to a number. The statues, the forms, the shadows always presented the recurring numbers 3, 4, 7, 8. The

67 Lao Tzu, *Tao Te Ching* (New York: Golden Flower 1966), 55.
68 Baudelaire, "Windows," *The Poems in Prose*, 93.
69 Michel Foucault, *Madness and Civilization: A History of Insanity in the Age of Reason* (New York: Vintage 1973), 99.

broken-off busts of women numbered 8; the phallic tooth, as I have said, had three stones and four holes; the forms that became volatile numbered twelve, etc.

"I repeat, if someone says that these forms are natural, I shall not argue; it is their repetition which is not natural."[70]

65 THE DANGER OF MIRRORS

The museum proliferates with the mythology of twins, a monstrosity typically born of an immortal father and a mortal mother. Castor and Pollux demonstrate the relationship of memory to representation. Killing one's double is akin to rebirth, hence the blood association of twin fratricide with remaking or creative action, flowing from Cain and Abel to Romulus and Remus. The arts of dissimulation and mimicry breed in the space between Jacob and Esau; those of recirculation between Hypnos and Thanatos.

66 THE MONSTER IN THE MIRROR

Travelling the museum as a labyrinth, on the quest which is a question, on the journey toward the monster – death in the mirror is an omen of transformation. For the long threshold of the museum the trick is simple: not to sacrifice the aim – the sense – for the goal.

The monster, which retains its separate elements within the amalgam, in order to be classified as such, indicates memory; more specifically, the monster was, and continues to be, the sign for the symbol – the recognition of the self in the other, and the monstrous link of self-and-other itself.

70 Antonin Artaud, *Selected Writings of Antonin Artaud* (New York: Farrar, Straus and Giroux 1976), 381.

67 PARALLEL LINES NEVER MEET

The museum is a cultural institution, and yet is the consumer of culture, much as a life is a consumer of life. The sphinx's riddle is simple: it asks you to recognize yourself in the universal. If not, you shall be consumed by the monster. Life lives on death. The medium is the message.

"my peace is there in the receding mist
when I may cease from treading these
    long shifting
thresholds
and live the space of a door
    that opens and shuts."[71]

68 THE ECHO OF NARCISSISM

The maxims of the oracle at Delphi: *Know thyself*, and, *Nothing to excess*.

The seer who was asked whether Narcissus should live long replied, Yes, if he does not come to know himself. Narcissism is a stage between auto-eroticism and object-love.

"The fetishism of the object and the subject's infatuation with itself find their correctives in each other. Each position passes over into the other."[72]

The hermeneutics of suspicion: a gnostic quest for the quality of latent content in the heterogeny of the world – order or chaos at the microcosmic level.

History is created by viewing time in the museum as superior to, and detached from, an original time of unselfconsciousness. Previous productions and artifacts are seen as naturalized by contextualization: a

71 Samuel Beckett, "my way is in the sand flowing" in *Collected Poems in English and French* (London: John Calder 1977), 57.

72 Adorno, "Valéry Proust Museum," 183.

symbolic device of semiotic control. The museum contains the object of study: the artifacts that man has created, which are now the only way to understand and (re)produce – culture itself! The work in the museum becomes linguisticized and decontextualized; it has ambiguous meanings, and several points of reference and cross-reference. By implication, so does the building itself: the reconstruction of intentions through formal interpretation (and the possibility of reconstructing a ruined or fragmented form through interpreting the intention behind it.)

69 SMOKE AND MIRRORS

The contents of the museum supersede the need for imitation; mimetic art proceeds from an act aimed toward possessing the object of desire. Possession through the museum is really a (re)collection of the universe, and through this, control of it, as if by history's Wizard of Oz.

"The artist is never fully aware of the work. Between his intention and the realization, between what he wants to say and what the work actually says, there is a difference. This 'difference' is, in fact, the work. Between the two works, between what the artist wanted to do and what the spectator thinks he sees, there is a reality: the work. Without it, the re-creation of the spectator is impossible."[73]

70 PLEASE DO NOT TOUCH / ALARM WILL SOUND

When you see this sign you should carefully touch the object in question. Close your eyes and caress it gently using all the fingers of one hand.

Prohibition is an indication of potential pleasure,

73 Octavio Paz, "The Castle of Purity," in *Marcel Duchamp: Appearance Stripped Bare* (New York: Arcade 1990), 85.

and hence the desirability of touching the thing. The museum should spring to life in an interactive way that you may not have witnessed in the past.

71 THE CARE OF THE SHELF

The responsibility of the curator. (see *editor*)

"The whole of history is still action and action already history. History is the same whether we contemplate it as a spectacle or assume it as a responsibility. The condition of the historian is not very different from that of the acting man. History could ... be said to be imaginative action."[74]

72 DREAMING THE MUSEUM

The curator is the new maker, along with the editor. Recreation works through destruction, a separation of the elements of matter, followed by juxtaposition, or frictional rearrangement, bricolage as a form of creation. Making is an act of judgment on the part of the bricoleur. The undertaking has an echo in rhetoric, where objects or words retain their own identities and simultaneously engage with other similar objects in dialogues. Irony, for example, requires an attentive, engaged subject.

73 IN THE WAKE OF INSOMNIA

"Dreams are the guardians of sleep – not its disturbers."[75]

Museums at night: why do works of fiction contain passages describing the illicit nocturnal occupation of museums? *Foucault's Pendulum*, by Umberto Eco, takes the stage in the Conservatoire des arts et métiers in Paris, previously an abbey.[76]

74 Merleau-Ponty, "The Crisis of the Understanding," in *The Primacy of Perception*, 194.

75 Sigmund Freud, *The Interpretation of Dreams* (New York: Penguin 1984), 82.

76 "On 25 Brumaire of the year III, the Convention authorized its Comité d'Instruction Publique to have the complete works of Bacon printed. And on 18 Vendémiaire of the same year the Convention had passed a law providing for the construction of a house of arts and trades that would reproduce the House of Solomon as described by Bacon in his *New Atlantis*, 'a place where all the inventions of mankind are collected.'"

The subtext may be the programmatic resonance of social psychic unity in places of public gathering. The Conservatoire, although a museum by day, is still the place of esoteric collective ritual by night. There is an echoing of Walter Benjamin's suspicion in his "Theses on the Philosophy of History":[77] that within history, theology lies concealed. The museum's unconscious side, its dark-time, hides a dormant potential for a realm of political assembly, collective authority.

"To dream of living in an unknown city means imminent death. In fact, the dead live elsewhere, nor is it known where."[78]

"How much I admire those men who decide to be shut up at night in a museum in order to examine at their own discretion, at an illicit time, some portrait of a woman they illuminate by a dark lantern."[79]

74 CROSSING OVER

"There was a crack, a slender chink, that had developed in the party wall between their two houses, when it was being built. This fault had gone unnoticed for many years, and the lovers were the first to find it; nothing can escape the eyes of lovers. They used it as a channel for their voices. They used to exclaim: 'Jealous wall, why do you stand between lovers?'"[80]

How does light travel in a vacuum?

75 CULTURE IN RUINS

"Proust knows that even within works of art themselves, history rules like a process of disintegration. 'What is called posterity is the afterlife of the work.'

77 Benjamin, *Illuminations: Essays and Reflections*, 253.

78 Gerolamo Cardano, "Somniorum Synesiorum," cited in Umberto Eco, *Foucault's Pendulum* (New York: Harcourt Brace Jovanovich 1989), 369.

79 André Breton, *Nadja* (New York: Grove Press 1960), 112.

80 Ovid, *The Metamorphoses* (New York: Penguin 1981), 96.

In the artifact's capacity for disintegration Proust sees its similarity to natural beauty. He recognizes the physiognomy of decomposing things as that of their second life. For him it is only the death of the work of art in the museum which brings it to life."[81]

76 CLOSED ON MONDAYS

"The slaughterhouse and the museum (religion and art), from this point of view, are two sorts of enclave within the economic continuum; the sacrificial nature of the first, and the fact that it is on a Sunday that one visits museums, connect both to a sabbatical or a Sunday rhythm, that is, to how one spends time on the seventh day. (What should one do when work is forbidden?)"[82]

77 THE SPACE OF PUBLIC APPEARANCES

"The theatre of the muses is the museum, an architectural monster that immortalizes and glorifies the human production of things and thoughts."[83]

"Every second of time was the window through which the Messiah might enter."[84]

78 CHANGES IN THE PROGRAM

Evidently, the reason Marcel Duchamp was the most infamous program revisionist of the twentieth century is that his famous first installation, a urinal, was mistakenly installed in the exhibition area of the museum where, needless to say, the public refused to use it.

The program of a building does not "refer to" its function any more than a man's spirituality "refers to" his physiological needs.

81 Adorno, "Valéry Proust Museum," 181–2.

82 Hollier, *Against Architecture: The Writings of Georges Bataille*, xiv.

83 Marco Frascari, *Monsters of Architecture: Anthropomorphism in Architectural Theory* (Savage: Rowman and Littlefield 1991), 6.

84 Benjamin, "Theses on the Philosophy of History," in *Illuminations: Essays and Reflections*, 264.

79 THE MUSEUM AND RHETORIC

"Reality ... gives to architecture a set of rules and productive techniques while, in its turn, architecture gives back to reality an imaginary coherence that makes reality appear natural and eternal."[85]

"Knowledge and communication sublimate rather than suppress our incarnation, and the characteristic operation of the mind is in the movement by which we recapture our corporeal existence and use it to symbolize instead of merely to co-exist."[86]

80 GAMES TO PLAY IN THE MUSEUM

Hide and Seek
I Spy
Charades
Broken Telephone
Hopscotch (contingent on floor surface)
Categories
Hunt the Thimble
Statues
Blind Man's Bluff
also faking of blindness, madness, death, etc.

81 WHAT BECOMES FULLER THE MORE IT IS EMPTIED?

"I never saw an exciting space. I don't know what a space is. Yet, I like the uselessness of the museum.

"I'm interested for the most part in what's not happening, that area between events which could be called the gap. This gap exists in the blank and void regions or settings that we never look at. A museum devoted to different kinds of emptiness could be developed. The emptiness could be defined by the

85 Demetri Porphyrios, "On Critical History," in *Architecture, Criticism, Ideology* (Princeton: Princeton Architectural Press 1985), 16.
86 Merleau-Ponty, "An Unpublished Text," 7.

actual installation of art. Installations should empty rooms, not fill them."[87]

The fullness of certain rooms was simply the result of the ascension of the void toward the periphery, and thereby explained neither the splendid miracle of natural vacuums, nor the incredible persistence of gravitational attraction.

82 WHERE IS THE MUSEUM?

"Aristotle replieth: it is in itself. The convex surface of the primal heaven is universal space, which being the primal container is by nought contained."[88]

83 THE ARCHITECTURAL MODEL

Representation in the museum proceeds from universal systems to specific concrete models, from complete symbolic systems based on the correspondence between representations and things, toward those which are based on indexical or evidentiary significance, which are necessarily incomplete. Reality then falls inside the thing itself rather than outside of it.

Where architecture diverges from symbolic representation to become an imposed model, society represents the influence of architecture rather than vice versa. Where architecture has prioritized formalism, society must follow suit.

84 THE WORK IS THE DEATH-MASK OF ITS CONCEPTION

"The height of a pyramid is related to the length of its shadow just as the height of any vertical, measur-

87 Smithson, "Some Void Thoughts on Museums," 58.

88 Giordano Bruno, *De l'infinito universo e mondi*, cited in Alexandre Koyré, *From the Closed World to the Infinite Universe* (Baltimore: Johns Hopkins University Press 1991), 46.

able object is related to the length of its shadow at the same time of day."[89]

"To measure the inaccessible consists in mimicking it within the realm of the accessible ... The point is to transpose some unreachable figure into a more immediate realm in the form of a miniaturized schema. The inaccessible is that which I cannot touch ... Instead of letting the pyramid speak of the sun ... he asks the sun to speak of the pyramid ... Thales stops time in order to measure space.

"What it announces, for the first time, is a philosophy of representation. The tale of inauguration is that interminable discourse that we have untiringly repeated since our own dawn. What is, in fact, an interminable discourse? That which speaks of an absent object, of an object that absents itself, inaccessibly."[90]

85 AT WHAT SCALE IS THE MUSEUM?

1: 0
The "real" museum is a fragment of the *museum without walls,* which is a fragment of the imaginary museum of all things existing in the universe, which is a fragment of the ideal museum of all that is possible in the universe, which is a fragment of the infinite.

1: 1
Homogeneous space is now populated by events (strangeness) which demarcate it in the historical paradigm

1: 2
In the West, the riddle, a "charm in reverse," is a

89 Plutarch, quoted in Michel Serres, *Hermes: Literature, Science, Philosophy* (Baltimore: Johns Hopkins University Press 1992), 84.

90 Michel Serres, "Mathematics and Philosophy: What Thales saw," in *Hermes: Literature, Science, Philosophy* (Baltimore: Johns Hopkins 1992), 85.

part of the poetic tradition of mythology, drama, and play.

1: ∞
Abstract representation must be a theatre of memory. We locate co-ordinates in infinite space, never depicted as infinite, but always modelled on the place of play, and like a game, delimited and separated from everyday life.

86 TOURS OF BABEL

"One must take into account the fact that the halls and the art-objects are no more than a container of which the content is formed by the visitors; it is this content which distinguishes a museum from a private collection."[91]

87 RITUAL INHABITATION

"Furthermore, the confined space of the compartment and the relatively brief duration of the journey expand in the way ceremonial space and time can expand when a series of events whose theatre was supposedly the mythical world are reproduced in a ritual subjected to narrow limits of site and duration. Yet what is happening is not that symbols – whose not immediately perceptible truth is the most important thing – are being ground down but that polyvalent elements operating on several levels are being brought into play (through a very delicate spatial and temporal network), elements none of which could claim to take precedence."[92]

Anthropologists speculated that the real reason that playing cards derived from the Tarot deck were banned from the time of the French Revolution was

91 Bataille, "Musée" in *Œuvres complètes*, vol. 1:239–40.
92 Leiris, "Michel Butor's Mythological Realism," in *Brisées: Broken Branches*, 211.

not the potential discovery of Hegelian fallacies, but the fear that, through divination, the people would refound the city of Paris using symbolic geometry.

88 CROSS-REFERENCES

The program is the possibility of orientation in the world, by understanding the resonance of phenomena in time and space. Exhibits in different rooms and halls should be qualitatively cross-referenced to one another with signs, arrows, notes, string, guides, etc.

89 *MONSTRUM IN ANIMO, MONSTRUM IN FRONTE*

"In the cultural perception of the madman that prevailed up to the end of the eighteenth century, he is different only in so far as he is unaware of difference; he sees nothing but resemblances everywhere; for him all signs resemble one another, and all resemblances have the value of signs."[93]

90 DUST BREEDING

The accretion of dust on surfaces is evidence of the passage of time, and of inutility; hence the significance of footprints and fingerprints. Dust accretes, exists, is erased by paths of desire; hence the traces of presence that remain in the museum.

The accumulation of traces of all kinds is dependent on inhabitation.

91 ST JOHN SOANE

"Our body is not in space like things; it inhabits or haunts space."[94]

93 Foucault, *Madness and Civilization*, 105.

94 Merleau-Ponty, "An Unpublished Text" in *The Primacy of Perception*, 5.

92 THE WANDERER

"The flâneur initiates excursions which never entirely resurface ...

"The flâneur is still on the threshold, of the city as of the bourgeois class. Neither has yet engulfed him; in neither is he at home."[95]

To dwell is to wander; to be in error. The answer is, the origin is on the interior.

93 PROOF OF THE NON-EXISTENCE OF ARCHITECTURE

Why were they seeking origins? Perhaps because they had begun to suspect the worst.

"Architecture cannot be shown in museums. Exhibitions of architecture cannot exist because true architecture is monstrous and museums are architectural monsters that successfully house any other kind of monsters except monsters of their own kind. Metonymically speaking, a labyrinth cannot conceal another labyrinth within itself because persons lost in the maze will never realize when they are leaving the meanders of the container-labyrinth for the maze of the contained-labyrinth."[96]

Amor fati – to love one's fate is to live with presence of mind.

94 WHAT IS THE SAME EVERYWHERE AND NOWHERE?

The museum spatializes time as a journey to the underworld, to the centre of the labyrinth. Answer

95 Walter Benjamin, "Paris: Capital of the Nineteenth Century," in *Reflections: Essays, Aphorisms, Autobiographical Writings* (New York: Schocken 1986), 156.

96 Frascari, *Monsters of Architecture*, 77.

the riddle, pass through. The past eclipses the future like the after-image of a light in darkness.

95 INSIDE THE MUSEUM, INFINITY GOES UP ON TRIAL

The heterogeneity of the museum cannot become a master-pattern for history, because it contains within its hermetic identity a secret preface to mortality: the inevitability of failure, and the necessity to persevere in the face of chaos.

"This very cogitation carries with it I don't know what secret, hidden horror; indeed, one finds oneself wandering in this immensity, to which are denied limits and centre, and therefore also all determinate places."[97]

96 HOW TO UNDERSTAND TAXONOMY

a) By similitude, which is in turn subdivided into similitude of substance (man as a microcosmic image of the macrocosm), quality (the ten figures for the ten commandments), by metonymy and antonomasia (Atlas for astronomers or astronomy, the watch for time, the beheaded snake for order, Cicero for rhetoric). b) By homonymy: the animal dog for the constellation Dog. c) By irony or contrast: the fool for the sage. d) By sign: the photograph for the camera, or the mirror in which Lacan admired himself for Lacan. e) By a word of different pronunciation: *sanum* for sane. f) By similarity of name: aristocracy for Aristotle. g) By type and species: ape for animal. h) By pagan symbol: the sun for Apollo. i) By peoples: the Cretans for labyrinths, the Egyptians for tomb furniture, the Phoenicians for the alphabet. j) By signs of the Zodiac: the sign of the

97 Johannes Kepler, *De stella nova in pede Serpentarii*, quoted in Alexandre Koyré, *From the Closed World to the Infinite Universe* (Baltimore: Johns Hopkins 1991), 61.

twins for the constellation Gemini. k) By the relationship between organ and function. l) By a common characteristic: the raven for writing-desks. m) By hieroglyphics: the frame for knowledge. n) And finally, pure ideolectal association, any monster for anything to be remembered.[98]

97 THE SECTION

The section – in the sense of the architectural convention – is a science of symbolic order: the deliberate cut into the universe that separates *res extensa* from *res cogitans*, the serpent's head from her body, the invention of the guillotine and the rise of surgery. Unification by division.

History is a kind of section – a master narrative which explains the presence of traces in the perceptible world by organizing them into a coherent whole. Dreams and interpretation operate on this principle. History has replaced the architect with the detective. The museum is a section of history, a meta-section. This, however, does not imply that meaning becomes frozen:

"Given a perpetually new natural and historical situation to control, the perceiving subject undergoes a continued birth; at each instant it is something new."[99]

98 *DEUS EX MACHINA*

History is a history of exceptions, monsters, things "out of order" – as if nature had a *purpose*.

"The transition from the cathedral, the palace, the

98 Interpretation of Cosma Roselli's *Thesaurus artificiosae memoriae* (Venice 1589), original quoted in Umberto Eco, *Interpretation and Overinterpretation* (Cambridge: Cambridge University Press 1992), 46.

99 Merleau-Ponty, "Unpublished Text," in *The Primacy of Perception*, 6.

nomad's tent, the boudoir of the courtesan, and the witch's cave to the museum was a magico-religious transmutation: objects turned into icons. Art inherited from the old religion the power of consecrating things and endowing them with a sort of eternity; museums are our temples, and the objects displayed in them are beyond history."[100]

99 EVERYTHING IS PREGNANT WITH ITS CONTRARY

In the practice of Zen Buddhism, the *koan* is a kind of riddle or paradoxical question asked of the novitiate in order to help him attain *satori*, or sudden enlightenment.

While language remains our most enthralling device, the koan's paradoxical nature is intended to eclipse the prejudices of logical thought, and free the fluid lateral powers of the embodied mind.

100 WHY WE NEED MUSEUMS

Two reclusive brothers were found dead in their inner-city apartment last night. Police had trouble investigating the cause of death, due to the high piles of thousands of copies of the Times which filled the apartment – for forty-nine years they had saved every single copy. Because the papers occupied so much space, the twin brothers had created burrows tunneling through the print-infested dwelling.

Police detectives speculated that the reason none of the papers had been thrown out is because the brothers had not finished reading them.

100 Octavio Paz. "Seeing and Using: Art and Craftsmanship," in *Convergences: Essays on Art and Literature* (New York: Harcourt Brace Jovanovich 1987), 52.

12.6

12.7

ILLUSTRATIONS

12.1 Papyrus, ca. 1400 B.C.E. *The Seven Doors of the Egyptian Underworld, seen as a Maze*, from Jung, C.G., ed. *Man and his Symbols* (London: Aldus Books 1964), 22.

12.2 Boullée: Plan of Museum at the Centre of which is a Temple of Fame (top); Section of Boullée's Museum (bottom), in Jean-Marie Pérouse de Montclos, *Etienne-Louis Boullée 1728–1799* (Paris: Arts et Métiers Graphiques 1969), 77–8.

12.3 Plan (top) and Section (bottom) of Durand's Museum, in Werner Szambien, *J.-N.-L. Durand 1760–1834 De l'imitation à la norme* (Paris: Picard 1984), 225.

12.4 Le Corbusier's Museum of Unlimited Extension (lower left) and Musée Mondial (lower right), in *Œuvres complètes*, W. Boesiger, ed. (London: Thames & Hudson 1964–70), 1:193.

12.5 Elevation of the Louvre, from S. Leclerc, *Traité d'architecture* (Paris: P. Giffart 1714), 186.

12.6 Joseph Cornell's workshop in Dore Ashton, *A Joseph Cornell Album* (New York: Da Capo Press 1974), 99.

12.7 Personal possessions of Jews, confiscated by Nazis and stored in a synagogue. "The Camp" by Josef Polák, in *Terezin* (Council of Jewish Communities in the Czech lands: Prague 1965), 32.

About the Authors

Gregory Paul Caicco
Gregory Paul Caicco was born in Bridgeport, Connecticut, in 1962. He obtained a bachelor of architecture degree with high distinction in 1987 from Carleton University in Ottawa, and in 1989 a master's degree in the history and philosophy of architecture from Cambridge University in England. He was a member of the Jesuit Order from 1989 until 1993 where he studied languages, philosophy, spirituality, and the Spiritual Exercises at Ignatius College in Guelph and at Loyola University in Chicago. He has worked in various architectural offices and most recently was the editor of *Refugee Update* as well as an educator and network co-ordinator with the Jesuit Refugee Service in Latin America and Toronto. Gregory is currently at McGill University researching a doctoral thesis entitled *Ethics and Poetics: The Early Franciscan Contribution to Architecture.*

Lily H. Chi
Lily Chi is assistant professor of architecture at Cornell University. She received a bachelor of architecture degree with high distinction from Carleton University in 1984, and a master's degree in architectural history and theory from Cambridge University in 1987. She is completing a doctoral dissertation at McGill University on the idea of character in early modern architectural theory.

Jean-Pierre Chupin
Jean-Pierre Chupin was born in France in 1960. He received professional degrees in architecture from Nantes (France) and Portsmouth (England), as well as a master's degree in history and theory of architecture from McGill University in 1990. He taught design studio and history at the Université du Québec à Montréal and has practised architecture in Montreal with Léa Zeppetelli and Nicolas Reeves. Jean-Pierre is currently pursuing doctoral studies at the Université de Montréal. His dissertation on the potential of analogical thinking considers a definition of project pedagogy. Since September 1995, he has been teaching in Toulouse, France.

Terrance Galvin
Terrance Galvin is an adjunct professor of architecture at McGill University and is currently pursuing doctoral studies at the University of Pennsylvania. He is a graduate of the architectural history and theory graduate program at McGill University, having previously studied at the Technical University of Nova Scotia and at the University of Toronto.

Karsten Harries
Karsten Harries is professor of philosophy at Yale University. He has also taught at the University of Texas (Austin) and the University of Bonn. He has published widely on Heidegger, early modern philosophy, and philosophy of art and architecture. He is the author of three books, *The Meaning of Modern Art* (1965), *The Bavarian Rococo Church: Between Faith and Aestheticism* (1983), and *The Broken Frame: Three Lectures* (1990). With Christoph Jamme he has edited *Martin Heidegger: Politics, Art, and Technology* (1994). *The Ethical Function of Architecture* is scheduled to appear in 1996.

Donald Kunze
Donald Kunze was born in North Carolina, where he received his bachelor of architecture degree in 1970. He later received a master's and a doctoral degree in geography. He teaches architecture theory and general arts courses at the Pennsylvania State University. He has lectured and published on the subjects of architecture's relationship to language theory, philosophy, and perception. Dr Kunze is currently studying the structure of artifacts of travel and tourism, developing interactive courses for distance education, and completing a book on architecture theory. He lives with his wife and three cats in Boalsburg, Pennsylvania, the birthplace of Memorial Day.

Joanna Merwood
Joanna Merwood graduated from New Zealand's Victoria University of Wellington in 1992, gaining a bachelor of building science and a bach-

elor of architecture degree with honours. She taught design studio at Victoria and was engaged in architectural practice in Wellington. She has recently completed a master's degree at McGill University in history and theory of architecture in the area of mid- to late-nineteenth century architectural representation.

Dagmar Motycka Weston

Dagmar Motycka Weston has lectured in the history and philosophy of architecture at the University of Toronto and at Carleton University. She is currently teaching architecture at the University of Newcastle upon Tyne, while completing a book on the space and thematic content in early Le Corbusier. One of her continuing concerns is to explore ways in which an understanding of cultural tradition can be a source of authentic meaning in today's architectural practice.

Stephen Parcell

Stephen Parcell is associate professor of architecture at the Technical University of Nova Scotia and an external advisor for the graduate program in architectural history and theory at McGill University. He previously taught at Carleton University, after receiving a bachelor of architecture degree from the University of Toronto and a master of architecture degree from the Cranbrook Academy of Art. His research on natural history dioramas is part of a series of representational studies involving other perspectival institutions – panorama buildings, stereographic images, and a late Renaissance perspective treatise. He is presently doing research on temporal representations in architecture.

Alberto Pérez-Gómez

Alberto Pérez-Gómez has taught at the universities of Mexico, Houston, Syracuse, Toronto, and Carleton, and is now the Saidye Rosner Bronfman Professor of the History of Architecture at McGill University, where he has directed the graduate program in history and theory of architecture since 1987. He was also the director of the Institut de recherche en histoire de l'architecture from 1990 to 1993. He is the author of two books, *Architecture and the Crisis of Modern Science* (MIT Press 1983), and *Polyphilo or The Dark Forest Revisited* (MIT Press 1992). His numerous articles have been published in North American and European journals. At present, he is working on a major book on the history and theory of modern European architectural representation, with special reference to the role of projection in architectural design.

Bram Ratner
Bram Ratner was born in Montreal in 1964. He received a bachelor of architecture degree from McGill University in 1987 and a master's degree in history and theory of architecture in 1992 at the same institution. He lectured and published papers on Jewish-related architecture, including most recently "The Symbol of the Western Wall." He is currently employed at Moshe Safdie Architects in Jerusalem.

Alain Robbe-Grillet
Writer and filmmaker Alain Robbe-Grillet has for the last forty years been one of France's most prominent authors. In 1954 he received the Fénéon award for his novel *Les Gommes*. Among his most celebrated titles, translated into many languages, are *Le Voyeur, Jalousie, La maison de rendez-vous*, *Projet pour une révolution à New York*, and *Topologie d'une cité fantôme*, as well as numerous essays on the *nouveau roman*, and more recently a series of autobiographical texts. In 1961, M. Robbe-Grillet wrote the scenario and dialogue for the film *L'année dernière à Marienbad*, directed by Alain Resnais. He subsequently directed other films, such as *L'immortelle*, *L'homme qui manque*, *Glissements progressifs du plaisir*, and *La belle captive*.

Tracey Eve Winton
Tracey Eve Winton has a bachelor of architecture degree from the University of Waterloo and is pursuing graduate studies in the hermetic arts in the history and theory of architecture program at McGill University. Her lucky number is 42.